The
SCREENWRITER'S GUIDE
to
AGENTS
and MANAGERS

JOHN SCOTT LEWINSKI

ALLWORTH PRESS
NEW YORK

05   04   03   02   01   00   5   4   3   2   1

Published by Allworth Press
An imprint of Allworth Communications
10 East 23rd Street, New York, NY 10010

Cover design by Douglas Design Associates, New York, NY

Page composition/typography by SR Desktop Services, Ridge, NY

ISBN: 1-58115-079-2

Library of Congress Cataloging-in-Publication Data
Lewinski, John Scott.
    The screenwriter's guide to agents and managers / by John Scott Lewinski.
        p.   cm.
    Includes bibliographical references and index.
    ISBN 1-58115-079-2
    1. Motion picture authorship—Vocational guidance.   2. Television authorship—Vocational guidance.   I. Title.
    PN1996.L44   2001
    808.2'3—dc21   00-053124

Printed in Canada

Dedication

I dedicate this book to Sarah and Beth Lewinski, my sisters.
They were my first, best friends and the only people on Earth who
make it OK for me to act like a kid. That has nothing to do with agents,
I know, but it's my book. So there. Nyah!

Table *of* Contents

Acknowledgments

I would like to give special thanks to the following outstanding individuals who made this book possible:

Tad Crawford at Allworth Press for the opportunity; Glenn Sobel for the patience; the Academy of Motion Picture Arts & Sciences Library; the Writers Guild of America; *Daily Variety*, Shelly Mellot at *Scr(i)pt Magazine*; and all the agents, managers, and assistants who graciously gave their time to share their experiences and passions.

About the Author

JOHN SCOTT LEWINSKI

John Scott Lewinski writes sketch comedy, books, screenplays, interactive games, and magazine articles out of Los Angeles, CA.

Lewinski started out researching, writing, and producing public affairs programs for WMVS/WMVT—PBS in Milwaukee, WI. After moving to Hollywood, he got his first job as a writer's assistant for Steven E. de Souza (*Die Hard, 48 Hours, Tomb Raider*) and for the Black Entertainment Television comedy series, *Comicview*. He worked his way up to staff writer and wrote several sketches for the Comicview Players.

A one-time new media columnist for Earthweb, Writers Club, *Cream Magazine On-Line*, *Inphobia Magazine*, and *Nautilus CD-ROM Magazine*, his book, *Developers Guide to Computer Game Design*, is available from Wordware Publishing in Texas. His second book, *Screenplaying*, is now available at Amazon.com from Random House/Xlibris Publishing.

Lewinski's feature script, *Darwin's Game*, won the 1996 Mel Brenner Award for Risk Taking in Screenwriting and entry into the 1997 First Annual Telluride Independent Film and Video Festival. His next script, *Forced Perspective*, won a 1999 Award from the Wisconsin State Film Commission and Screenwriter's Forum for Best Screenplay Set in the State. That script also qualified as a quarterfinalist for the 1997 Nicholl Fellowship, the 1997 Austin Heart of Film Festival and the 1998 Empire High-Value Screenwriting Contest. Finally, he was a semifinalist for the Chesterfield Screenwriting Fellowship in 1998, 1995, and 1994.

As a journalist, he covers the motion picture industry for *Scr(i)pt Magazine*, *Creative Screenwriting Magazine*, and *Hollywood Scriptwriter*.

A veteran Hollywood story editor, Lewinski served as Creative Executive Story Editor at Trimark Pictures and was closely involved in the development and production of the critically acclaimed "Ernest Hemingway's After the Storm" for USA Networks and "Summer of Miracles" for CBS. He was also a story analyst for Fox Family Channel, Saban Entertainment, The Wallerstein Company, Evolve Entertainment, Val D'Oro Entertainment, and *Scr(i)pt Magazine* Screenplay Analysis Services. In 2000, he served as a judge for the $1 million Kingman Screenplay Contest.

Lewinski's interactive writing includes contributions to the multimillion selling CD-ROM games LucasArts' "Star Wars: Demolition," Broderbund's "Riven, The Sequel to Myst," "Command & Conquer II—Tiberian Sun," "Command & Conquer—Red Alert," and "The Journeyman Project 3, Legacy of Time." His feature articles on game writing and interactive industry trends currently appear in *Amazing Stories Magazine* and *Game Developer Magazine*. Lewinski also edits online forums covering interactive writing for Earthweb, *(http://discussions.earthweb.com/)*.

Lewinski holds a Master of Fine Arts degree in screenwriting from Loyola Marymount University in Los Angeles and a Bachelor of Arts in journalism from Marquette University. He completed his study of English literature at Exeter College, Oxford University.

Born in Milwaukee, WI, Lewinski enjoys a good debate, movies, reading, music, college basketball, college football, boxing, fencing, horseback riding, photography, painting, computer art, cooking, and volunteer teaching.

Finally, he is no relation to Monica Lewinsky! Just look at the spelling! It's obviously different! He has nothing to do with her, whatsoever. Never did. Never will.

Unless such a connection might help his writing career . . .

INTRODUCTION

THE 10 PERCENT SOLUTION

As a writer, an agent hires you as a client so she can work for you.

They all asked me the same question. Writers, agents, publishers, journalists, friends—everyone! Why write a book about screenwriting agents? Aren't they the forgotten part of the creative equation in Hollywood? The Oscars honor the best screenwriters alongside the producers and directors that brought their scripts to the screen. But there's no award for the agents who put all those people together and handle the deals.

There are plenty of screenwriting titles on the market. They handle everything from conceiving and writing a script to marketing and shooting it. Some might even briefly discuss agents and how to get one to market a given story. But I thought it was time we really examined the roles of agents and their professional relationships with their clients.

Other than perhaps a parent or a teacher, no single individual plays a more important role in a screenwriter's development than his literary agent. However, there is no single entertainment industry professional less understood by writers than agents. Young writers want to impress them. Struggling writers berate them. Successful writers struggle with them. Retired writers often warn aspiring students away from them.

Writers too often treat agents and managers like possessions or objects. Just as writers know they need to buy a word processor and a three-hole punch, they believe they need to get an agent because every established professional has one. Nevertheless, few film and TV scribes truly know what agents and managers do every day, what they go through on behalf of their clients, or why the agents choose to tackle such a tough job. No wonder so many writers struggle to earn and keep an agent's attention and support.

In my preliminary research for this book, I spoke to scores of aspiring and working screenwriters. I met them at screenwriting conferences from Chicago and Austin to Glendale and San Francisco. Some wanted to break into features or television writing. Others already had a credit under their belts and wanted an agent who could keep their career going or a manager capable of pushing them to the next creative or financial level.

They all wanted a new agent, but many confessed that agents absolutely mystified them. They wanted to know how agents thought. How do they choose material? What kinds of writers get their attention? Do query letters serve a purpose? How can you make an agent take you seriously? The questions never stopped coming. Together, we'll find the answers and discover how to deal with top agents and managers—with those same professionals providing the lessons.

Newcomers will learn what an agent does and what a writer needs to do before even considering contacting them. Screenwriters with a few scripts already under their belts will discover how to approach and catch an agent's eye. More importantly, those writers on success's doorstep will learn that agents and managers are human beings doing a job, not monoliths to be hunted or worshiped. Finally, active writers already established in the business will gain insights into what happens in their own agent's head. The working pro can better interact with his current representation one on one after hearing what agents and managers have to say about their careers, ambitions, and hopes. The usefulness of the information herein is simply boundless.

Now I wouldn't expect you to simply take my word for any of this or rely on my stellar entertainment industry wisdom. Let's go over my head to the real experts. This book will include featured interviews with prominent agents and managers offering their insights and experiences. I will focus on presenting these professionals as human beings with dreams, ambitions, anxieties, victories, and defeats. Many writers seem shocked to learn that agents have a sense of humor. Well, they will get a chance to share their wit and wisdom on these pages.

Writers will learn what qualifications agents look for in new clients and what experiences scribes need before they should even consider pursuing an agent. Chapters will cover the different levels of representation (boutiques, management, the Big Houses, etc.), what kind of spec scripts get the attention, how to write a professional and effective query letter, and how much is too much when pursuing representation. Also, agents and managers will get the chance to explain reasonable expectations for aspiring writers and how to best build and maintain a strong representative/client relationship.

Finally, we will confront the screenwriters' Catch-22. They cannot sell a script unless they have an agent, and they cannot get an agent unless they sell a script. There are solutions to this dilemma, and the agents and managers will unveil them.

When did I first come up with the concept for this book? I was writing an article on agents for a popular entertainment magazine and realized two things:

- Agents are real people.
- Agents don't believe that anyone realizes number one is true.

As I did a series of interviews for the magazine piece, I discovered how personable these much-maligned professionals could be. Yes, part of their job requires them to schmooze, but I mean the agents I spoke to seemed like genuinely good-natured and approachable people. That surprised me because (as one agent put it), you can take any lawyer joke, substitute "agent" and it would work just as well within the entertainment industry.

So, to offer you a road map for this book and to prepare you for the kind of material we'll deal with on these pages, I wanted to include that original article in its entirety. It'll let you in on why I wanted to write about these misunderstood professionals and give you a good primer for this book's subject matter.

Many of the professionals featured in it were kind enough to offer a second, more extensive interview later in the book, so, we'll see them again. But, for now, settle in and look at a sort of *Cliff's Notes* for this book.

Managing Your Agent or Manager

Agents and managers are a different breed. That's not much of a news flash—there are so many well-worn stereotypes of both that you can take any lawyer joke and simply substitute "agent" and end up with the same punch line!

All aspiring screenwriters want an agent or manager, but not everyone knows precisely what role they play in a writer's career. A strange relationship develops between writer and representative because it is one of the only employment situations in which the employee (the agent) decides if the employer (the writer) is worthy of the employee's work. As a writer, an agent hires you as a client so she can work for you!

Did you follow that? Well, stay with me, because the whole deal is just crazy enough to work in Hollywood. Still, it's important to understand the relationship between representative and client so you can get the most out of your agent.

First, let's look at the difference between an agent and a manager. The individual screenwriter must gauge his own needs to determine which one he needs, but some generalities remain for the categories of representative.

Both may bring an attorney's education and experience to the table, but at the very least, they bring a skill for contract negotiation and a list of industry contacts to whom they can submit your material. While an agent usually focuses on one particular arm of the entertainment industry (film or episodic TV, for example), a manager can oversee all facets of a writer's career. A manager can even work with an agent if the writer has the skills to warrant enough work.

For the purpose of this article, we will assume that you have an agent or manager. But once you have representation, how do you work with the agent or manager and keep her as a professional advisor?

The best way of examining the agent-client relationship is to go right to the source and discover how professional agents and managers interact with their clients.

What is going through the agent's head? To find out, we start at the top. Rob Carlson, of the venerable William Morris Agency, is one of Hollywood's hottest literary agents. Working with his partner, Alan Gasmer, Carlson represents some of the biggest A-list writers in the motion picture industry. He and Gasmer are the undisputed kings of spec script sales, and they also keep their clients busy with a mix of assignments and rewrite gigs.

Carlson says his relationship with his successful clients is not that distinct from that of a small boutique agency and its lesser-known, aspiring writers. The agent-client or manager-client relationship still depends on working with each other to determine the best course for a writer's career.

"The dealings are not significantly different," Carlson says. "The stakes are simply higher in our case.

"It's interesting, because Alan Gasmer and I started out differently than most motion-picture literary agents. We were both TV agents and weren't representing writers in the film industry. But we had TV writers who wanted to move into writing for movies. They wrote spec scripts, and we set out to sell those specs." Carlson says he and Gasmer steadily gained momentum and built their reputations as top motion-picture agents. But it all started by working with their clients' wishes and encouraging those clients to develop their material.

"I've always said, 'You don't write a spec script to get it sold. You write a spec script to get a job.'" Carlson says. "So we agents need our clients to keep writing spec scripts, because we need that selection of material to market a writer."

Carlson explains, "We often hear from companies where we've submitted material—something like, 'We loved it! What else do you have from that writer?' So even if a writer is A-list talent making $1.5 million a script, we still need spec material in those situations. Plus, if we're still trying to establish a lesser-known writer, it can often take four or five specs before he hits."

Carlson offers some hope to struggling writers who must constantly prove themselves with spec after spec. He says that even well known scribes need to go out on a limb if they want their careers to branch out in new directions.

"If you're a drama writer, and you want to write comedy," Carlson said, "you need to write a spec comedy. We always try to encourage our clients to pursue those kinds of challenges, but even an A-list writer still needs to prove he can write material for a new genre."

While smaller-scale agents and managers might seek to option or sell a script to a independent production company to build some heat for a lesser-known writer, Carlson looks to hook up his clients with top directors to forge hot movies. Also, he enlists his stable of writers for production rewrites, involving their top-shelf talents in the key phases of a movie's development.

Still, Carlson stresses the necessity for writers to write simply for the sake of creating new screenplays. "We have clients at the top of their games getting big money for assignments," he says, "but they still write scripts simply because they feel a need to get a story told."

"As agents, we always encourage that for the client's sake," Carlson adds. "Plus, it's great for us as agents because it gives us more material to enter into the marketplace."

Adam Shulman, a literary agent for the Beverly Hills firm APA, builds many of his client relationships with the writers of low-budget, experimental independent films. While his agency remains a Hollywood player and maintains ties with the studio system, Shulman is comfortable guiding the careers of more independently minded scribes, creating a supportive environment for his clients.

"A significant part of my business is the independent film industry," Shulman says. "I still work within the studio system as well because I like both." Shulman encourages his clients to pursue whatever artistic course they feel compelled to follow.

"There are some agents like me who work in both the independent and studio worlds, and there are a few who actually work only in the indie world. But most agents have a problem with directing their clients in that direction because there simply isn't as much money to be made in that area. Or those agents simply might not enjoy those kinds of film. I appreciate both worlds." Shulman adds, "I will submit material to the big studios, but I have always been very open to representing people in the indie world. It all depends on the individual client's work and interests."

Michele Wallerstein of the Wallerstein Company represents established, working clients as well as up-and-coming writers of multiple screenplays looking to make a mark. Her boutique agency handles fewer clients than a Big House like William Morris and can offer developing writers more personal advice and attention.

"These days, no one is looking to write the Great American Novel," Wallerstein says. "Everybody wants to be a screenwriter! So they write a screenplay, pass it around to their friends for some comments, and then send it to an agent."

However, Wallerstein stresses that she is not a writing coach and is not in the business of critiquing the work of aspiring writers. "My job is to look for and develop talent; talent that I can market, talent that I can sell," she explains. "I am looking for ability that I can make into an entity in the Hollywood entertainment community. When I forge a relationship with a client, it helps if that writer brings professionalism and a wider range of material to the table.

"There are very few rules in the entertainment industry," Wallerstein adds. "But the ones that exist you must pay attention to."

One rule Wallerstein stresses is that, before finding an agent or manager, a writer must be personally and professionally ready to work with that representative to build a career. "This is a business," she says. "Writers are professionals who deliver a product. I want to work with my clients to make sure they produce the best material possible and develop the most successful career they can."

Tammy Stockfish of Broder, Kurland, Webb, Uffner represents established television writers of hour long dramatic series, sitcoms, and movies-of-the-week. Most of her clients come to her through referrals—from clients, other agents, or producers.

Stockfish says that the qualities that build a positive relationship with her clients are often the same qualities that attract her to them as a representative in the first place. "One of the hardest things to accomplish as a writer is getting an agent," she says. "I work best with writers who distinguish themselves as dedicated professionals."

Stockfish advises writers to treat their agents with as much professional respect as anyone to whom they might submit their material. Don't pester your agent or manager with too many phone calls.

Both Wallerstein and Stockfish stress that they work best with writers living and working in Southern California. "I don't necessarily limit myself to writers in L.A., but it is definitely an advantage to live here," Stockfish explains. "Out of sight is often out of mind, and if you're not here, you miss out on a lot of opportunities. For example, big meetings can happen here in a snap. A writer needs to be here to take advantage of that meeting."

While most representatives prefer to work with more established writers because they are already making money, Stockfish is quick to add that good agents and managers look to develop and nurture new talent. "We also need to have baby writers as clients. One day, those writers will be in the business," she says. "I feel for young writers. I know how tough it can be, but this is a business of persistence and aggression. Stick with it!"

Stockfish's advice to writers—whether they're searching for an agent or manager or forging a relationship with their representative—is simple but essential: "The professional willingness to pay your dues is important. You need to get out there and fight with or without an agent because experience, information, and knowledge are the keys."

Both Wallerstein and Stockfish also urge writers not to rely solely on their agents and managers for career developments. "An agent or manager can help you get work, but you need to do your own research and work with your rep," Stockfish says. "Prepare yourself like you would for a job because being a writer is a job. Watch the changes in the business. Follow your market. Know what you want to write and what genre you want to work in before you begin writing your spec screenplay material.

"Most importantly," Stockfish concludes, "write your passion. If it's on the paper, it will find a home and give your agent the best opportunity to sell it in the marketplace." All over Hollywood, this writer found agent after agent who support their clients' writing interests and desires while offering their business acumen to guide career paths.

If you are lucky enough to overcome that first major hurdle of finding an agent or manager to help you build your career, be sure to prepare yourself for dedicated, professional behavior. You need to bring your own contacts, your own research, and your own plan to the table when working with even the best agent or manager. Never expect your representative to display more concern, respect, and ambition for your career goals than you show. You set that tone.

Your agent or manager should offer advice and suggest alternative strategies as you build your contacts and work options. However, she should not stand in the way of your passions, but rather allow you to create the screenplays you most enjoy developing. The representative should support your wishes and want to see you succeed how and where you wish. If an agent or manager is legitimate, she will more than earn her percentage. But the relationship between you and your representative is a partnership. Work harder than your agent to promote your own work and you will enjoy a fruitful partnership with your rep when payday arrives.

I wrote that original piece as journalist relaying information and the opinions of experts, not as a screenwriter trying to teach someone how to hunt and hoodwink agents. I will approach this book as a reporter, a conduit for the information you need to learn to enter the screenwriting arena and find a representative who works for you. Some of that data will overlap, and still more will contain outright contradictions between the different agents and managers.

I will share my experiences, opinions, and predictions wherever I can, but you and I will learn agents' and managers' secrets together as we move from agency to agency, expert to expert. Wherever we can draw on the wisdom of the most established industry professionals around the business, we will. Trust me! Agents love to talk about themselves and their work. I'll get them started. They'll do the rest. And you'll reap all the benefits!

1

Agents and Managers at Work

*The agent gets 10 percent because the writer is
still doing 90 percent of the work.*

It's the great Catch-22 facing struggling writers in Hollywood: You need an agent to sell your script, but you need to sell a script before you can get an agent. That's the wall so many young (and not so young) aspiring screenwriters face as they try to break into film or television writing.

I attended several screenwriting workshops and seminars across the country over recent years, and I've seen countless writers bemoan that very problem. They watch movies and develop their story sense. Maybe they pick up a few volumes from the ever-growing library of books for screenwriters. They write their scripts and hone their craft. They might build up a few samples before deciding they've finally written a story for film or television that warrants production. When I come across these writers at conferences, they share a collective refrain: "What's next?"

That plaintive cry leads to an even more daunting challenge. Writing the script is hard enough. It takes many long, lonely hours of sweat and frustration to get an artistic, narrative vision on the page. But that act in and of itself demands that someone take notice of the effort. Any writer who says he writes stories of any genre just for his own enjoyment is lying or deluded. Writers write to express themselves to others. Screenwriters write in hopes of getting their stories up on the screen or into that little plastic box with the remote control.

Those writers need to get their work to the producers or executives in Los Angeles, New York, Chicago, Canada, wherever, that translate written work into the movies and television shows we enjoy. While the scribes might get a chance to meet a few producers at a screenwriting seminar or entertainment convention, such hectic venues are rarely appropriate for anyone to drop off a finished manuscript. Most eager writers coast to coast could grab a *Creative Directory* or *Hollywood Reporter Blu-Book* and compile a list of production companies to which to submit a script.

The Dark Mantra: No Unsolicited Manuscripts

Unfortunately, those producers cling to a great and very reassuring Hollywood tradition of never accepting "unsolicited manuscripts." This protects the producers in a couple of ways. First, it prevents them from receiving endless piles of scripts or book manuscripts that they could never read in a lifetime. More importantly, the policy protects producers from receiving material that they could later be accused of stealing.

Why would these fine, upstanding professional folk be cursed with such an accusation? If you consider that there are only so many stories possible from the human collective psyche, you realize that some overlapping is unavoidable. That's a fancy way of saying that many stories are similar. A writer might sincerely believe that he conjured up the most original and touching story in the history of human endeavor . . . until something with heartbreaking similarities wins the race to press or projector.

Now imagine if a writer submitted just such a rare, unique, and original manuscript to a producer who coincidentally was already producing a very similar project. It can happen at any time, as Hollywood often chases its own tail while pumping out strangely similar projects. If a writer wrote a project eerily similar to something he saw at the local theatre, a lawsuit could result.

So unless producers want to send out a legal release form for every project they receive, they need agents and managers to act as safe, professional channels through which materials will flow into their offices. Literary agents and managers represent the writers hoping to get their material read throughout the industry. As they go about their business, there are certain conventions that agents and managers follow to run an honest business:

- They are expected to deal honestly and fairly with their clients—both the writers represented and the producers on the receiving end.
- The agent should never derive personal gains at the expense of his/her clients.

- Agents should treat relationships with clients in a confidential manner.
- They should not encourage or induce an artist to breach an existing representation contract; nor should they represent an artist while the artist is under a valid contract to another agent.

So, with those principles in mind, you try to impress them, to get their attention, to earn their respect. You know you need their assistance, their resources and their expertise. But, do you really know what agents and managers do and why they do it?

For an insider's look at an agent's role in the industry, we turn to Alex Sanger, Director of Development at Trimark Pictures in Marina Del Rey, CA, and Ann Zald, cofounder and owner of The Screenwriters' Room.

Alex Sanger, Director of Development, Trimark Pictures

As the professional most directly responsible for bringing new material into the company, Sanger works with several agents on a daily basis.

"I think there are two different breeds of literary agents," he said over coffee near his Marina Del Rey office. "There are the agents at the UTAs, ICMs, and William Morris types. Then, you have the next tier, such as the Paradigms, the Writers & Artists, and those less blockbuster-obsessed firms.

"Of course, they're all trying to track talent and cover their territories. They all keep an eye out for the new, fresh, up-and-coming writers, in addition to representing well-established writers.

"But, the CAAs and the other Big Houses are dealing with the biggest names—the best established talent. I assume they don't have as much time to develop new talent or to work for writers not already bringing in high six- or seven-figure paydays.

"Unfortunately, there a lot of good writers out there whom the business refuses to pay attention to," Sanger explained. "They're not bringing home a huge amount of money, so they don't get the attention of the bigger agencies. That's why I look to deal with slightly smaller and more intimate agencies like Gersh, Writers & Artists, or Paradigm because they have time to deal with up-and-coming writers."

From Sanger's point of view, an agent's job is to call attention to talent: "Agents and managers are supposed to be out there as well as doing what development executives like me don't have time to do. They need to find talent—not only new talent, but to cultivate or recreate pre-existing clients into whatever the marketplace demands."

Sanger realizes how hard it is for the writers not yet in the millionaires' club to get an agent's attention. Even worse, if a writer can't get his material to an agent and gain that representative's support, he will never know if Sanger or someone like him might green-light the story on the page.

"There's a wall a writer has to go through if you want to deal with agents," he said. "It might seem easier to skip agents and managers and go right to the source (a producer or executive), but I need agents to bring me material. That's just the way the business goes."

Sanger added that it was not an absolute necessity for a writer to have an agent, but it definitely helps:

"It is that same Catch-22! Every writer believes he has something to say. They all believe their material is good and that they're ready to look for an agent. But it's going to end up being the agent who decides what material is of quality and what's not ready to go out. The manager will decide which writer shows some promise. The rep might hip-pocket (represent without signing a binding contract) and cultivate a writer until he is ready—sort of bringing him up through the learning process.

"A writer also has to realize that agents are as inundated with material as development executives. They can only take on so much stuff at any one time. So, it's as hard for agents as it is for us to find new talent."

Sanger explained that one of the most important functions any agent can serve is to "cover a territory." For example, regardless of whether an agency is a boutique, mid-size, or Big House, the firm assigns one or more agents to monitor the studios and larger production companies. Those agents need to learn what genre or form of material a company is looking for so the agency can provide suitable stories or talent on demand.

"A good agent knows what kind of stuff I'm looking for before sending me anything," he said. "Certain production companies or studios might have stronger relationships with one agency or another. As a development executive, it can seem sometimes like covering agents are staying in contact with you as much as they should.

"It's a two-way street. I work to build relationships with the agents who bring me the best talent. We should all maintain contact with each other. I need to know who they represent, and they should know what I need to read."

As you'll see later in this book, Sanger's take on the agent/execu-tive relationship conflicts with what some agents believe. Many man-agers and agents urge writers who are looking for agents to contact pro-ducers and executives in hopes of earning a referral. The conventional wisdom holds that an agent will take a writer more seriously if he comes packing a positive review or friendly word from an industry professional.

Sanger didn't completely agree: "The only way I can see that work-ing is for the agent's benefit. They go to the same markets and pitch fests that I go to across the country or in town at UCLA and such. Writers come in and pitch their ideas to you, but it's the first time you see these people. And, it's their introduction to pitching in some cases. It could be that you find a good writer in the crowd, but there are so many to meet, it's complicated.

"If you find that writer at a pitch fest, you might tell your favorite agent about it with a, 'I found someone you should be aware of.' For an agent, that's a good way to go about it. But, it's not the job of every devel-opment executive to be out there pounding the pavement looking for people for the agents to represent. I think that's ridiculous."

WHAT MAKES A GOOD AGENT?

So, what makes a good agent and a bad rep, from Sanger's point of view?

"Obviously, it's subjective. I've never worked at an agency, so I don't know what the standards are in every case for the hiring and devel-opment of junior agents out there who pound the pavement for new tal-ent. I know it's not the agencies' job to serve us (executives), but a good agent knows to build a strong mutual relationship. That agent or manag-er makes an honest effort to connect with the people to whom she wants to sell material.

"There are circumstances in which bad agenting can hurt a good writer," Sanger added, "so any screenwriter should pick their rep careful-ly. If an agent sends a script out before it's ready, that can do damage.

"Also, if a writer really trusts the wrong agent and grooves his writ-ing in the wrong direction, he can be pigeonholed. Maybe the writer only writes action stuff, and it gets lost that he's really a much better comedy writer."

Sanger offered an example from his own daily experience of an agent not tackling his job correctly:

"A few days ago, we were trying to purchase a piece of material. We were moving past the option phase to an outright purchase, so it was an important decision. There was another offer on the table for this agent's client from another production company.

"So, just to see if the agent would say anything, we asked what this offer was like. He actually took out the offer and read to us the exact terms of the other offer from the competing studio! That's the dumbest thing I've ever seen in this business. It was bad for the client because it pre-empted our bid. The client lost money because we knew what the current offer was and exactly how much we needed to go back in with to make the deal.

"We ended up with the material for less than we probably would have paid for it in a bidding war."

Other potential agenting gaffes include not making or returning phone calls and otherwise dropping the ball during follow-ups. Sanger stressed that some agents take on too much responsibility at a young age. They might need some mentoring before going out to make deals in their youth.

As for who should make the first move in calling an executive's attention to a script, Sanger admitted there is never one clear-cut rule of thumb.

"It can be completely different for every situation. It depends on the talents and personalities of the writer, the agent, and the development executive involved. With three different people involved with each different project, it's a question of chemistry. If the writer, agent, and executive get along and can work together, it can be a great time.

"But, if the agent's really touchy about being in control of a deal and maybe wants to keep the writer and development executive apart for whatever reason, it can make everything more difficult. I would prefer to work directly with the writer and not have to use the agent as a mediator."

A LACK OF SUCCESS CAN MAKE YOU POPULAR

Sanger added that younger, less established writers are almost always more accessible than their wealthier, more established counterparts.

"I don't know if the bigger writers hide behind their reps," he said, "but the reps can act without their client knowing it. The agent might say, 'Don't talk to my client unless you consider this step (a scheduled, paid phase of the development process).' In that case, the writer isn't paid to worry about every stage of development."

Sanger was also quick to point out that almost all of the agents he deals with know their jobs. Writers should not step out into the representation market terrified that some agent might destroy their careers. They should simply shop carefully.

As for the writer, Sanger outlined a simple, but sound set of qualifications any writer should focus on before seeking representation. But he was quick to add that there is no clear-cut set of attributes that equal success.

"I think that writers must be literate—well read. It helps if they studied English in college or attended writers' programs. They should join writers' groups and know their markets. They should study their art and develop their skills. But, even all of that won't guarantee success. It's not how this business works."

He added, "Some people make it after doing nothing of significance, and others never make it after working at it their entire lives.

"I would love to go to my bosses and say, 'This writer has a classically trained background. Let's work with her.' But, it wouldn't necessarily help. There are people out there selling material the first time out of the gate, without education or experience. So, sometimes it's not a component in the process."

Sanger urged new or up-and-coming writers to contact a mid-size agency or a boutique if they're looking for their first agent:

"I'd look to a Writers & Artists or a Gersh. You'll get more attention, and they're just as respected as anyone else around town. That's a good level to start out. Maybe, at some point, you move up to a bigger agency—or stay where you are—if it's working for you. Remember: It's the agent's job to work for you. They need to do their jobs throughout your career and build your résumé, or move on to someone else."

Finding talent and developing scripts at a smaller studio like Trimark offers aspiring screenwriters unique opportunities and challenges compared to the same process at the giants (Paramount, Fox, Universal, etc.). Sanger suggested that many of the bigger agencies fail to grasp Trimark's needs and goals.

"To make sure material keeps coming in, you have to proceed on an agent-to-agent basis," he said. "Or, I take a general meeting at an agency and explain to a roomful of agents what we look for in a script. Since every production company seems to change constantly, I give agents credit for staying up on everything going on around town. It seems like there are a million production deals, and it's hard to keep up with all of that.

"Since Trimark is a smaller territory for the agencies, sometimes it seems like agents assume there's less opportunity to make money here.

Maybe that's generally the case, but it doesn't mean there aren't more opportunities to get movies made here than there are at other companies. We could get a hold of a *Teenage Mutant Ninja Turtles* like New Line, or a *Blair Witch* like Artisan, and we'd be booming. It's always a step away."

Ann Zald, Cofounder and Owner, The Screenwriters' Room

Turning to Ann Zald, we can view the business from the perspective of a professional who lists as one of her skills the ability to develop writers and refer them to the appropriate agent at the right time. Zald was a development executive for Interscope Communications and a creative executive for the then–Universal-based Alphaville. She was a development assistant for Robert Lawrence Productions and Twentieth Century Fox. She also worked in production and post-production. She was involved in the development of *Jumanji, Mr. Holland's Opus, Rapid Fire, Michael, Tombstone, Dazed and Confused, Heart and Souls, CB4, Snow White,* and *Dead Silence.*

Her company, The Screenwriters' Room, evaluates spec features, books, half-hour sitcoms, one-hour dramas, and MOWs. According to the company's literature, unsolicited screenplays (i.e., those not submitted by a recognized literary agency) are rarely accepted by production companies and agencies. The Screenwriters' Room says yes to those manuscripts in an effort to guide them into the right industry hands. If they do get in the door, they're read by assistants, interns, or novice readers and fail to attract the attention of the people with the power to buy it. Unsolicited screenplays are a low priority. Zald and her partners work to make a script a high priority.

The Screenwriters' Room offers experienced feature film executives who read and consult on screenplays for all writers and can provide personal referrals to agents, producers, and studio executives.

For beginning screenwriters, these services can help develop basic writing and editing skills in their quest to become professional writers. For established screenwriters, The Screenwriters' Room can provide objective feedback before a writer exposes a screenplay to the spec market and the rigors of development. The Screenwriters' Room works to maximize a screenplay's artistic and commercial potential to get Hollywood executives to give the work the time and attention it deserves.

The Screenwriters' Room services (no pun intended) include telephone, written, and comprehensive consultation. Phone Consultation is the most affordable service. After reading a screenplay, one of the service's executives will schedule a telephone consultation with the writer. The executive will provide that writer with an objective assessment of his script's potential and suggestions for how to improve it, as well as answers to questions that the writer may have about the industry. For example, a writer could ask how to get an agent, what types of spec screenplays are currently selling in Hollywood, and the like.

Written Consultation might serve a writer if he can't absorb all the story notes during a phone call. The screenwriter can receive the same in-depth written assessment that professional writers receive from Hollywood studios (three to five pages in length). After reading the work, a Screenwriters' Room executive will provide story notes containing specific suggestions that can dramatically improve a screenplay and enhance its commercial prospects.

If a writer wants both options covered, he can sign up for the Comprehensive Consultation. This in-depth analysis includes innovative suggestions on how to refine a screenplay and provides an opportunity to brainstorm new ideas with a professional. This option includes both Phone and Written Consultations.

After all of this work, The Screenwriters' Room executives draw on years of professional experience to identify original and marketable screenplays. If any of Zald's executives think a script is technically and artistically ready for Hollywood, The Screenwriters' Room can develop it with the writer, find a respected agent, and help sell the screenplay to a studio or production company.

This optional service is available free of charge. Any writer who purchases any service from the company is eligible to be considered for this opportunity.

AROUND OR THROUGH THE WALL

According to Zald, the idea for her unique service developed while she was working her way up in show business:

"After I graduated from college, I moved to Washington, DC, and worked in documentary post-production for about four years. We had all kinds of different clients, including the government, public service announcements, congressmen, documentaries for *National Geographic*, etc. But I decided I really wanted to be in feature films.

"I came out to LA, knowing nothing about the business, and decided to attend the Peter Stark Producing Program at USC (a graduate-level, MFA program). The most wonderful thing about the program, besides the fact that all of the instructors worked in the business—so there was no academic vacuum—was that they placed you in an internship during the summer between the program's two years. They put me in as intern/second assistant with Michael London, who was at that time senior vice president at Twentieth Century Fox.

"At that time, Michael was supervising *Alien 3, Sleeping with the Enemy, Class Action,* and *29th Street.* I got to go in and watch everything. Michael was great because he always encouraged me to, say, go over to post-production, watch everything, and ask questions. He'd set up meetings for me all over the lot. I'd spend half a day with marketing or publicity. I could take papers over to business affairs and ask, 'This deal memo came across Michael's desk. Could you explain what $10 million against 10 percent of the gross means?'"

From there, Zald went to work for Robert Lawrence, a producer on the Fox lot. She moved to Alphaville at Universal soon afterward. Finally, she headed to Interscope to set up their story department. She worked as an executive there, bringing in and supervising projects that she worked on such as *Terminal Velocity, Jumanji, Mr. Holland's Opus, The Ties that Bind, Operation Dumbo Drop,* and others.

"While I was at Interscope, and anywhere else I worked, it became clear to me that every company would get letters from aspiring writers. The companies would have a blanket policy of not accepting these letters for legal reasons. Alternatively, they might accept them. But, who has the time? If I'm getting fifty of these letters in a week, I don't have time to go through them. Even if I did go through them all and found one or two promising scripts, I could request it and have a reader or assistant read it for me. Usually, I'm going to pass on it without the time to sit down with the writer and make it a production experience—to help them understand why I passed.

"All the writer gets in that situation is a pass without an explanation as to why I passed. That's a closed-door system. Even though people in the industry, be they agents or producers, are looking for new writers, they face a 'needle in a haystack' search. Agents and managers can't take the time. It's too bad, but the reality is most of those writers won't be up to snuff and ready to get an agent."

Zald explained that she and her partners saw the need for a service that would help writers improve and to contact insiders:

"We wanted to help writers reach people in the system who've been in the meetings and can push a program forward. And, we wanted to make sure the writers and their work were ready for them. For those people who have a script that was professionally done and ready for selling, we wanted to provide them that all-important personal call to an agent or production company.

"That's the way it works for most writers. They know a producer or a friend in the business who refers them. Or, they know another client at that agency who can ask an agent to read a script. For those people without those connections, we can be the conduit for them."

YOU DON'T KNOW WHAT AGENTS DO . . . YET

Zald confessed that many of the clients who come to her company don't have a complete understanding of what agents do. (So it's a good thing I included her in this chapter, don't you think?)

"I think some understand more than others. What is generally believed is an agent has to sell a writer's script, and an agent may try to get a writer work. What writer's don't understand is that you're not just trying to sell your spec, you're usually trying to option a script first for a set period of time with a buyout price set.

"Most writers also don't grasp the concept of writing assignments," she said. "Your script may not sell to a studio, but that script then becomes a writing sample that an agent can give to companies looking for a writer to do project X, Y, or Z. If the production company likes the sample, they can have the writer in for a meeting."

Zald believes the biggest misconception many writers have is that they only need to get an agent to start making a living in the business. Too many writers who actually get representation rely on it too heavily for their own career's good.

"They sit by the pool and wait for the phone to ring because the agent is out there hustling on their behalf. Hopefully, an agent will be out there working for you, but the agent has a lot of other clients with higher profiles than you as a newer writer. The agent can get the high-profile clients more work with less effort and make more money doing it."

So, the new writer needs to keep writing and keep hustling, especially if a writer is in New York or LA where he can network. Whether it's going to conferences or parties, writers need to sell themselves. Later in the book, we'll look at some of the conferences writers who are not located on the East or West Coast can attend.

Zald added, "I invariably hear from new writers, 'I got this great agent and got this great job.' I also hear, 'I got this great agent. I was at a party and heard about an assignment. I called my agent, and he got me the assignment.' The agent didn't get that writer the job. The writer flagged it for the agent. You can't expect the agent to do everything for you because agents don't have time to do it.

"The agent gets 10 percent because the writer is still doing 90 percent of the work. That 90 percent is not just the writing; it's marketing and networking. That's a hard concept for a lot of writers to grasp. They say, 'I'm a writer. I'm supposed to sit alone in my room at my computer.'"

PICKING YOUR MOMENT, NOT YOUR AGENT

According to Zald, writers need to consider very carefully precisely when they are ready to seek representation. Suffice it to say, one script is not enough. You'll hear that repeatedly from several experts throughout this book.

"A writer needs a body of work, more than likely more than one script," Zald said. "It needs to be of a professional quality so an agent can actually show it to people. A writer wants an agent or manager who can hustle on his behalf with good material.

"In addition, you need to consider that an agent has a pipeline of material. She has a client list. That agent will have a new script going out maybe once a week. So, when an agent calls a producer to read a script by a new writer, that producer will respond in a timely manner because producers don't want to upset the agent. They want whatever the agent may be sending out next. A new writer doesn't have that leverage to get any producer to read it. Ideally, you want an agent or manager who will get after people and say, 'Read this script.'"

Zald strongly cautioned the writer against going to any agent or manager with material that isn't ripe yet: "The biggest mistake you can make is going out with material that isn't ready. You will get only one shot with that agent or manager. If you give these people something that they really think is amateurish, or if the idea is not right for studios or independents, they're not going to read your next script.

"I know writers are eager," she said. "They've seen such-and-such spec sell for a million dollars. So, they're thinking, I want to get my stuff out there. The reality is that they might sabotage themselves. They don't understand that the script that they love may not be enough. When I go around and ask my friends who are working writers how many scripts they wrote before they sold a script or got a writing assignment, they never say one or two. They say four to seven. A learning curve happens in the developing of their skills and ideas."

Zald cited the example of one unnamed friend who boasts several outstanding credits and countless writing assignments. This screenwriter was a novelist before he got into the movie business. When she asked this writer how many scripts were in the can before that first assignment came along, he confessed to penning twelve to fourteen samples.

"He had to keep hammering away at it before he broke down the wall. I think too many writers suffer from impatience. Even though there are a lot of junk movies out there, you have to be inspired to do really good work so somebody says, 'I want this writer who can do something better than this hack.'"

Once you have four or five scripts under your belt, Zald suggests looking for an agent that you like and feel good about having involved in your career.

"The personal relationship is most important. You want an agent whom you can get on the phone and talk to. Someone who will give you the straight scoop, and not just what you want to hear.

"It can be really satisfying to be at a Big House agency, but a new writer's value to that firm compared to a hot actor or director is comparably minimal. At a smaller boutique agency, the writer might have more currency."

Zald urges all writers to go with a legitimate agency in Los Angeles or New York. She warns that there are a small number of agents who don't try hard to get their clients' work into the marketplace. However, most professionals at the legitimate agencies will work for their writers.

"Like I said, writers needs to hustle on their own behalf. But, ideally, you want an agent who can work for you and with you. Until you find that agent, maybe take what you can get. It's better to have some representation than to have none at all."

ZALD'S GENERAL ZUGGESTIONS

As a general rule, Zald recommends that new writers work on material set in the present day. Also, the genres of comedy, action, thriller, or romantic comedy open the most doors. She suggests staying away from period pieces and dramas. In the studio world, those genres are based on books or plays—stories with an established pedigree. You don't see many completely fictitious period pieces and dramas getting made. Obviously, most new writers should offer their own original work, except on those rare occasions in which they somehow optioned a quality story from another medium.

"What the agent wants to evaluate is what the writer brings to the table. It's very hard to tell how well you handled an adaptation unless they read the original material."

Even though science fiction or World War II epics might be a popular genre these days, Zald advises against writers delving into those areas to impress an agent or manager. Those pictures can cost upwards of $100 million–plus to produce. That's a big risk to take on a rookie.

"It's not impossible to make a sale in sci-fi, say," she added, "but that might make them take pause. Write something in a genre that's very popular and can make lots of money, but is not incredibly expensive to make."

If you would like to make further use of Zald's expertise, insight, and advice, you can contact her and her firm online at *www.screenwritersrm.com.*

BONUS SECTION

Agent/Writer Speak

We're going to deal with a lot of serious business in this book. Actually, we already have. So, I thought we should at least have a little tongue-in-cheek fun before we get in too deep. Before we move on to speak with some of the best agents in the industry, I wanted to set the mood and paint the picture of the lonely writer facing the entertainment industry giants, with only the single agent to watch her back. More importantly, I wanted to start introducing some of the terms a writer comes across while sitting in an agent's office.

So consider the next portion of this early chapter a sort of foreign language course. The subject of our lesson? Agent/Writer Speak.

Screenwriters strike other professionals within the entertainment industry as cynics. Perhaps some of us are—especially those who claim Hollywood is a town built on lies.

You can see where such an impression might come from easily. After all, movies aren't real. Their narratives create worlds where you want to live. But, deep down you know that the world is simply made of wood flats on some studio backlot. Just offset, out of view of the camera and the magic within its lens, there's some sweaty, smelly focus-puller named Earl who would immediately break the fictional mood.

These movies introduce you to beautiful, wondrous people. Their heroism and complexity transform them into beings you'd like to know—people you'd like to be. However, they're only actors. After the shoot wraps for the day, they sit around Jerry's Deli all night, resisting the urge to sample the cheesecake while smoking cigarettes and complaining to their friends about the casting supervisor that got them this latest lame gig.

It's no grand insightful scoop, but nothing is at it seems in Hollywood. Even the area itself is a myth. Hollywood is more of a state of mind than a city; a convenient label for the entertainment industry headquartered in Los Angeles. There really isn't much moviemaking going on in Hollywood anymore. It swarms with tourists comparing their shoe sizes to John Wayne's at Mann's Chinese Theater. It's choked with drifters scouring Hollywood Boulevard in hopes that it's really paved with gold. Most of that famed Hollywood glamour moved to a higher rent district like Brentwood. (Then the whole O. J. disaster happened, and I have no idea where the glamour moved after that.)

Whether you, the screenwriter, want to be a cynic or not, the fact sticks to your shoe like the chewed gum you kicked up outside the Chinese Theater. (It was stuck down inside John Wayne's bootprint.) The entire film industry is a beast built not on lies, but on make-believe.

If nothing in Hollywood is as it seems, it's because we prefer the artificial to the real. If the entertainment industry thrives on vague half-truths and broken partial promises, then perhaps the problem lies not in the stars lining the Walk of Fame, Horatio—but, rather, in ourselves. Real life offers comparatively little magic compared to the silver screen. The truth hurts—while the sort of woolly thinking the movie world and its minions offer feels much more comfortable when worn next to the skin.

Screenwriters turn to agents to guide us through the Hollywood fog. The problem is that the agent-screenwriter relationship can prove tenuous. Why? Writers are artists; agents are business people. Writers create stories. Agents sell the stories and the given writer's services as a client. Writers produce material, and agents deal in the selling and marketing of that product and the skill required to produce it.

That is not to say that agents can't be creative individuals in their own right. Quite the contrary. Agents must have some aesthetic or artistic sense. They need it to tell you as a would-be client apart from the hopeless scribblers of the world. If agents lacked any sense of storytelling or taste— or just a deep-seated love for entertainment media—they'd be off managing investment portfolios or working as assistant district attorneys somewhere.

But writers and agents are different breeds, and they often speak different languages. The writer spouts off about act breaks, character arcs, and beat structures. Agents go on about advances, royalties, and residuals. While these two separate professionals continue trying to communicate in their own languages, there are always the producers out there who speak in their equally cryptic code.

No one in the entertainment industry encounters more vagary and double talk than screenwriters and their agents. Everyone swirling around them separates their meaning from their actual words with a rich blend of pseudo-intellectual babble and clichéd buzzwords.

Entertainment industry professionals like the swirling, psycho, intellectual babble—all that cozy industry jargon. They enjoy it. It demonstrates their shared world view as screenwriters, agents, producers, directors, etc. It airs out the collective, three-act unconscious. Hollywood jargon serves as the passwords that allow writers and others to get inside the showbiz tree house. A turn of a phrase here and there can gain a pro access to the exclusive "writer's club"—next door to the Sacred Order of Water Buffaloes' lodge where Fred Flintstone hangs out.

But, for our purposes, we need to focus on Agent/Writer Speak— the amusing and atmospheric give and take that takes place between the two camps daily. While I'm not the absolute authority on Agent/Writer Speak, over the past few years I've immersed myself in a detailed study of some of the more common examples of this foreign language. OK. Actually, I just sit around and listen to it. However, it strikes me that, if you're a newcomer to the screenwriting game, you might find yourself lost as Agent/Writer Speak begins to swirl around you. As an aspiring newbie, you could easily run for the hills (and probably a more peaceful life) if you allowed the various double meanings to overheat your nervous system.

Writers are especially fond of and susceptible to the ups and downs of Agent/Writer Speak. Since everything in their world has a double meaning, writers must really sift through the various industry messages to figure out what's going on in their careers.

Writers like words too much to use Agent/Writer Speak all the time. They like to use words to communicate truth. But Agent/Writer Speak has nothing to do with truth. It's much too important for such trivialities. We as writers register the literal interpretation of "You did a great job" or "Who cranked out this stink burger? A typing chimp?"; all the while, we might be missing the subtle nuances truly intended in Agent/Writer Speak.

Ten Prime Examples of Agent/Writer Speak

Therefore, I prepared a brief primer on this mysterious professional foreign language. The following ten occurrences are not the only possible samples of Agent/Writer Speak. However, they do represent some of the more common sightings of this mysterious verbal animal. I will include the actual words, who is most likely to use them, why they're used, and what they really mean.

Before I begin, I include a brief and convenient disclaimer. Each one of these examples can, every now and then, mean precisely what they say. I'll demonstrate that in a couple of these examples. When the boring, old truth surfaces in Agent/Writer Speak, it's really not much fun and should be immediately buried by baffling bull quickly.

1) "We enjoyed reading your script, but it's not quite what we're looking for; it's not for us."

What does this mean? Possibly exactly what it says. Agents must use this line very often. If they're looking for the next *The Rock* to package and pitch to the major studios and you send them the next *How to Make an American Quilt,* you're out of luck. It's their job to tell you so.

Also, this line can be used to soften the blow. The agent deserves a little credit in this case. Nowhere in the script readers' handbook does it say you have to let the writer down easy. If the agent really thinks you don't so much write as type, she could really ruin your day by telling you so.

If you wrote a genuine landfill of a script (and all of us have that potential deep within us, waiting to burst forth), the reader has the First Amendment right to suggest that you take up flower arranging to avoid a life of panhandling on the Santa Monica Promenade! But we don't want to hear that. And no one with a single ounce of compassion or humility wants to say such a thing. So, they can use the old, "not quite what we were looking for" line to preserve your ego for the next go-around. If every rejection went for your artistic jugular, you'd take up something comparatively simple and lucrative—like writing books about screenwriting.

2) "I've optioned a couple of screenplays, and I'm ready to take the next step and seek representation."

This one is obviously used exclusively by writers. What does it mean? It's quite simple. He optioned more than one script to production companies for anywhere from one to several thousand dollars.

The subtext? The poor writer had just enough success to stick with screenwriting—but not nearly enough to make a living at it. Without an agent to push their careers along to the next step, writers are trapped—

not making enough money to feed themselves by writing, but making just enough to feed the dream. Someone in a position to make the big decisions decided the scripts were good enough to take at least a little risk. That immediately fuels the hope that a lucrative career in screenwriting lies just ahead for the scribe, just over the next rewrite.

You know what? Great! Enjoy the dilemma! It's really dramatic! It's the cynic's job to give up now! Fuel that dream! Feed the hope close to your bosom! Someone has to have the talent to succeed at this gig. It might as well be you. If you have to sling coffee at the Barnes & Noble (a proud retail outlet offering this fine book) for a while, so what? Do you want to have a real job, or do you want to write?! Get out there with your work and beat the bricks for the agent who can help propel your career out of this gray area.

3) "I think you should take another pass at it."

What does this really mean? You can probably figure this one out for yourself. Sorry, chief, but this script just ain't making it.

Simple words can replace this bit of Agent/Writer Speak: bad, vile, base, gross, poor, wretched, grungy, gruesome, measly, execrable, awful, shoddy, tacky, crummy, pathetic, unsatisfactory, faulty, flawed, incompetent, mangled, spoiled, scruffy, filthy, mangy, gunky, yucky, icky, foul, fetid, rank, unsound, tainted, corrupt, decaying, disordered, infected, envenomed, poisoned, septic, diseased, toxic, irremediable, incurable, depraved, accursed, heinous, sinful, shabby, contemptible, shameful, scandalous, disgraceful, woeful, grievous, unendurable, onerous, burdensome, fetid. (Oops. I used "fetid" twice there, didn't I? Sorry.)

Now, it's your job and your professional duty not to take any of these comments personally. The agent isn't saying any of those terms applies to you. You merely struck out on this draft. Hank Aaron didn't hit one out every time up either . . . though no one ever saw him hit a single and asked him to "take another swing at it." Face it. Screenwriting is strictly home run or strikeout. You nailed the screenplay, or you didn't. If not, try again.

4) "I haven't written anything lately. I'm waiting for the flow."

Don't get me started on this one. It's used exclusively by screenwriters and has nothing to do with agricultural irrigation! It really means the scribe in question is seriously deluded by artistic mumbo-jumbo—sophistry, rationalization, self-deception. There I go again! Sorry. Such pretension can easily lead to self-induced writer's block.

Sometimes, writing is work. That's why we get paid to do it! Fortunately, we all experience times when the work seems to come from beyond what we know. The words do indeed flow across the page, taking shape into scenes that really dance and characters a hundred times more interesting than we are! Hours pass like minutes in this ecstatic writer's trance. When finished, you bask in a sort of carnal afterglow. You feel genuinely wonderful about who you are, what you do, and how well you do it. At least I hope every writer experiences that. Otherwise, I may need to be tested for manic depression.

However, those moments of artistic bliss come somewhat infrequently. That's why we remember them so vividly and work in hope that such a moment will come down from on high again soon. The rest of the time we spend in front of our word processors comes down to struggling to find the right phrase and figuring out how to make the scenes work.

Writing (and rewriting) requires professional discipline to get something on paper. If it was an easy, always pleasurable, intellectual process, everyone would do it, not just "we few . . . we happy few!" Agents expect their writers to do that kind of work, not to simply write when the "flow"—or the muse, or whatever—decides to materialize.

5) "Follow your bliss."

I have no idea what this means. I've heard agents say it to me on occasion. If you know what it means, then here's your chance to contribute to my analysis of Agent/Writer Speak! Simply write Allworth Press with your analyses and bask in your brilliant analytical ability. (No, you don't get a dime for your letter! In fact, let's just forget the whole thing so my editors don't yell at me. Thank you.)

6) "I think the script should reflect more of the hero's journey."

Writers and agents both might let this one slip. It merely means that the reader of a particular work might have read Joseph Campbell's many books and believes his analysis of narrative. It might mean the reader read just one of Campbell's books. It might mean she saw a few minutes of Campbell interviewed on PBS by Bill Moyers while waiting for *Seinfeld* to come on. Finally, it could also mean that the reader once had a bowl of Campbell's Chicken & Stars soup and just wants to sound smart while rejecting your script. I usually opt for the last possibility.

7) "The script bogged down a little in the second act, right around beat nine."

Simply take my analysis of example six and substitute Syd Field for Joseph Campbell. No, Syd Field was never interviewed by Bill Moyers. Otherwise, the same idea applies—except for the soup. There is no Syd Field brand soup . . . yet. Maybe I'm onto something there! Get Syd Field on the phone!

8) "I was unable to identify the hero's praxis and hubris."

Oh, boy! Now, instead of Campbell or Field, the reader migrated over to Aristotle. Same cause and reason. Agents and writers! Stop reading all this analysis and just stick to the scripts! Sheesh!

9) "The writer sold out his/her vision in this script."

First, it often seems to me that writers are the only Hollywood professionals not allowed to make money with a clear conscience. It's an irony that writers are often teased for being the moody artists in the entertainment business—unable to view events with the proper business sense and detachment. When we adopt that brand of shrewd professional attitude, we're often accused of "selling out."

Fortunately, agents do not share this narrow view of writers' rights. In fact, it's their job to make sure writers make as much money as they can, as often as they can.

As for the sellout tag, anyone in the industry can say this particular line at one time or another. It means that your screenplay sold. You made a nice little bundle on it. Now, other writers might use this Agent/Writer Speak if they resent your success. Also, if the film that results from your script really bombs, the director, producer, or executive can use this one to blame you for tainting the process right out of the gate. If your agent uses it for some bizarre reason, it's time to move on to a new representative who wants your work to sell for as much as possible. It's a good thing you picked up this book!

Just remember that we write these things for an audience. After a script comes off your printer, cut it loose. It's not your kid. Hopefully, you can sell it and use its revenue to live while you produce more entertaining stories. If a script gets chewed to pieces, you can smile to the reader and say, "Eat all you want. I'll make more." Just be prepared to pay a royalty to the Frito-Lay Corporation.

10) "I think we've got a winner here."

What does this mean? Somebody likes your work!

Now you're in trouble. I chose this particular phrasing of approval because I've heard it applied to my work. I was writing on assignment for a production company. My agent approved the fruits of my labor. When I submitted my latest draft to the project's producer late in the pre-production process, I got back the very words you see above written in happy letters on the first page. The producer and I passed it along up the line to the executive producer and waited for the clouds to open up and allow the praise to rain down on our heads. I called my agent and told her to prepare for the onrush of big money deals to pour my way.

When I got the same "winning" script back from the executive producer, the first page was crossed out in red ink with "lousy" written over the producer's praise. Moral? Today's hero is tomorrow's pariah. Your work can drift in and out of favor depending on budgetary restraints, market trends, or whatever the reader had for lunch. A producer might love a script. The director could find the need to rewrite half of it. An actor could then get it and wonder what the producer and the director were thinking. Then, the actor can take it back to Jerry's Deli and rewrite it in cigarette ash while waiting for his agent to answer the phone.

Your agent needs to be the one source of constant support for your work. Once you sign with an individual rep, you should not have to worry that she will be yet another source of criticism and rejection. Yes, reps can give you notes on your work to improve the stories, but you should not fear a cold shoulder from your agent when so many other folks in the industry will be more than happy to offer you that chilly body part. No, an agent will not hold your hand, but her criticism should always be constructive.

The best you can do is fiercely hang on to your sense of humor and roll with the constant stream of notes and suggestions. If you're too thin-skinned for screenwriting, you can always go into politics.

So, as these ten examples of Agent/Writer Speak fade into the mist of Movie Land, we are again faced by the cynics among us. They shake their fists and protest that every one of these examples is exactly what they charged them to be—lies! It seems no one writing or reading scripts really says what they mean! Lies! Lies! Lies! (Wait . . . One more!) LIES!

I can only respond, "Sure . . . if you insist on being literal about everything!"

That's what's so wonderful about out professional lexicon! It's an art and an abstraction—like the task of screenwriting itself. It's a mystery wrapped in riddle covered by an enigma. It's not to be taken literally! What fun would that be? I wouldn't want to trade in the vague facts and figures swirling around our chosen careers in showbiz! Other professions don't get to play the way we do. That's why I write books about showbiz!

If your dentist pokes that stainless steel hook in your mouth and says, "You have a deep cavity in your right bicuspid," he's not making a comment on modern social ills! That's what he means! If your accountant tallies up the receipts for the last fiscal year and can't get any words out between the fits of bitter, pitying laughter, she's not revealing a deep-seated psychological insecurity brought on by an overprotective mother! She means you'd better take that second job at Barnes & Noble! (I love those fine people, so put this book up high and centered on the shelf!)

No double meaning to be found anywhere in this example! Literal. Factual. Serviceable. Boring. We need double meaning and symbolism in our scripts—and in our business lives. That's what makes what we do more fun that performing root canals or doing taxes.

In the end, if you don't buy any of this, if you think it's all nonsense, or if you're convinced that there has to be some other, more eloquent explanation, congratulations! Now, you're starting to catch on.

CHAPTER REVIEW

- For a beginning writer, signing on with a boutique or smaller mid-size agency is usually better than pursuing representation with the big name agencies.
- Agents have territories or companies they focus on so they know what producer or executive is looking for what kind of material.
- Some agents and development executives disagree about whose responsibility it is to refer talent. Agents would like producers and executives to refer talent to them, but producers and execs would prefer agents to do the talent hunting.
- One of the biggest mistakes writers can make is pursuing representation before they are ready. They need to have enough spec material of a high enough quality before making any inquiries.
- Referrals are unofficial recommendations from industry professionals that can make an agent stand up and take notice of you and your work. Referrals are the lifeblood of this business.

MOTION PICTURE AGENTS

No matter what agency you're from, your reputation rests on the material you send out and the writers you represent.

During the days of the multimillion-dollar spec sales in the mid 1980s, selling a motion picture screenplay became the writer's Holy Grail—that one-shot, e-Ticket ride to lifelong financial freedom and artistic affirmation. Even though those sorts of spec sales are very rare, writers gave up trying to tackle the next great novel or play and flocked to screenwriting in droves.

So, how do the agents who represent motion picture writers deal with the rarified air of the screenwriting market? We turn to two busy and successful agents for their insights: Mary Kimmel and Steven Fisher.

Mary Kimmel, Preferred Artists Agent

Mary Kimmel represents feature writers and long-form television scribes out of the Encino offices of Preferred Artists. We met over breakfast at the homey French Bistro, Chez Nouz, in Sherman Oaks.

Kimmel became a motion picture agent because she loves the movies. She collects movie memorabilia, scripts, and other knickknacks. She expects her clients to bring the same kind of passion to their work and career because the spec market is perhaps the toughest, most exclusive literary field. Spec sales are few and far between when compared to the sheer number of people writing feature screenplays.

"There are so many Internet sites and chat rooms dedicated to the movies and the business," Kimmel said, "In addition to reading the trades, writers need to keep tabs on those resources. They should treat it as research—but they should also enjoy it because it is their chosen field.

"One of the most interesting things for me with writers is that they have an incredible idea to write a great script, and they may finish it and pull it off brilliantly," she said. "But, they might run into the hard truth that there are five out there like it. Maybe there's no market it for it—especially now when spec sales are tougher than ever. You need to have access to information to answer those questions."

Even if a writer makes a sale, Kimmel cautions against worshiping the power of one's own prose. Spec scripts are invariably rewritten, especially when they come from first-time writers:

"If you don't want your story rewritten, write a stage play or a novel. You can't forget the business side of screenwriting."

And that business is headquartered in Southern California. While some movie agents will work with out-of-town clients, Kimmel keeps her clientele local.

"If you don't live here, it's very difficult to stay up on the industry and know the ins and outs. Yes, you can get a subscription to *Scr(i)pt Magazine, Creative Screenwriting Journal, Scenario* or something like that, but it's not the same. I see out of town people not only ill-informed on the business, but ill-informed on formatting, genre, and other key issues."

Overeager = Underqualified

Kimmel says the lack of foreknowledge by first-time writers can come from their own overeager desire to break in. They work so hard on their writing and want so much to make their mark that they fail to pick up on some industry lessons.

She cites one example in which a writer sent a script to a small agency. Rather than reject the material, the agent in question held onto the script, promising to work with it, and steer it to the right producers in the future.

"I had to tell that writer, 'It's a pass.'" Kimmel said. "If the agency wanted to do something with the script, it would. But, as a writer, you're looking for any positive sign.

"The truth is that agents get so much material that a feature writer really has to know how to pitch. Get your idea out there quickly and passionately and make an agent really take notice. Make your material stand out from all of the rest."

Kimmel bemoaned how few writers understand the necessity of good pitching: "Once you finish the writing process, you must change hats and become a marketer. You need to develop a sales presentation.

Make it exciting. Get to the point. Don't go over back story; get to the story itself. Distill it down to the essence.

"The whole idea of a pitch is to get someone's attention quickly and completely. I'll sometimes ask would-be clients to pitch for me before I sign them to see how they handle it—and how they handle making and taking comments from other people."

Kimmel added that she needs to know her writers are on the ball before she settles in to work with them:

"Before I go out with a script, and I start making my calls, I have to have my sixty-second pitch ready because I don't want my script to arrive someplace and just sit. If my writers can help come up with a good way to pitch a script, I'll use it! I'll involve them as I come up with my strategy. If I like their ideas, I'll use them. If I don't, I won't—and I'll tell them why not.

"If the writer isn't able to provide a hook, it makes it that much more difficult for me. When a writer has that captive audience and can't explain what the story is, that's the worst. They should know their work better than anyone else and be able to show that."

She added, "That's part of the problem when a writer sets out to find an agent way too soon. Your body of work has to be ready, but your understanding of the business and the professional skills needed have to be there as well."

Kimmel does work with some new writers to help them develop their story and marketing skills. For example, she listed a school teacher and an attorney that each wrote a couple of scripts. She identified talent in their work and decided to "hip-pocket" them. That practice allows Kimmel to develop a writer's work without officially signing the writer to an agency contact. It offers both parties the advantage of working together without being legally tied to one another—sort of like an engagement between a fledgling couple.

"Hip-pocketing allows me to help more writers than I could possibly sign. I can offer advice and assistance, developing the writers' work and guiding their career. But, if I signed every writer that I assist in that manner, my client listing would be too large. When an agent hip-pockets and works with someone like that, you just hope the person busts out and finds success.

"Then, you also have to trust that people will stay with you when they're hot because they could go to a bigger agency. It's happened in the past that smaller agencies lose clients like that to bigger agencies. If successful, a writer should expect to be seduced. Bigger agencies call the practice cruising or coasting. It will always happen. There was a time in which the big agencies and smaller companies operated under an understood code that the big fish would not go after the small house's clients.

"It's different if the client decides to pursue other representation, but you hope other firms don't try to steal away talent you've worked for sometimes years to develop. Unfortunately, these days all bets are off. We have one big-name client who is constantly wooed by other firms. Fortunately, he's stayed loyal to us."

Kimmel explained, "I had a client who wrote and directed an award-winning short that got into Sundance. He made his living making industrial videos, but they were so funny. With one camera and no money, he could make wonderful films. Warner Bros. was interested in him as result of that work. Even though we got him into a position to warrant that studio interest, we lost him to ICM.

"If there's heat on you, every agency wants to be in a position to field offers for your services. So, the interest is from the outside. You're not generating it. It's coming from other people, and agencies want a piece of that. If you're not generating that kind of buzz, a bigger agency has less reason to keep you around. A smaller firm is more willing to build a career and work with you through the ups and downs."

So, in the end, Kimmel urges writers to consider that an agent is taking a risk and making an investment when agreeing to take on a new client:

"No matter what agency you're from, your reputation rests on the material you send out and the writers you represent."

Steven Fisher, APA agent

Steven Fisher served for years with Renaissance, a Hollywood-based literary agency for which he represented film and television movie writers, as well as authors. In recent years, he moved to the larger and more prestigious APA overlooking fabled Sunset Boulevard.

When I asked Fisher how he answered the classic Catch-22 we mentioned earlier (no agent until you get work, no work without an agent), he was kind enough to compliment me on my insightful question. He didn't have a magic bullet answer to get around the dilemma, but he did have a couple of useful suggestions.

"There are a few ways to overcome it," Fisher said. "One way is to place highly in a screenwriting contest. You can drop names if you even placed in a competition, and that can open a door.

"Also, use anyone you know, or anyone who knows anybody. Get them to read your script and ask for recommendations of agents you can send it to with their approval. With any luck, they'll make the call for you. That sort of referral is the most useful and the quickest way to an agent.

"I signed my most recent client off a referral by an entertainment attorney who I knew in the past. I let him know I was looking to sign people, and he recommended someone."

Finally, Fisher suggested contacting production companies directly. Some will read unsolicited material, and, at the very least, they might give you good feedback.

"If you get any sort of positive notes or responses," he said, "you can contact agents with copies of those letters the show the strong points of your work. If it's a gushy enough letter, and it's someone I know, it'll get my attention."

As an agent, Fisher represents his clients with one hand while he feeds the industry with material with the other. But whom does he serve first and foremost?

"My primary responsibility is to serve my clients. I see my role as facilitating my clients in any way I can to make their career goals happen.

"Conversely, if I feel the client is asking for something unreasonable for where they are in the business, I need to discuss my concerns with the client. While my primary goal is serving them, it's also important for an agent and agency to maintain integrity in their relationships. Agents are prevailed upon a lot by clients with out-of-whack expectations. In that case, I need to think long and hard how to get around that."

Sometimes that overblown expectation can be as simple as a hack thinking he can write. There is no way that would-be artist will believe his own incompetence, yet the agent has to confront it on occasion to clear a desk. What does Fisher do in that ugly circumstance?

"I've read some awful, abysmal material. But, I'm not going to be that blunt with the writers because there's a difference between honesty and cruelty. Your script is your baby when you send it out into the world. I don't want to be cruel with people because, with writers, a little criticism goes a long way. So I use criticism sparingly. I won't say something is good if it's not."

Fisher added, "The tricky thing is when I ask myself, 'Is it equally cruel to feed a delusion?' I don't think it's up to me to tell people what to do with their lives and careers.

"When I'm reading a script and don't like it, I put it down after forty or fifty pages because it's not going to get any better. Is it up to me to tell that writer that he doesn't have a career? No. Maybe it's an early script for him and he's really progressed since then. Maybe he can get much better and jumped the gun by sending something out too early. It's not fair for me to say or even imply that someone was in the wrong career. I'd have to be much more acquainted with a writer."

Fisher is not so slow to shoot down ideas or pitches that are not ready for the screen or that lack some key dramatic element. If a pitch lacks originality, irony, humor, or other appealing attributes, Fisher will shoot it down and let the writer move on to the next idea. So, it helps if you, as a writer, have that next idea to jump to in any situation.

BONUS SECTION

Ageism

Throughout this book, we will encounter the ugly term "ageism." It refers to a subtle form of discrimination in Hollywood that prevents writers of advancing age from getting work. This sort of numbers-based prejudice might make it easier for young writers to get ahead in the business, but it drums out experienced and talented men and women before their prime.

If you ask many industry professionals, agents only want to help writers under forty-five years of age. Some agents have a few clients who are older because they earned the right to grow older along with their representatives. Otherwise, ageism makes no sense because what has age got to do with writing, other than improving it?

Steven Fisher agreed with the logic behind the "an older writer is a better writer" theory, but he said it has its pitfalls:

"So much of this business is relationships and the connections people experience when they're sitting in that pitch room. If it was just a guy sitting at home working on a word processor and sending pages into his agent, it wouldn't be a problem. But, part of building a career as a writer is getting writers out there and having them meet all of the people. When you're putting them in a room with someone ten to fifteen years younger than they are and they don't have the chemistry, it's an uncomfortable and unfortunate mix."

According to the Writers Guild, 56 percent of its membership is older than forty. That's 4,500 members. Many of those members find it difficult to get an agent to read their material if it is known that they are that age.

Older writers can find themselves rejected by agents solely because of their age. Imagine the feeling of hearing your preexisting agent say she could no longer represent you because you passed forty. Most writers understand the agent's problem from the agent's P.O.V. The agent's attitude is that if she represents an older writer and invests time and talent in promoting that writer, the writer might be too old to have a long and fruitful career ahead of him. The agent might not get a big payoff, but the agent needs to understand that the older writer brings some important assets to the table: experience in life and writing skill, maturity, and, perhaps, useful and practical experience in other aspects of the entertainment field. The writer's vast experience in other entertainment industry fields provides him with greater depth and insights into the craft of writing.

There is an ongoing effort in the industry to end ageism. I urge older writers to keep trying to make their mark, as we all hope this unfortunate prejudice will continue to fade from industry practice.

CHAPTER REVIEW

- The spec market is the toughest literary field in the entertainment business. Seemingly, everybody writes features and wants to write for the movies. You and your agent need to make your material stand out from the crowd.

- Agents genuinely rely on referrals, so you're doing them and yourself a favor when you use such a reference to make contact.

- Approach an agent with more than one script and even more ideas so you always have a backup if your initial pitch fails.

- Make your agent's job easier by preparing a good pitch and helping her to market your material.

- Hip-pocketing allows an agent to work with writers without signing them to a contract.

- Agents take a risk when they sign a new client. Make your work and professional behavior worth your agent's effort.

Television Agents

*The people who keep writing and develop their passion
are the winners who get an agent and get a job.*

There are more TV shows on every
season than movies released throughout an entire calendar year. So,
many writers think TV can serve as more steady, if less lucrative, employment. Other scribes remember watching the *Six Million Dollar Man* or
Wonder Woman in awe back in the seventies and want to see their talent
streaming out of that little glowing box in the living room.

TV agents face an entirely different set of challenges and practices
compared to straight motion picture agents. Their work can prove more
seasonal and often more pressured as they face limited time windows to
get their clients work every TV season. Tammy Stockfish and Beth Bohn
were kind enough to take a breath with such deadlines looming to share
their views on TV lit agenting. The staffing season runs from about
March to mid-May (though cable and syndicated shows staff earlier), and
every TV agent scrambles to find work for her stables. Both Bohn and
Stockfish graciously agreed to interviews during that busy time.

Tammy Stockfish, Agent with Broder, Kurland, Webb, and Uffner

During an interview at her Beverly Hills office (under the long and
unlikely shadow of the Playboy HQ), Stockfish discussed the daily ins
and outs of a TV agent's life.

Rather than go through a blow-by-blow description of how she
signed her entire client roster, I simply asked how she signed her most
recent writer:

"Through a referral by an ex-client, immediately before staffing season," Stockfish said. "It was a 'right-place-at-the-right-time situation' in which I signed an unproduced, baby writer following the referral. That said, most of my clients come to me through referrals—from pre-existing clients, other agents, or producers."

Acknowledging that it can often seem as difficult to get such a referral as it is to find actual representation, Stockfish tackled my favorite Catch-22: "can't get anywhere without an agent . . . can't get an agent without getting anywhere."

"The truth of the matter is it's one of the hardest things to accomplish as a writer—getting an agent. Rather than merely writing a good query letter, which can help, it's more often a matter of standing out from all the other writers looking for representation. Do you have anything already produced? Have you managed to get on staff somewhere already?

"I also look for education on a résumé. I admit not every agent does that or cares about that, but I consider that very important. Do you have a track record rooted in English, journalism, or film school? That can make a difference."

Still, how does a TV writer get such an experienced rep to return a phone call—let alone read a spec script? Stockfish offered a handful of unlikely, yet very clever tricks that could help any writer at least get a foot in the door:

"Endear yourself to the agent's assistant. The assistant is in charge of the script slush pile and call-sheet. She can do you a favor if she likes you, believes you're sincere, and wants to help."

It's important to add that many agent assistants will also become agents one day themselves. Indeed, an assistant position is often the first, best path to a career as an agent—especially at the Big Houses. So, while you might not catch the eye of a certain established agent, you might earn the respect of that assistant. If the assistant's career path leads to a corner office someday, she might want to add you to the stable.

Stockfish added, "Out of sight is out of mind for an agent because there is so much going on all the time. The assistant can help you out of that problem.

"Also, I advise prospective clients to learn an agent's work patterns. For example, most agents make calls in the morning and return and receive calls in the afternoon. If an aspiring writer makes a call to an agent (and writers better not make too many calls to any one agent), he should do so when most likely to reach the agent."

What was that about making too many calls? We'll visit this topic more than once on these pages, but your passion for progress and success can often inadvertently turn you into a first class pain in the neck. You want to seem dedicated and professional—but never at the cost of becoming an insecure pest.

MY OWN PERSONAL OVEREAGER "OOPS"

I offer an example of "going too far" from my youth. I was trying too hard to earn my first agent for some video game scripts I was writing for a couple of different companies. I thought I had a good shot at earning the attention and favor of a top-flight news media agent from one of the Big Houses. (No, that agent does *not* appear in this book).

So I wrote that agent a query letter, sent along some samples, and started making calls. The agent explained that he liked my work, but had nothing for me at that time. He invited me to get back in touch soon and remind him that I was out there in case anything came up.

So I called the following week. Twice. I was too young and too eager. I failed to realize that by "stay in touch," the agent meant maybe give him a call in a month or so. I knew I had gone too far when he mentioned, "Why do you call me more often than my actual clients?"

Ouch. This guy wouldn't be signing me now. He wouldn't hip-pocket me. He wouldn't dump water on me if I was on fire. I went from promising young writer to unprofessional pest, and I was dead in the water. Don't make the same mistake. Later in the book, we'll look at contact etiquette, but try to keep your cold calls to maybe one every couple of weeks.

Stockfish agreed with my take on the thin line between passion and pest. She experienced more than one would-be client who seemed just too eager—and a few who almost crossed the line to literary stalker. It's easier for writers in the Los Angeles area to cross that line because all they need to do is pick up a phone. It's one of the few areas in which a writer outside LA might have an advantage over an in-town talent. He might save a dime or two by not making so many long-distance calls, relying more on letters and an occasional phone check-in—thus, becoming less of a pest.

Otherwise, Stockfish had a couple of different takes on whether or not a writer needs to live in Southern California to make it in Hollywood:

"Anyone who's dedicated enough doesn't necessarily have to live in town, but it is definitely an advantage to live in LA. As I said, out of sight is out of mind, and if you're not here, you miss out on a lot of opportunities. For example, big meetings can happen here in a snap. A writer needs to be here to take advantage of that meeting."

So it helps to live in LA. But prospective TV writers need to keep another issue in mind when considering moving into the business. Novelists or playwrights can write at any age. In fact, barring failing health, they probably improve with age, like good brandy. Poets or journalists can work well into their twilight years. But there does tend to be an ideal age for a television writer.

"Most successful television writers tend to be younger," Stockfish explained. "You can be a little older and still write features, but it's easier for me to find opportunities for a younger writer. It doesn't mean that an older person can't be a writer, but he might have to re-evaluate what kind of writer he wants to be."

HOW YOUNG IS YOUNG?

For example, most top sitcom writers are fresh out of college. It seems the entire staff of *The Simpsons* just fell out of Harvard. They polish some spec sitcom work before they hit LA, or find a gig as a writer's assistant, and work their way onto staff before the age of twenty-three. One-hour episodic writers can run a little older, but the hard truth is that, oftentimes, a TV writer is considered washed up by thirty-five. So if you're staring thirty or forty in the face and thinking about writing for TV, you might want to consider rolling those ideas into feature scripts or novels. TV networks and producers look to attract a young audience with disposable income to lure lucrative sponsors. They fear that older writers won't communicate well with the kids out there, so the kids get the TV writing gigs.

But, if you still fit the age requirements, or you simply don't care what the supposed restrictions are and you want to break the age craze's glass ceiling, how do you best go about attracting a TV agent? Stockfish's response was right on the nose, even if potentially unpleasant for some TV writers to read:

"*Pay your dues!* Experience, information, and knowledge are the keys," she said. "Watch the changes in the business. Follow your market. Use the Internet. Join writers' groups. Know what you want to write and what genre you want to work in before you begin writing your spec material."

Also, would-be TV writers can break into the business as writer's assistants. They literally work side by side with working TV scribes, almost as an apprentice works beside a carpenter or plumber. Following this discussion with Tammy Stockfish, we will take a brief look at the life of a writer's assistant and the value it might offer you as an aspiring television writer.

Once writers have done all that intense work and know exactly what kind of television program they want to crank out, then the real toil starts. Stockfish insisted that a young TV writer needs more than one good spec script to get an agent's attention.

"You need three or four good specs for the top shows in your genre," she said. "Specs from mainstream shows—and those specs have to shine because there are smaller writing staffs on shows now. Budgets are always tight, and some producers now keep fewer writers on staff and assign those writers more work. So spots are tight.

"Most importantly, write your passion. If it's on the paper, it will find a home."

So Stockfish would seem to indicate that there is a legitimate opportunity for aspiring writers to find that agent who will push their careers to the next level.

"Most agents want to work with more established writers for the most part. This *is* a business. We all have to make a living, but we also need to have baby writers as clients, too. One day, those writers will be in the business, too.

"I feel for young writers," Stockfish added. "I know how tough it can be, but this is a business of persistence and aggression. Stick with it. Keep in touch. Watch the industry." Like everything else in this business, you need to outline a game plan. Don't be afraid to ask for advice in preparing yourself and deciding how best to go about getting an agent. Get your spec scripts ready. Prepare yourself like you would for a job, because being a writer *is* a job.

"Finally, tell the truth. Don't blow smoke, because an agent can smell it!"

For years, Stockfish has appeared at writers' conferences to talk with aspiring writers on how to develop their work and career—and, of course, how to get an agent. Why does she give her time to advise aspiring writers like this?

"I think it's important to give back to the business. I see how many aspiring writers are out there. The more we can give them from inside the industry, the better their work looks when it finally comes to the industry."

Beth Bohn, APA

A native of Wisconsin, APA's Beth Bohn earned a degree in nursing from the University of Wisconsin. After deciding that nursing was not the career for her, she went into sales and marketing.

She explained, "I really didn't know what I wanted to do, but I knew I liked food. So I went into sales for the food industry. They were looking for someone who wouldn't cost them too much. So it was a great opportunity for me to learn. From there, I went to a cosmetics company and did the same sort of work.

"I was always searching for something that I was passionate about, and it wasn't that job. So I went to a seminar that dealt with how to find a career that you love. I loved watching TV and really wanted to watch TV as part of my job. I also loved doing sales and deals on the telephone. From there, I determined that becoming an agent would be something to look at further.

"In the early nineties, I negotiated out of my corporate job and started temping in the entertainment industry. I temped at the Agency in the casting and literary divisions. I decided I preferred literary and moved to the Irv Schechter Agency as an assistant."

From there, Bohn's path took her to the Turtle Agency, the Paul Kohner Agency, and eventually to the budding Big House firm, APA. Now she represents television writers, directors, and producers for one-hour series, sitcoms, and reality-based shows.

"I think one of the most important things for any agent is to be able to juggle their duties," Bohn said. "There are so many demands on an agent from her clients and the firm's management. A successful agent can push all the distractions aside and really focus on who they need to call, submit to, and what priorities they need to be on top of that particular day.

"My days can really vary, depending on the season and what the follow-up needs. The important things to remember are who I already submitted to, who I should follow up on, and who I need to call and introduce clients to around town. Also, an agent needs to make sure that they are totally focused when the time comes to negotiate the deals."

Surprisingly, Bohn said there isn't a significant difference in business practices as she moves from one-hour drama to sitcom to reality shows:

"The sales principles are the same. It's hearing what the producers (or buyers) need and seeing who you have that fits that need. In the reality TV world, it's a smaller community. Most started out as runners or PAs for Dick Clark or Merv Griffin. They all know each other.

"With primetime half-hours, they obviously look for people who are funny and can write funny material. In one-hour dramas, they look for someone who can write for the medium because it really depends on what the show needs. Across the whole realm, it comes down to the writers having material that matches the individual show."

While looking for new clients that fill those ever-present needs, Bohn looks for writers who are truly prepared for the rigors of the writing life.

"People who are prepared have more than one sample. I find that when new writers get to their third spec script, that's when the business starts making sense to them with regard to their writing. By the same time, they have pulled together their support group of people who they can trust to read their work and give them good notes.

"One difficulty that I have when people send me their work," Bohn said, "is that they're writing their specs hoping to please others. Their voice doesn't come through. When I read something original, it'll be wonderful, creative, and unique. For writers, it's important that their spec script stand out the same way."

Bohn offered the example of a glut of *Ally McBeal* and *Frasier* spec scripts received over recent months. They all feature similar plots and offer no surprises. While, without a doubt, the writers each believed they'd finally found a truly original angle, their fellow scribes were on a similar wavelength because none of them was writing from the heart. They were all writing what they thought the market wanted.

"A spec script has to stand out. When you read it, it has to be different from any of the other specs I've read of that show. When producers read an original spec script, they'll want to meet the writers that have the fresh ideas. They need someone to come up with really creative ideas."

THE REFERRAL CONNECTION

As for how to contact and best earn an agent's attention, Bohn said it sometimes happens on its own:

"Writers who really want to write, as they travel through their journey of writing, never giving up their networking. They will somehow eventually create a relationship with an agent or producer who can refer them. The writers who don't encounter those opportunities haven't been doing it long enough or focusing on their networking skills. Maybe they haven't been going to seminars or writers' groups.

"It always amazes me that the people who keep writing and developing their passion are the writers who get an agent and get the writing jobs."

Bohn admits that her schedule does not allow her to take on new writers. She doesn't take unsolicited material. Writers are usually referred to her.

"Writers need to watch and study the shows they want to write. They must become students of the craft. As new writers, they need to experiment with different writing styles. Write a show you love, not a show you hate because your agent or friend suggested it. You really need to explore the marketplace and discover your voice in it."

Bohn brushed aside the question of ageism, again citing dedication as the secret to success:

"The people who really throw themselves into the business are the people who will get ahead. I find people right out of college who are not serious about what they're doing, so they screw up and hurt their career. On the other hand, you might find an older writer who really knows his craft and has made the connections he needs. It comes down to the desire and the talent."

She insisted that the same standards carry over to agents as well. A writer wants to find a rep who is passionate about him and will put in the time:

"It takes a tremendous amount of work to introduce a young writer around town," Bohn said. "Whatever size agency you sign with, you need to find someone who loves your work and gets your writing so that they will be passionate and fight for you. There are a lot of calls an agent has to make to guarantee a writer is read and considered."

IF YOU WANT A JOB, SMILE

Bohn added that personality can play a huge role in the entertainment business. No one likes to work for or with someone who's unpleasant—especially in "La-La-Land." So it helps to have a personality people enjoy being around.

"My assistant will tell me when someone is rude or hostile to them. No one wants that sort of behavior around them. You select people who you would enjoy talking to and working for."

Bohn agreed with Stockfish that most TV writers need to be here. She wouldn't say it's the end-all of TV writing, but it obviously helps. With so much television production now going on in Canada for budgetary reasons, many TV writers relocate North of the Border, rather than slugging it out in Southern California.

Bohn closed with, "I'm more impressed with writers when they are not focusing on, 'I need an agent.' They should focus on what they're working on. When writers are talking about writing, it's the coolest thing to see how excited they are. It gives me a good idea of the kind of person they are. That helps me determine if I want to represent them.

"When I start hearing a writer talking about his story ideas, as an agent, it gives me an idea of whether or not I want to represent him."

BONUS SECTION

Writer's Assistant

Hollywood is full of aspiring writers. Every one of them thinks he has that one great spec script inside him that will kick in the studio doors and allow him to quit his job making copies in the mailroom or slinging java at Starbucks.

In reality, writers need to pay their dues in Hollywood like every other entertainment industry professional—unless they have a famous relative tucked away somewhere in the business. Baby writers usually need to gain experience in the different aspects of Hollywood writing and marketing before they can execute a top-shelf script. But how do they get that kind of insight while busting their ink-stained tails to keep body and soul together?

One of the most direct routes to that insider's scoop is grabbing a job as a writer's assistant to an already established film or TV writer. An assistant gets to play a small part in the creative process while watching over a veteran writer's shoulder as big-time Hollywood marches past.

Throughout this book, agents (especially those in the television field) cite a gig as an assistant as a useful path into the industry. Assistants learn how scripts come together from the inside out, and that experience often makes those assistants more reliable as young writers.

What exactly does a writer's assistant do? It depends on the writer employing the assistant. Duties can range from interesting creative tasks and involvement to clerical tasks to personal business. On television series staffs, the assistant sits in on writers' meetings and takes notes so the others can kick ideas around more freely. For feature or MOW writers, an assistant would work more one-on-one with the screenwriter in charge, tracking drafts or copyediting scripts. It's all based on how the writer handles his work and life.

The most interesting and challenging duties a writer's assistant can hope for are revisions and research. The latter is obvious. If a screenwriter is making six or seven figures per script, writing time is money—a lot of money. It's much easier for that writer to pay someone else to examine historical texts, list types of modern weapons, or discover if this week's script title has ever been used before.

As far as revisions go, don't think "creative." Think "saving the writer work." When A-list writers perform a script revision, they are pulling down a hefty check to rewrite a screenplay. As a writer's assistant, when you perform revisions for that writer, you're catching typos, misspellings, or continuity errors.

In some cases with older writers, revision means conquering the veteran writer's technophobia. Some current screenwriters at the tail end of their careers came into the business composing their work on typewriters. Some even wrote their first drafts by hand and let someone from the studio typing pool or a "Kelly Girl" bang it into script format. Writer's assistants are this era's answer to the typing pool. The veteran writer may write his scripts in some old-fashioned form and ask you to type them into the computer.

When older writers look at a Mac or a PC screen and see word processing software like MS Word or WordPerfect (or even specific screenwriting programs like Final Draft or Scriptware), they may need you to make sense of it for them. Do it—quickly! You'll spare the wizened scribe a mild panic attack, and you'll save yourself the story of how, in the old days, you didn't need these newfangled computers to write a picture, and how the writer used to walk to the studio in the snow every day, uphill, both ways, etc.

Some of a writer's assistant duties can stretch into the clerical realm. You could be asked to take notes at meetings for studio execs. Or, if they tape the meeting, you might have to transcribe the notes. This requires screenwriters to think on their feet—and allows them to look important in front of the studio execs. They all have assistants, and if a writer wants to be a player, he has to have one, too! Whether or not you want one when you make your break is entirely up to you.

If a writer is working on a single spec or writing on assignment, a writer's assistant's life can prove fairly smooth. However, more often than not, a writer is working on multiple projects. Any one of a number of stories in various stages of development could be submitted all around town. It's often the assistant's job to track all those submissions to make sure the right title and correct draft go to the right producer.

In some rare, dreaded cases, a writer's assistant's duties slide into the sordid realm of personal assistant duties. The jobs are separate, and in a perfect world, they stay that way. Still, on occasion, even the most skilled writer's assistant will be asked to make a delivery, order lunch, or pick up a Prozac prescription.

Those duties can be a blow to an educated assistant's fragile ego, but perform them anyway. Consider them favors for someone helping to pay your bills. If you're spending more time taking care of personal business than handling creative tasks, you may want to think about looking for a new job.

So a writer's assistant position is a true "pay your dues" sort of gig. But what's in for you besides a paycheck ranging from $10 to $15 per hour? Hopefully, you can pick up some vital firsthand education on how the industry really works. An assistantship allows young writers to watch the slings and arrows of writing for Hollywood from the battle's sidelines without having to wield a weapon before they are ready. It's sort of like playing squire to the established writer's knight.

You can pick up insight on the draft and revision process, the pitch routine, writing on assignment, and the screenwriting marketplace. You can also prepare yourself for some of the less pleasant aspects of professional screenwriting, such as dealing with impatient, inconsistent producers and the endless mill of studio notes.

If your boss likes you (which is never a given if you consider how temperamental writers can be), he might be willing to read your work and refer it to producers and agents looking for new talent. But don't fool yourself. No writer will take bread off his table in order to give your career a break. You will get the crumbs the established writer doesn't want, but those are crumbs you are probably starving for, and wouldn't get without such an opportunity.

Finally, if you end up working for a writer you admire, you may find inspiration or technique in his craft that improves your own screenplays. No writer's assistant holds such a job for the sheer joy of assisting! You take the support role in hopes that it will enhance your own writing opportunities down the road. If you're lucky enough to fall in with a writer willing to serve as a mentor on the side, the job might just make you a better writer.

BONUS SECTION
Television Series Contact List

In addition to its other outstanding services, the WGA also publishes a contact list for television series. If you're still struggling to find your personal representation, but you have your TV specs piled up alongside a desire to share your work with the industry, this list offers a good start on the road to making your own production contacts.

Many shows will not accept unsolicited scripts. But some will answer the phone and show a little friendliness to an aspiring TV writer. At the very least, they may offer you a submission agreement allowing you to submit your spec work for consideration. According to the WGA, the information in this list is the most current information available. The person named as the contact for each series is not necessarily the one empowered to make commitments to writers. Information listed on the TV Market List is current as of the date of publication. Information is subject to change without notice.

- *3rd Rock from the Sun*
  Comedy   30 min.   Tue   8:30 PM   NBC
  www.3rdrock.com   Carsey Werner Productions, LLC
  Orit Schwartz, (818) 655-6057

- *7th Heaven*
  Drama   60 min.   Mon   8:00 PM   WB
  www.thewb.com   Spelling Television, Inc.
  Jonathan Schnack, (323) 634-3761

- *Ally McBeal*
  Drama   60 min.   Mon   9:00 PM   FOX
  www.fox.com   David E. Kelley Productions, Inc.
  Pam Jackson, (310) 727-2100

- *Angel*
  Drama   60 min.   Tue   9:00 PM   WB
  www.thewb.com   Twentieth Century Fox
  Meredyth Smith, (310) 579-5225

- *Becker*
  Comedy   30 min.   Mon   9:30 PM   CBS
  www.cbs.com   Paramount Pictures Corporation
  Chris Porterfield, (323) 956-2700

- *Buffy the Vampire Slayer*
  Drama   60 min.   Tue   8:00 PM   WB
  www.buffy.com   Twentieth Century Fox
  David Goodman, (310) 579-5100

- *Charmed*
  Drama   60 min.   Thu   9:00 PM   WB
  www.thewb.com   Spelling Television, Inc.
  Deborah Greaney, (818) 673-1100

- *Chicago Hope*
  Drama   60 min.   Thu   9:00 PM   CBS
  www.cbs.com   Twentieth Century Fox
  Henry Bromell, (310) 369-2180

- *City of Angels*
  Drama   60 min.   Wed   8:00 PM   CBS
  www.cbs.com   Steven Bochco Enterprises, LLC
  Maureen Milligan, (310) 369-2400

- *Cosby*
  Comedy   30 min.   Fri   8:30 PM   CBS
  www.cosby.com   Carsey Werner Productions, LLC
  Elaine Martinelli, (718) 706-5701

- *Dawson's Creek*
  Drama   60 min.   Wed   8:00 PM   WB
  www.thewb.com   Granville Productions, Inc.
  Holly Henderson, (310) 979-8735

- *Dharma & Greg*
  Comedy   30 min.   Tue   9:00 PM   ABC
  www.abc.com   Twentieth Century Fox
  Donna Sahli, (310) 369-7174

- *Diagnosis Murder*
  Drama   60 min.   Thu   8:00 PM   CBS
  www.cbs.com   Viacom Productions, Inc.
  Geoffrey Colo, (818) 756-1272

- *Drew Carey Show, The*
  Comedy   30 min.   Wed   9:00 PM   ABC
  www.abc.com   Warner Bros. Television Productions
  Kris Marvin, (818) 954-3380

- *Early Edition*
  Drama   60 min.   Sat   9:00 PM   CBS
  www.cbs.com   October Holdings, Inc.
  Robin Haddad, (310) 342-7727

- *ER*
  Drama   60 min.   Thu   10:00 PM   NBC
  www.nbc.com   Warner Bros. Television Productions
  Carol Flint, (818) 954-3826

- *Everybody Loves Raymond*
  Comedy   30 min.   Mon   9:00 PM   CBS
  www.cbs.com   HBO Independent Productions
  Jason Gelles, (818) 954-7770

- *Felicity*
  Drama   60 min.   Sun   8:00 PM   WB
  www.felicity.com   Walt Disney Pictures & Television
  Jennifer Levin, (310) 558-5200

- *For Your Love*
  Comedy   30 min.   Fri   9:30 PM   WB
  www.thewb.com   Walt Disney Pictures & Television
  Julie Di Cataldo, (818) 954-3638

- *Frasier*
  Comedy   30 min.   Thu   9:00 PM   NBC
  www.nbc.com   Paramount Pictures Corporation
  Peter Ferland, (323) 956-3100

- *Friends*
  Comedy   30 min.   Thu   8:00 PM   NBC
  www.nbc.com   Warner Bros. Television Productions
  Jamie Montville, (818) 977-7943

- *Futurama*
  Animated   30 min.   Sun   7:00 PM   FOX
  www.fox.com   Twentieth Century Fox
  Christine Shinn, (310) 966-6184

- *Grown Ups, The*
  Comedy   30 min.   Mon   9:00 PM   UPN
  www.upn.com   Montrose Productions, Inc.
  Barbara Brace, (310) 202-3383

- *Jag*
  Drama   60 min.   Tue   8:00 PM   CBS
  www.cbs.com   Paramount Pictures Corporation
  Shari Ramsey, (323) 956-8660

- *Jamie Foxx Show, The*
  Comedy   30 min.   Fri   8:00 PM   WB
  www.thewb.com   Warner Bros. Television Productions
  Drew Brown, (818) 954-5264

- *Judging Amy*
  Drama   60 min.   Tue   10:00 PM   CBS
  www.cbs.com   Twentieth Century Fox
  Yolanda Lawrence, (323) 956-1600

- *Just Shoot Me*
  Comedy   30 min.   Tue   9:30 PM   NBC
  www.nbc.com   Universal Studios Network Development
  Becky Clements, (818) 655-5760

- *King of Queens, The*
  Comedy   30 min.   Mon   8:00 PM   CBS
  www.cbs.com   Montrose Productions, Inc.
  Trevor Dellecave, (310) 244-3588

- *King of the Hill*
  Animated   30 min.   Sun   7:30 PM   FOX
  www.fox.com   Twentieth Century Fox
  Dave Boucher, (310) 229-2476

- *Law & Order*
  Drama   60 min.   Wed   10:00 PM   NBC
  www.nbc.com   Studios USA Television, LLC
  Dena Morean, (818) 777-1236

- *Law & Order: Special Victims Unit*
  Drama   60 min.   Mon   9:00 PM   NBC
  www.nbc.com   Studios USA Television, LLC
  Nick Kendrick, (818) 777-1236

- *Mad TV*
  Comedy   60 min.   SYN
  www.madtvonfox.com   Girl Group Company
  Scott Sites, (323) 860-8999

- *Malcolm & Eddie*
  Comedy   30 min.   Mon   9:30 PM   UPN
  www.upn.com   Montrose Productions, Inc.
  Shawna Levin, (310) 202-3540

- *Malcolm in the Middle*
  Comedy   30 min.   Sun   8:30 PM   FOX
  www.fox.com   Regency Television Productions, Inc.
  Wendy Wilkins, (818) 655-6099

- *Martial Law*
  Action   60 min.   Sat   9:00 PM   CBS
  www.cbs.com   CBS Broadcasting, Inc.
  Bill Cluverius, (818) 909-6675

- *Moesha*
  Comedy   30 min.   Mon   8:00 PM   UPN
  www.upn.com   Big Ticket Productions, Inc.
  Rocky Staten, (323) 468-4800

- *Nash Bridges*
  Drama   60 min.   Fri   10:00 PM   CBS
  www.nashbridges.com   Paramount Pictures Corporation
  John Wirth, (818) 238-2200

- *Norm*
  Comedy   30 min.   Wed   8:30 PM   ABC
  www.abc.com   Warner Bros. Television Productions
  Steven Gabriel, (818) 954-7542

- *Now and Again*
  Drama   60 min.   Fri   9:00 PM   CBS
  www.cbs.com   Paramount Pictures Corporation
  Dana Schoenfeld, (718) 786-9456

- *NYPD Blue*
  Drama   60 min.   Tue   10:00 PM   ABC
  www.abc.com   Steven Bochco Productions, Inc.
  Dayna Kalins, (310) 369-2400

- *Once and Again*
  Drama   60 min.   Mon   10:00 PM   ABC
  www.abc.com   Once Again Productions, Inc.
  Josh Gummersall, (310) 840-7477

- *Pacific Blue*
  Action   60 min.   Sun   9:00 PM   USA
  www.pacificblue.com   North Hall Productions, Inc.
  Rick Okie, (310) 558-5040

- *Pensacola: Wings of Gold*
  Action   60 min.   SYN   Stu Segall Productions, Inc.
  www.pensacolatv.com
  David Balkan, (818) 506-9591

- *Politically Incorrect*
  60 min.   M–F   12:00 AM   ABC
  www.abc.com   Incorrect, Inc.
  Jonathan Davis, (323) 575-5000

- *Practice, The*
  Drama   60 min.   Sun   10:00 PM   ABC
  www.abc.com   David E. Kelley Productions, Inc.
  Elisa Todd, (310) 727-2200

- *Providence*
  Drama   60 min.   Fri   8:00 PM   NBC
  www.nbc.com   NBC Studios, Inc.
  Heather Hemmer, (323) 468-3400

- *Roswell*
  Drama   60 min.   Wed   9:00 PM   WB
  www.thewb.com   Twentieth Century Fox
  Breen Frazier, (323) 956-1710

- *Sabrina, The Teenage Witch*
  Comedy   30 min.   Fri   9:00 PM   ABC
  www.abc.com   Viacom Productions, Inc.
  Matthew Goodman, (323) 956-2600

- *Seven Days*
  Drama   60 min.   Wed   8:00 PM   UPN
  www.upn.com   Paramount Pictures Corporation
  Adrienne Ferguson, (323) 956-5861

- *Sex and the City*
  Comedy   30 min.   Sun   9:00 PM   HBO
  www.hbo.com   HBO Films Div HBO Time Warner
  Amy Harris, (718) 472-5377

- *Simpsons, The*
  Animated   30 min.   Sun   8:00 PM   FOX
  www.thesimpsons.com   Twentieth Century Fox
  Debbie Stolpp, (310) 369-1910

- *Sopranos, The*
  Drama   60 min.   Sun   9:00 PM   HBO
  www.hbo.com   HBO Films Div HBO Time Warner Ent. LP
  Julie Ross, (718) 786-7500

- *Spin City*
  Comedy   30 min.   Wed   9:30 PM   ABC
  www.abc.com   Dreamworks Television, LLC
  Steve Rose, (212) 336-6420

- *Sports Night*
  Comedy   30 min.   Tue   9:30 PM   ABC
  www.abc.com   Walt Disney Pictures & Television
  Lauren Carpenter, (818) 560-6636

- *Star Trek: Voyager*
  Sci-Fi   60 min.   Wed   9:00 PM   UPN
  www.upn.com   Paramount Pictures Corporation
  Michael O'Halloran, (323) 956-5799

- *Steve Harvey Show, The*
  Comedy   30 min.   Fri   9:00 PM   WB
  www.thewb.com   Universal Studios Network Programming
  Leo Clarke, (818) 733-0653

- *Then Came You*
  Comedy   30 min.   Wed   8:30 PM   ABC
  www.abc.com   Twentieth Century Fox
  Kate O'Donoghue, (310) 369-5292

- *Touched by an Angel*
  Drama   60 min.   Sun   8:00 PM   CBS
  www.touched.com   Caroline Film Productions, Inc.
  Jim Evans, (818) 508-3420

- *Two Guys and a Girl*
  Comedy   30 min.   Wed   8:00 PM   ABC
  www.abc.com   Twentieth Century Fox
  David Hartle, (818) 655-5008

- *VIP*
  Adventure   60 min.   SYN
  www.sony.com   Lafitte Productions, Inc.
  Lorianne Tibbetts, (818) 255-0515

- *Walker, Texas Ranger*
  Drama   60 min.   Sat   10:00 PM   CBS
  www.cbs.com   Amadea Film Productions, Inc.
  Galen Tong, (818) 752-9292

- *Will & Grace*
  Comedy   30 min.   Thur   9:00 PM   NBC
  www.nbc.com   NBC Studios, Inc.
  Michelle Spitz, (818) 655-5642

- *Xena: Warrior Princess*
  Action   60 min.   SYN
  www.mca.com/tv/xena/   Studios USA Television, LLC
  Lu Abbott, (818) 754-8800

- *X-Files, The*
  Drama   60 min.   Sun   9:00 PM   FOX
  www.fox.com   Twentieth Century Fox
  Mary Astadourian, (310) 369-1100

CHAPTER REVIEW

- Television writers compose spec scripts of currently airing series to use as samples in seeking employment.
- Television agents have busy seasonal periods (staffing or pilot season) in which they seek steady work for their clients.
- To write for television, you need to know the shows you like backwards and forwards.
- Make certain your spec scripts are strong and highly polished before sending them out as your industry calling cards.
- Like feature agents, television reps rely on referrals instead of query letters to locate new clients.
- Becoming a writer's assistant is a useful step along the path of writing for a television series, and may help you obtain those all-important referrals.

4

THE BIG HOUSE AGENCY

You never want to turn talent away because you never know
where the next David E. Kelley will come from out there.

Big House agencies offer the theoretical pinnacle of representation for any writer. They have the biggest offices, represent the biggest name talent, negotiate the biggest deals, and cut the biggest checks. But do they have anything to offer the less accomplished, but still eager writer?

Unfortunately, each of the traditional Big House agencies systematically refused to take part in this book. I called them all: William Morris, ICM, CAA, United Talent Agency, and Endeavor. They all declined to give me any information or access to any of their agents. Apparently, they considered this writer and his agent-friendly book to be some sort of threat or danger prying into their inner-workings.

More likely, they simply don't want or need to seem friendly to aspiring writers. Rob Carlson shared his insights in the article that inspired this book, and I thank him for that, but the agencies otherwise dodged my dogged pursuit. Also, Stefanie Henning granted me an interview at ICM for the chapter on interactive writing. However, I don't think she checked with the powers that be in the Beverly Hills firm before sitting down before my tape recorder.

Fortunately, I was able to speak with a top agent from one of the emerging Big House firms, Paradigm. At the time of the interview, the firm included twenty-eight agents on the West Coast and fifteen more in the firm's East Coast office.

Andy Patman, Paradigm

Andy Patman represents television writers. He works with the firm's feature agents to track both TV and feature films because of the regular crossovers between the two fields. After a short career in the light-fixture business, Patman started out in the William Morris mailroom and worked his way up from there as an agent trainee to a junior agent.

"Any Big House has an advantage over, say, a boutique in terms of resources and inside contacts. The smaller agency does not have access to the information that an agency of greater size and stature has.

"Some agencies can be so big that there's no synergy between agents and departments. They can be so big and have so many clients to service that only so many of them get any attention, while others get lost. Some agencies are too small because they don't have access to people. Paradigm has the advantage of avoiding the pitfalls of the big agencies."

Larger agencies rely on packaging to assemble and sell projects. Patman defined the process as "what green-lights a project and causes you to roll film":

"You take elements and assemble them to make sure a project goes forward. It could be a writer and/or an actor who is talented and powerful enough to make a project go. But you may have to add another element to get the project going."

Even though Big Houses tend to favor more established working writers, Patman said that doesn't mean they necessarily turn away up-and-comers:

"You never want to turn talent away because you never know where the next David E. Kelley will come from out there. So we keep an eye out, though most of our clients have had some success in the business before getting here.

"Quite frankly, the big agencies cannot look for up-and-comers because it's easier to steal them from smaller agencies. As much as big agencies would like to take someone and groom them to the next level, you're looking at a very long commitment—sometimes ten years of hard work. It's sometimes easier to find an established client who's unhappy with their current agency and is ready to move up.

"When you cruise [or steal] a client from another agency, they're unhappy with their current situation."

Most of Patman's new clients come from referrals. He rarely signs talent from a query letter:

"A manager or an attorney will refer writers to me. On occasion, a producer will pass on a name. There are too many query letters coming in for me to respond to on a regular basis."

Developing the Referral Approach

According to Patman, the best way to earn that precious referral is to find a spot as a writer's assistant on a weekly series. That allows a young writer access to producers and agents. Quite often, it's the writers' assistants who are given that first job. They're friends of the executive producer or the supervising producer. They get their shot through that connection.

"So, you don't need an agent to break in, but you need some sort of access to somebody who would get you work. An agent is a necessary aspect of a career, but it's not impossible to move forward without one. It's part of the game in which you have to be meeting people, establishing more and more relationships—building that foundation."

Patman also stresses that life experience can help any writer get a job or an agent:

"If you're an ex-cop, that might help you get a job on a *NYPD Blue* or *Law and Order*. They're looking for doctors on the medical shows. It would help to set you apart."

If writers want to set a long-term goal of earning a Big House's reputation, Patman recommends that they get in touch with someone within a big agency or someone who has a buyer's relationship with that agency:

"Form relationships with anyone who can offer you that referral because every agent at every Big House receives stacks of query letters every week. There's just no way to read them all because we need to read other material. Periodically, there will be a referral that will lead us to read someone new who's seeking representation here."

As for Paradigm's developing status as a major agency on a par with William Morris, CAA, ICM, UTA, or Endeavor, Patman says his firm has never been shy or intimidated by the big guys:

"We are going to compete with anyone in this industry. We'll go toe to toe because we want to be better and grow into whatever size fits the company."

CHAPTER REVIEW

- Big House agencies wield the most power among Hollywood firms and are less likely to help build an aspiring writer's career from scratch. They want a guaranteed piece of money before they sign up new talent.

- Big House Agencies often "package" talent, fitting scripts with directors and actors they represent to collect all the commissions involved in the project. Under these circumstances, if the package doesn't fit together, a script may disappear.

- The newest arrivals to Big House status, like Paradigm, reject the traditional role of Big Houses and work with their clients to ensure success.

- Representatives of most famous, Big House agencies (William Morris, UTA, CAA, ICM, and Endeavor) declined to take part in this book. Since this book is designed to benefit young and aspiring writers, I assume they would decline to deal with them as well.

- This just in: Referrals help you get an agent.

5
The Mid-Size Agencies

*Obviously, those people who can't find agents will always feel
negative about it. If they should finally get representation,
they'll immediately jump to the other camp.*

The mid-size agency falls snugly in the gap between the Big House, with its scores of agents and armies of assistants, and the boutique, with its single principal or a small group of reps looking after a small pool of clients. The mid-size agency enjoys a few advantages over both the other categories. As these are often better known than the smaller boutiques, earning a mid-size's representation can often bring a writer much-needed prestige. Also, with fewer agents and fewer clients than giant, packaging-oriented agencies like William Morris or ICM, mid-size agencies are less likely to lose a writer in the shuffle.

With more individual attention paid to writers than is possible at a larger agency, and more resources to bring to bear than a boutique, the mid-sizes are gaining prestige and status every day in Hollywood. Consider the wise words of some key players in the mid-size agency game.

Angela Cheng, Writers & Artists
Angela Cheng is a feature and long-form television agent at Writers & Artists in Beverly Hills. Born in Washington, DC, she graduated from Brown University with degrees in semiotics and French. Cheng headed west immediately after college and started working with talent (actors and actresses) for about a year. She described that experience as "working with models who want to act."

"That was just not for me," Cheng said. "It wasn't that I was opposed to working with actors, but I felt more predisposed to working with writers."

Cheng moved to the Gersh Agency, a mid-size company representing both above- and below-the-line artists. She worked for one of Gersh's senior agents for film and TV literary. About eighteen months after serving that apprenticeship, she become a full-fledged agent.

Now that she has moved to Writers & Artists, Cheng represents book authors and journalists for film and television, as well as traditional screenwriters for features and television movies. Cheng believes that working with such a varied clientele gives her a distinct advantage.

"For me, it's really about being passionate about the writer," she explained. "If I read something that just captures my imagination, then it's my job to find a market that will take in that writer.

"Obviously, for television, it's all about determining if a writer has the right spec screenplay for a particular job. Beyond that, the best part for me of having different kinds of writers as clients is that I get to think outside of the box. I'm not confined to thinking only about TV series or feature films. I'm working on taking an article in the *Los Angeles Times*, written by one of my clients who's nominated for a Pulitzer, and making it into a television series."

Cheng added, "My writers are also creators. So, whereas you might have a TV writer who climbed the ladder from freelance writer to story editor to executive producer, my writers come into a situation and are already executive producers because they were the ones who came up with the original idea for the series."

Cheng does not take unpublished manuscripts to major book publishers: "About 99 percent of the material I represent in book form already has a publisher. But I work on material simultaneously with book agents. I see proposals early in the creative process and manuscripts as they develop. When we arrive at a finished book, reviews are usually already in place all over the media."

The same afternoon that I interviewed Cheng, she was meeting with a writer who had just become her newest client. The writer had recently adapted into a screenplay a book that Cheng had sold about eighteen months earlier.

"He did a tremendous job," she said of her new client. "It was one of the few instances in which the author of the book was thrilled with the adaptation. The screenwriter had instincts for the material that were just second nature. He incorporated nuances into the adaptation that the original author wanted in his novel until his editor convinced him otherwise. So I had an ongoing business relationship with that writer for more than a year before I signed him."

Cheng agreed that it's hard to get an agent without generating some action in your career first, but she doesn't believe that it's an absolute, unbreakable law that you must sell a script before an agent will consider you:

"When you're looking at the huge iron curtain of agencies and managers, I know that's what people think," Cheng explained. "But good writing is good writing. I read my query letters, and if the writing jumps out at me, I'll request that piece of material."

If you submit such a letter to Cheng, you need to get her attention immediately and avoid any mistakes in your verbiage: "I'll pick a letter up and read it really quickly. If I see typos or spelling mistakes, or if it is in any way badly written, I just will not give it a second look. I really am anal about that sort of stuff."

To compose a really standout query letter, Cheng suggests that you personalize your letter and follow the basic practices of mailing it with a SASE.

"You'd be surprised at what I get," she said. "I do not respond to anything addressed to 'To whom it may concern' or 'Dear Sir or Madam.' I don't think anyone else would, either. And I won't look at anything handwritten.

"Really, all a good query letter has to do is convey a quality synopsis concisely. It's about being able to show, perhaps, that you have a sense of humor. You need that query letter to serve as your vehicle. It becomes an art form to write a really good query letter because it's incredibly rare that I receive one."

She added, "I have asked for material from maybe one out of fifty or one out of a hundred query letters I receive. Unfortunately, I only signed one client from a query letter. But I was able to sell that piece of material, so the letter fulfilled its function. It made it possible for us to find that writer and that material. We were able to find that proverbial needle in a haystack or diamond in the rough, or whatever cliché fits."

As a screenwriter working to make a positive impression on Cheng, it helps if you follow basic, considerate agent-contact protocol:

"I don't like receiving queries via e-mail. I don't like being contacted that way because I'm really bad at erasing messages from my mailbox. It's best to reach me via traditional mail with a return SASE. The agency receives tons of query letters, and if we were to respond to every one sent in without that SASE, the company would go broke."

AGEISM, 'SCHMAGEISM' . . . MY WORDS, NOT HERS

Fortunately for many veterans, Cheng does not immediately dismiss queries or calls from older writers, as many agents do.

"Ageism is rampant, and it's awful," she admitted, pulling no punches. "There's no cutoff age, but we've all heard the story of the thirty-year-old woman who had to lie and say she was nineteen to get a writing job. That's just ridiculous. The woman was an actress who starred in a major feature film, and she had to pass herself off as a teenager to get work.

"I admit there's something intriguing about finding someone right off the playground who can write a great screenplay and make a millions dollars. I certainly know that my boss read a screenplay by a Beverly Hills High School senior that sold for a million dollars. Unfortunately, that production was botched, overdeveloped, and never made.

"My boss came to me and said, 'You're the youngest person at this company. How come you haven't found the sixteen- or seventeen-year-old who can write a great screenplay and be precocious?!'

"So my mission became to find someone. Of course, it's incredibly rare to find someone that young with that talent who can achieve any kind of longevity. More often than not, they can become one-hit wonders. They can't sustain the quality of their work under the glare of recognition and attention."

Obviously, age, wisdom, and character still have a part to play in the screenwriting business—at least as far as Angela Cheng is concerned.

In addition to keeping her eyes open for writers with maturity, Cheng also considers talent from outside California's sunny confines:

"The book authors I represent don't need to be here. Writers can live and work anywhere because I act as the conduit between them, the New York publishing industry, and Hollywood. Also, screenwriters can live anywhere they want as long as they can get to LA at a moment's notice—at least within twenty-four hours. As for television, you need to live in New York, LA, or wherever the show is shooting.

"Look, there is a genuine opportunity for a writer to find a good agent," Cheng insisted. "Obviously, those people who can't find agents will always feel negative about it. If they should finally get representation, they'll immediately jump to the other camp.

"If you work really hard on your craft of writing on a daily basis, it'll pay off. I look very seriously at published short stories. If someone has shown some semblance of writing skill, I will take them seriously."

As for Writers & Artists' status as a premiere mid-size agency, Cheng believes her firm has a few special advantages over a Big House, such as the personal touch.

"The reason I came to Writers & Artists is that I certainly felt we were not a machine. It is not all about the agenda of the agency here. So often, that agenda is to use talent."

She explained, "All of the bigger agencies claim that they can 'package.' What that means is, if a writer has a good enough piece of material, the agency will serve it up to its hottest actor, and the writer ends up getting shafted. For that kind of agency, it's not about the longevity of the client's career, it's more about the agency's need.

"Coming here, I got to work with all of the other agencies because we avoid that weird kind of competitiveness. There's more of a collaborative spirit like that with a medium-sized or boutique agency. Meanwhile, CAA, ICM, and William Morris will never speak to each other." (Or to this author, for that matter!)

Cheng said the big agencies call her all the time looking for material. The Big Houses reach out to her if one of their producer or actor clients is looking for a certain kind of script or book. Cheng lays out what she has and plays the literary agent's version of *Let's Make a Deal*.

Cheng was generous enough to offer a few pointers on how to contact, impress, and otherwise please an agent any writer wants to target as a possible representative. She said prospective writers should make sure to have a selection of spec scripts ready before composing those magical cover letters:

"It's incredibly rare that I sign any client as a result of one screenplay," she said. "I always ask how many specs a writer has, and it's best to have at least two to show. If you earn a mention because of your first script, but no one wants to sign you based on that screenplay, you need to have another one to show."

As for the type of spec a writer needs to hit the market running, Cheng advises anyone just to write his passion:

"It's all a matter of desire. I find that when I read any material in which a writer is really trying to seem commercial, it shows. I would rather read something smaller and more character driven, something very well written with a lot of emotional investment. I want to see that instead of a *Lethal Weapon* ripoff.

Cheng also urged scribes not to base what they write solely on what they see at their local theatre.

"Clients and potential clients always ask me what to write next, and all I can say is what's hot today is never hot tomorrow. I think it's ridiculous to track and follow fads. If you were to try and follow, for example, the *Scream* slasher comedy in hopes of achieving success with a script considered *Scream*-esque, days later, people are already onto something else. The original may have made a lot of money, but about the time I'm ready to sell the new script, it's no longer fresh and has already been seen by millions."

Cheng sits on screenwriting panels at national writers' conferences regularly because she looks to educate (and perhaps even inspire) fresh talent. She hasn't signed any writers she met at such conferences, but she hopes her insights provided some guidance to the writers in attendance. She urged writers at those gatherings to view them as learning opportunities, because those venues don't necessarily provide the best opportunity to pitch your material.

"When I handle a pitch session at one of those conferences," Cheng explained, "it's ninety minutes or two hours of working through a line that queues up out the door to talk to me. They end up with thirty seconds to pitch to me, and I can't give them any feedback. I end up with no idea what they've written—or how well they've written it.

"At the biggest conferences, hundreds of writers show up. As a featured guest, you're put into a huge holding room with all those writers at the same time, so there's no privacy. Imagine you're a writer who waited all this time to speak to an agent, and you end up with people pressing against you, making motions for you to hurry up. It's tough to pitch under those circumstances.

"You may wait patiently for your moment, but at the end of two hours, you may only have spoken to two or three professionals. Writers might have very commercial material, but if they haven't pitched it properly in the short time they had, it doesn't matter at the end of the day. With the way the market is today, no one is really buying pitches because the market won't support it."

She added, "To a certain degree, I think conferences can be a great way for aspiring writers to network with managers, executives, agents, and other writers. But it's not helpful for me in finding material."

ENCOURAGING ASIAN INVOLVEMENT

One passion that Cheng devotes special attention to is her desire to encourage and cultivate Asian American talent in the entertainment industry. She is a first-generation American; her mother was born in

Shanghai, her father in Hong Kong. Her parents immigrated to the United States in their late teens. While they support their successful daughter's career, they don't fully understand what she does they way the might comprehend the more traditional professions (doctor, lawyer, etc.). Since there is no equivalent to an agent in Asian business, Cheng's career path is additionally puzzling to her folks.

"All through college," Cheng explained, "I know my parents wanted to know why I hoped to work in entertainment. They would say, 'Don't you want to go to law school or become a doctor? Don't you want a real job?' Now, they have a little better understanding, and they love what I do."

When she moved to the ethnically diverse Los Angeles area, she found the strong Asian presence a benefit as she settled into Southern California and its most prominent industry. However, her heritage did not translate into a fast and easy ticket to a table at Spagos.

"When I first interviewed out here in Los Angeles, I encountered the sort of prejudice I was not prepared for—especially since I went to a progressive all-girls prep school and a very liberal East Coast university. I thought those kind of attitudes belonged to a different era."

For example, "There was a partner at one agency who told me that, as a woman of color, it wouldn't be hard for me to find a job because supervisors had to make hiring quotas and such."

Cheng added, "I never heard, 'Wow, you went to Brown!' or 'You seem intelligent and studied really hard.' It was, 'You'll have no trouble finding work because you're an Asian woman.'"

Cheng confessed that she encountered that kind of attitude often enough to teach her that she was in a tough business. So now that she achieved success on the basis of her hard work and dedication, she devotes some of her attention to helping other Asian Americans through the trials of that business.

"One of the greatest parts of what I do is that I get to work with Asian American authors. I'm searching for Asian American screenwriters. I have a specific agenda for those searches."

The emergence of widely accepted Asian film stars (such as Jackie Chan, Joan Chen, Jet Li, and Lucy Liu) should continue to open doors in Hollywood. But Cheng considers it offensive when the media tags "Asian" as a "hot" trend:

"I find that identifying of a trend as a perceived novelty," she said. "That's outright offensive. That's seeing color first, not ability."

Some critics and media reporters hyped the choice of Lucy Liu as the third Angel (in the film adaptation of *Charlie's Angels*). Cheng cited Liu as an example of warranted success, not en vogue Asian chic:

"Lucy is empirically beautiful and very smart, so her time has come. Her success is simply long overdue."

In the end, Cheng encourages talent with diverse heritages to try their luck in Hollywood: "I certainly am very interested in mentoring young Asian American college graduates who want to try this industry. I don't think that there are enough in the business."

Cheng suggested that talent of any ethnicity can find support in the industry to mentor and educate them. There are people across the board who look to shepherd eager young talent, without regard to individual race or heritage. Maybe the entertainment business isn't as cold and scary a field as so many believe.

Finally, Cheng promised to take this book and turn it into a $2 million movie deal, so I'll be getting in touch with her real soon.

Susan Shapiro, Shapiro-Lichtman

Susan Shapiro of Shapiro-Lichtman in Beverly Hills, built her seven-year career representing episodic television writers and interactive writers. Recently, she moved into motion picture features, adding a handful of new talents to her stable.

She is that rarest of creatures—a third-generation agent. Her maternal grandfather served as an agent during Hollywood's golden era, representing such silver screen stars as actor (turned leader of the free world) Ronald Reagan. He trained both Susan's father (Martin) and Mark Lichtman—founders of the thirty-year-old, mid-size literary agency that bears their names.

A 90210 native and a graduate of Beverly Hills High School, Shapiro grew up in the business and never doubted what direction her professional life would take:

"I knew I always wanted to be an agent," she said. "I always watched what my Dad did. I would sit at the dinner table and talk with my Dad about what he did that day. It was interesting. He had exciting things to do at work. He would bring scripts home when I was little. I knew it was for a TV show, and I'd say, 'Wow! Let me read it!' I didn't know it was only a spec, and I didn't care.

"He'd always be sitting and reading, and I love to read. He'd take me to screenings and such, also. It always seemed compelling to me. I realized that an agent was essentially a salesperson. When I discovered in school that I was good at selling, I realized I wanted to be an agent.

"As I got older, I knew I needed my own credibility. I didn't want to get into the business just as 'Daddy's little girl.'"

Shapiro decided to follow in her attorney mother's footsteps. She attended law school, but realized she had no real interest in practicing law. Rather than pass the bar exam, she took a pass on the lawyer's life and became an agent.

"After law school, I felt I had the credibility to be an agent. I've been at Shapiro-Lichtman for seven years—six as an agent and five years working with episodic television writers. I do features now, also."

Shapiro also works with new media, representing interactive writers and designers as well as online entertainment companies. She explained that it's a sign of the times that agencies look to emerging entertainment media to expand their business.

Such diversity is also an advantage for a mid-size agency over a boutique shop. While a smaller agency might only have enough resources to cover one market well, a firm with more resources, such as Shapiro-Lichtman, can handle features, television, print, and new media, opening its doors to more different breeds of writing talent.

For example, Shapiro's most recent client prior to our interview came out of the New York playwriting scene: "He had one play produced, which isn't a lot. He had no experience in Hollywood, but he attended law school at England's Cambridge University. I had something to talk about with him. Also, his spec was probably the best script I've read in five years. So that obviously helps.

"Another client was referred to us by an attorney. I read the material, and it was excellent. They have a pilot deal in the works, so I signed them. But I will occasionally read unproduced people. A writer needs to have something that catches my eye—that gives me something to talk about to producers or executives."

In addition to bringing some interesting personality traits or life experiences to the table, Shapiro urges writers to have at least two spec scripts completed before contacting any representative. That rule holds true for would-be feature film writers, sitcom staffers, or one-hour drama scribes.

"Try to make your specs as different as possible to show your range. Make certain to write shows you watch and really know because your spec needs to be even better than an actual aired episode of the show. Otherwise, you simply haven't done what you need to do."

Shapiro asserted that feature writers might need a larger body of spec work. However, they should never try to send a pile of scripts to any agent:

"You can describe all of your scripts, but only send your best work—your favorite thing that you've written. Or send whatever fits the genre that the agent is looking for at the time. If you send too much material at any one time, your stuff will go into a pile and will keep getting pushed to the bottom. If I have six TV specs and five features to read from existing clients, I'm not going to have time to work through three specs."

Once you have a body of work and a spec script you want to submit, Shapiro advises writers to contact her through whatever connections they have:

"If somebody comes with a recommendation from somebody I know or respect, I'm more likely to read the scripts. A good query letter can help. Such a letter has something other letters don't have. People get creative. It needs to get my attention and somehow stand out to me. Include any information about yourself that might make you special to me as a writer."

SET YOURSELF APART

"It helps if you can say in a letter or over the phone, 'Sure, I'm a new writer, but there are other things about me I can talk about. That set me apart. Whether it's in your background or experience, give me something to work with in your past."

Shapiro didn't list this as an example, but one recent signee sent her a dozen roses before signing his contract with her. They were still on proud display, even in their dead, dry condition. I don't suggest you send roses to every potential rep you contact, but if one actually agrees to work with you, show your appreciation with a personal touch.

However, don't pester the agent. Expect at least a month of turnaround time before you get a response. Yes, a mid-size agency gets less material to deal with than a Big House, but it's still more than anyone could work through quickly.

"If someone wants to know how often they should check back in with me," Shapiro suggested, "they should just ask me. I'll tell them. Then they need to stick to that timetable. If they're calling and calling and calling, they're pestering. If I'm not calling, I have nothing to say to them—which is unusual because I return my calls. My father taught me that."

Finally, never send any material (to an agent, manager, producer, or studio executive) without first receiving a request to do so. You will step into the deadly realm of "unsolicited material" where millions of perfectly good trees go to die. If 7-Up is the UN cola, consider this the screenwriter's UN-rule: Unsolicited scripts go Unreal Undoubtedly and Unavoidably.

"If you send in an unsolicited script, it'll never get to me. If I'm not expecting it, it's turned back at the door. That's a big no-no."

Shapiro said that it helps if a writer lives in Los Angeles, but it's not absolutely necessary. She again brought up the New York playwright who was educated in England and knew nothing about LA. He and other out-of-town clients must be willing to travel and perhaps engage in long-term temporary relocation to Southern California—especially if they want to write for a series shooting there.

"It's another Catch-22," Shapiro admitted. "It's easier to get writers work if they live here, but how can I ask anyone to relocate until I get them a job?"

Like other agents I spoke with, Shapiro was not quick to jump on the ageism bandwagon: "It's not a certain age that I'm looking for necessarily. In sitcom writing, they want younger people. Everyone knows that. The younger the better. If you're not that young, then you'd better look young because that's what they're looking for. That's funny because when you watch the Emmys and see who's winning the awards, they're all older professionals. The older you get, the better you get and the more experience you have."

For a beginning writer, Shapiro advises not starting too late: "It's hard to sell somebody who's been kicking around the business for a while without finding success. It's tough to rep a forty-nine-year-old housewife who just decided to start writing. She could be a fabulous talent, but it'd still be hard to sell her.

"I have a client in his late fifties who has unbelievable credits from all his work over the years, but he hasn't worked in a while. His credits included head writer, supervising producer, and co-executive producer. He got into animation (a lower-paying branch of the industry) because he wasn't working in live action anymore. Finally, he agreed to write an *NYPD Blue* spec. Because somebody already knew him on the series *JAG*, he got a shot."

Shapiro admitted that she knows how tough it is to get an agent. At a mid-size like Shapiro-Lichtman, the entire firm must get behind writers and their work before they will get a contract.

"If I don't have the support of everyone here before signing a person," she said, "I'm not going to succeed in representing them. That's doing someone an injustice."

Timing can play a part as well. When I interviewed Shapiro, she explained that the firm was not signing any new clients at the moment because the agency was restructuring. So even with a great script and strong referrals, a scribe would be out of luck after knocking on Shapiro-Lichtman's door. A writer might have a better chance of earning the agency's attention a few months down the road.

Shapiro will sometimes take a "one-shot" with a writer. If someone brings her a piece of material with interest from a producer or studio already built in, she will agree to handle that deal rather than turn away the potential 10 percent.

"The opportunities can be few and far between to get an agent," Shapiro added, "but they are there."

BONUS SECTION

The Agent's Assistant

The agent's assistant is one of the primary entry-level jobs in the movie and TV business. Agents work their way up from the mailroom through an assistant position (or some variant of those positions) before becoming junior agents. More than a few writers, producers, show runners, development executives, and studio chiefs all began their careers as agent assistants.

So what does such an assistant do, and how can that kind of position promote your career as an aspiring film and TV writer?

Brian R. Adams serves as Angela Cheng's assistant at Writers & Artists. He shared some insights into the daily work of an agent's right hand.

Beyond merely answering telephones, making copies, taking care of travel arrangements, and managing an agent's schedule, Adams described the other aspects of an agent's assistant's job. His experiences prove that such professionals are more than mere secretaries.

"One of the most important tasks for an assistant is to keep track of whom Angela is calling and who is calling her," he said. "I need to stay on top of all the comings and goings of material in and out of her office.

"She needs to know when somebody called, what they called about, and any other important details. She wants all of that information at her fingertips on demand, and I have to make sure it's there."

Adams added, "The other important task is to make sure the outgoing material gets out on time and to the respective parties correctly. I confirm that the material gets there and in good condition. Or I might have to make sure that it gets back to us, if need be.

"As much as possible, while performing those tasks, I try to listen in on some of the deal-making so Angela can have a second ear or someone to bounce ideas off of or to keep track of things. It helps me to stay on top of everything going on in the agency so I know where to look or whom to ask when the moment comes." So it's an understatement to say an agent's assistant needs to multitask.

Both Adams and Cheng agreed that a good way of getting on an agent's good side (or onto their call-sheet) is to make friends with the agent's assistant. It's a refrain often spouted by writers, producers, and other agents around the business.

Cheng explained, "I really rely on my assistant as a gatekeeper, so I definitely think you need to impress my assistant if you want to get to me. It helps."

How does someone make friends with an assistant like Adams?

He explained, "It's such small things, like saying 'Thank you,' or acknowledging a favor. It's nice if they remember your name, too.

"Say you needed to schedule a business meeting over lunch, and a client wants this, this, and that in fast order. It helps if the person calling in has the time cleared to set that meeting."

Adams also stressed that having a sense of humor will often help you along, since so many egos in the industry inflate their own self-importance.

Just as those "do's" should help you along, there are also definite "don'ts" to avoid when dealing with assistants.

Adams said, "No one likes being yelled at or belittled, so when someone calls up shouting at you, you're not going to be positively disposed toward that person—whether you're at fault for the incident or not!

"I suppose that, if that client is making the agency a lot of money, you have to put up with it, but most writers trying to make first contact are not in that position. It just helps to be treated like an equal, and not someone who's so unimportant that they can be abused."

In return for serving as Cheng's gatekeeper, Adams receives the opportunity to bring in good material and otherwise get involved in the creative process.

"Angela is great because she lets me read a lot of stuff that comes through the door. If I feel passionate about a piece of material, she trusts me enough to read it. That doesn't happen on every desk, so I'm fortunate."

Moreover, a writer is fortunate to find an assistant who enjoys that kind of respect from his boss because it's one more inroad for your material. Adams takes a couple of novels home with him every weekend in hopes of finding Cheng's next crossover client.

So a would-be agent's work is seemingly never done. Be nice to the poor guy.

CHAPTER REVIEW

- While harder to get into than the small agencies, mid-size firms can offer advantages in resources over the boutiques.
- Writers may receive more personal attention at mid-size firms.
- Did I mention that referrals are a good idea?
- Unsolicited scripts go Unread Undoubtedly and Unavoidably.
- Big news flash: Timing and luck play a major role in finding a Hollywood agent.

6

THE BOUTIQUE
AGENCY

Making a deal makes me feel great. What else can I say? I'm an agent!

The majority of talented, but unaccomplished writers usually find their first representation with a boutique agency. Made up of anywhere from one to perhaps four or five agents, the boutique offers more individual attention to writers because it represents a smaller client base. However, the boutique may lack some of the resources (and, in some cases, the prestige) of a larger or more well-known agency.

To examine the benefits and inner workings of the boutique agency, we turn to two top agents who lend their names to their firm's brass plates: Marcie Wright of The Wright Concept and Susan Grant of Soloway, Grant & Kopaloff.

Marcie Wright, The Wright Concept

Marcie Wright runs her prestigious boutique firm out of sunny offices deep within beautiful downtown Burbank. She had worked in the business for fifteen years before I wandered into her office (and promises to stick with it for another decade, at least).

"I still enjoy the work," Wright said, "and as long as I enjoy it, I'll keep at it. I started out by writing a couple of scripts back in the 1970s. And I got an agent."

Wright quickly added that she recently reread her early work and realized she wouldn't have represented herself: "I realized that I didn't want to be a writer back then because I just didn't have any talent. But I enjoyed being around writers. My husband's grandfather was the first American writer to make a million dollars writing, so I've always been surrounded by writers."

Wright went to work as an assistant to her own agent and realized that she could do the agent's job better than he could. She took a job with a small voiceover agency and built a new literary department under its banner. After a few lucky breaks, and meeting professionals who were kind enough to share their advice and knowledge, she grew the department into a successful division. When that agency closed its doors, rather than seek a position with another agency, Wright opened her own firm, The Wright Concept. A decade and a half later, the agency continues to thrive.

"Opening my own firm just seemed like the right thing to do," she said. "I had worked in corporate America in the past and never liked it. I work better on my own with self-motivation. I never even considered trying to get a job at a big agency."

While Wright relies on referrals to sign most of her clients, she doesn't require a contract to work with a writer. She receives query letters, like all other agents, but doesn't find them effective:

"I once received a great query letter—the best I'd ever received. I requested the material, and the script was terrible. But the letter was fantastic! We've received gimmicky queries. One letter came in a urine specimen cup. Another came with a can of tuna. I don't think gimmicks work. I think you need to find a hook that will catch someone's eye.

"Most important, don't be bitter. It's amazing how many query letters we get that are angry. It's not exactly the best way to impress somebody. If you're angry now, what are you going to be like when you get your rejection?"

PERSONAL RELATIONSHIPS MAKE THE DIFFERENCE

Unlike larger agencies that require signed agreements, she relies on personal relationships to keep her clients with her firm.

"I have had clients move on to other big agencies, but I've never had a client stiff me out of a deal that I made. Most of my clients realize that, by working with a boutique firm like mine, you get more specialized attention. I do all of my own reading. You can get me on the telephone. By having a smaller, specialized list, there's not as much competition for my time between clients. When I call a producer and ask him to read something, I'm only talking about one or two clients. I'm not going to send him a box of scripts.

"On the feature side," Wright explained, "I can represent ten comedy writers, and they're all going to have different styles. So when you're working on writing assignments, you're only going to have one or two writing samples that are appropriate for that assignment. Producers want to see projects that are close to what they're doing, but not too close."

It might seem possible for a small agency like the aptly named Wright Concept to disappear in the Hollywood shuffle while competing with 50 to 100 agent firms like William Morris or CAA. But Wright maximizes her firm's exposure with a Web site: *www.wrightconcept.com.*

"We get a lot of queries through the Web site," Wright explained. "Most of them are very unprofessional and not well thought-out. We rarely respond to a query letter off the Internet. That is not the purpose of my Web site. It's a tool for the development people and executives to go to and find out what my clients are doing. We have a newsletter on the site dedicated exclusively to scripts listed by genre. If they're looking for thrillers, they can go onto the Web site and find what they need. I also include upcoming scripts that we're going out with, so producers know what's coming down the pipe."

The Wright Concept also snail mails a newsletter around town to generate interest in its clients' projects. According to Wright, the response to that newsletter is often overwhelming.

"We send the newsletters out four times a year over a three-month period. We just sent the last batch out, and we've already had a request for more than 100 scripts."

You don't see the Big Houses sending out newsletters to development executives because they don't need to do so. But a boutique like The Wright Concept uses such clever promotional moves to compete.

Wright said, "Nobody else that I know of uses a Web site or a newsletter to promote their clients. I've had our Web site since 1996, so we got into it early. We've had more than 275,000 hits since then. We get 400 to 500 hits a day.

"Anybody who wants to know what I do or what my clients are doing can see it on the Web," Wright said. "It's right there.

"I know other agencies can be much more closed about whom they represent and what their successes are. But if you do research, you can learn as much about a boutique agency as you can about a bigger firm."

Wright urges writers to do that research for one simple reason: Just because an agency is licensed and it's a Writers Guild signatory doesn't mean it's properly connected or correctly operated.

"Anyone who wants to be an agent and doesn't have a felony background can become one. So it's best to find someone who knows the agent and does business with the agent and knows her reputation. Find out what kind of success the agent is having before you begin working with her.

"I marvel that, when I was getting started, people entrusted their futures and their careers to me. But of those first dozen or so writers I represented, I still represent six of them. We've all become successful together."

KEEP IT UP

That sort of developing relationship is perhaps the primary advantage of working with a boutique agency. The firm needs to make money, but it doesn't have the ever-present pressure for mega-success that a Big House requires. So the agents have more time and a greater ability to coach and build careers. If writers want to find that boutique agent and expand their careers with such representation, Wright said, "Persistence wins out over talent every time.

"Just keep at it. If you have any passion and talent for it, you can make it work. But writing something and sitting back or waiting will not make it happen. Find ways to get into the business somehow. There are all kinds of ways to get in and to find someone who will take a liking to you. Even cold calls to assistants can make it possible to send something in—if you're polite. Besides, most assistants are aspiring to move up in the business, so they're looking for nuggets to help them get where they want to go.

"You just have to keep at it and find someone who will welcome you."

Susan Grant, Soloway, Grant & Kopaloff

From her office overlooking the Miracle Mile along Wilshire Boulevard in midtown Los Angeles, Susan Grant added her insights on the role of the small agency in Hollywood. A partner at Soloway, Grant & Kopaloff, Grant started out as a below-the-line agent who made the transition to representing directors and writers.

"I bridged the gap between types of talent," Grant said. "Now I represent everything from directors of photography, to costume designers, to line producers, to directors and writers for long-form television and features. I'm eclectic in the sense that I represent that range of talent and a collection of international artists. So my business is literally all over the map, and that allowed me to enjoy some success in the business."

Back in the early 1980s, Grant was studying psychotherapy at Ithaca College, but she decided she did not want to pursue that career path. After attending a series of seminars presented by the great *Twilight Zone* creator, Rod Serling, Grant fell back on a past rooted in theatre and music.

"I ended up taking some film and television courses along with the liberal arts. That background gave me the ability to come out here and work as an agent. So I came out here in the 1980s—right around the time that the big Guild strikes hit the business."

During those strikes, Grant took a two-year detour and became a corporate headhunter for the biotech industry.

"I put a little money in my pocket that way until I went to work for a little agency out in the Valley with a director of photography who wanted to start a below-the-line agency. With my past in music, I used to hang around with rock-and-roll groups. I knew a lot of the techies and roadies. As some of them grew up and realized they didn't want to be on the road all the time, they decided they wanted to be in film. So at that start-up, below-the-line agency, I came in with the desire to represent professionals for the film industry."

IN THE OLD DAYS . . .

Back in those dark days before e-mail and fax machines, Grant had to make daily trips to the studios for meetings. She put thousands of miles on her car traveling to Disney, Universal, or Fox, but that gave her the opportunity to meet the executives and learn from them.

"I saw how the end buyers—the producers—were people who would be looking for my production designers, DPs, and, eventually, my writers and directors."

Grant's experience as a headhunter, making cold calls and researching, allowed her to build her below-the-line business quickly:

"There were maybe twelve or so agents in the business doing that sort of work. I asked them questions on how they did their jobs. I learned that, in making deals, both sides are your clients. Your clients are the people who are giving you the opportunities to make deals, and your buyers provide employment. As an agent, you service both."

While representing her below-the-line talent, Grant began reading scripts and studying the literary agenting world:

"I had always had a good story sense, and story was always important to me. I looked at my career and asked, 'Where does Susan Grant want to be in two years down the line?' I wanted to work in the whole filmmaking process. I am not the sort of person who enjoys freelancing, so moving into producing wasn't for me. I found it more appropriate for me to start working with directors and writers."

Grant finds her writer clients through referrals from producers, managers, and attorneys.

"Writers are referred here all the time, so we read a lot of material," Grant said. "We really have to discriminate, especially in this day and age because the spec market that we once knew no longer exists. Everything is done by attaching stars and developing projects.

"So getting an agent is about getting to know people," she said. "It's never about sending unsolicited materials. You don't want to take ten agents and send them your log-lines. Even query letters are a long shot. I know everybody believes their script is a strong pitch, but it's rare.

"It's about getting out there and meeting the industry and the people in it. It's about swallowing your pride, making no money, not being treated well, but building relationships. It's about knowing how to deal with people—knowing how to deal with the dynamics of human sociology and psychology. If I were to design curriculums in film schools, I would make sure the students had a heavy dose of liberal arts courses so they were covered in those areas."

To make those networking contracts, Grant recommends beginning with just one friend. "Perhaps you have a distant cousin who is a working screenwriter. You need the moxie to call that relative or friend and invite him or her to coffee. Through that person, you get to know a couple more people. Maybe you join a writer's group or an independent film group.

"You need to do that, even if you're an introvert—which many people in the film business really are," Grant explained. "You need to step aside and leave your shyness at the door and say, 'Hi! How are you? What do you do?' That can make the difference between working and not working."

One of the advantages of working for a boutique firm, according to Grant, is the ability to teach insights like this to her clients. She can guide her writers into useful situations and prep them with the skills needed to succeed. So Grant takes a larger role in building her clients' careers that an agent at a bigger firm might be able to play.

KEEP UP WITH THE TIMES

"I tell my writers to keep up with the times. See movies. Watch TV. Read scripts. Understand what the market is looking for. You don't want to be a good writer who has a style and taste that was desirable ten or fifteen years ago. You always have to understand that this business is about change. What is it about that year's movies or TV shows that made them hits?

"Also, know your markets inside and out. If you're looking at TV movies, and examining CBS, you're looking to write a nice, sweet story with a good hook with well-developed characters. If the characters aren't ready, you won't attract cast, and whichever medium or genre you're dealing with, it's all about casting and interesting actors. A writer needs to know that."

While discussing characters, Grant digressed for a moment and urged writers to avoid writing "hateful characters" because they turn off readers and could prevent a writer from ever being read again.

"In other words," she said, "if you write a character no one can latch onto, you lose an audience. You need characters an audience can identify with and sympathize with. I don't care who you have to go to, how many times you have to have your script read by professionals, or how many times you have to rewrite a script, make your characters likeable. Don't carry in a defensive attitude. Take criticism well and get the script in shape."

Back on the topic of coaching her writers, Grant said she urges her writers to determine what they are really comfortable writing:

"Some writers feel comfortable in action; some gravitate to comedy. If you're writing different scripts just to include a variety of samples, don't bother. Stick to a single genre."

If she could give advice to all the young writers out there, Grant would tell them to stick to their dreams:

"You need a dream. I had a dream coming out here. This is a tough time in the film business, and it has gotten progressively more so in the last decade. You could say, 'Forget about this business. I'll go find a job on a dot.com or in another field.' But I think that would be rather sad."

Grant added, "When I'm working with a writer who I think really has talent, and we're able to get somewhere with a script, it gives me a lot of excitement. Making a deal makes me feel great. What else can I say? I'm an agent!"

CHAPTER REVIEW

- Boutique agencies can offer more individualized attention and better build the careers of less-experienced writers.
- Small agencies need to use creative marketing and business techniques to compete with larger firms armed with greater resources.
- Just because an agency is smaller doesn't mean it receives inquiries from fewer writers hoping to find representation. You still need to make sure your specs and samples are outstanding before approaching a boutique agency.

- Boutiques use many of the same business principles as larger agencies, so you still need referrals and relationships to access them.
- Don't be bitter, angry, or defensive when approaching any agency. It's the fastest turnoff in the business.

7

From Book to Box Office

Personal investment for agents is more common than people think.

Lisa Callamaro did not go the easy route. The young woman behind the small, but well-respected Callamaro Agency in Beverly Hills traveled from coast to coast to slug it out in Hollywood's trenches. She brings a strong artistic sense and genuine affection for her clients into her office every morning.

Lisa Callamaro, The Callamaro Agency

Callamaro entered the publishing and motion picture industry when she enrolled in the Harvard publishing program. Even during her college years, she had an interest in the arts, including motion pictures. After completing Harvard's course of study, she decided to steer her life's work toward the business of art. Callamaro soon found herself recruited by The Elaine Markson Literary Agency in New York City. Entering the company as a bookkeeper, she worked her way into an assistant's position with Markson herself. From that assistant's position, it was a short jump for Callamaro to handling publishing rights for the agency's best-selling authors. When Hollywood came calling for the film rights to particular novels under the Markson banner, it fell on Callamaro to work out the details.

While she handled the film rights for the agency's novels, she also began building working relationships with a small list of screenwriters. Those writers became Callamaro's first roster of film and TV writers when she moved to LA to establish a West Coast office for the Markson Agency. She ran that sunny extension of the prestigious New York agency for a year and a half before going solo and opening her own boutique. The Callamaro Agency maintains a connection to Markson, co-representing books in Hollywood. Callamaro also represents her own prominent stable of writers and directors.

Entering the business through the literary New York publishing environment gave Callamaro an excellent literary sense. She loves storytelling and storytellers, often encouraging her clients to venture out into the independent filmmaking world instead of the studio system if it means remaining true to their narrative ambitions. A few agents would avoid such advice rather than see their commission dip, but Callamaro pushes her clients to succeed as hard as she drives herself to look out for their interests.

Right before sunset on an early summer evening, a battle-weary Callamaro kicked free of her desk, wrestled the headset out of her hair, and sat down to talk about the Hollywood literary war from the trenches.

"I was lucky to get hired by Elaine Markson after completing the Harvard program," Callamaro said. "At the time, she was one of the classic agents with a very good reputation. She became a great mentor for me.

"During the time I spent with Elaine, the publishing business didn't really want to deal with the film industry the way it does now. They just weren't that comfortable with it. So whenever the film people came to the office, the agents would scatter. I was the only one left! But I loved talking about the movies, and the deals were interesting and fun for me."

ON HER OWN

In April of 1993, Callamaro opened her own shop in an airy, French courtyard-style office amid the expensive shops and idle rich of central Beverly Hills. She never imagined she'd end up in those surroundings when she started in the agent business back in the Big Apple.

"I hated agenting in the early days because agents got so much abuse, and I really didn't like the idea of taking that. But the interest for me was that I looked around and saw that when publishers, editors, and producers needed to increase their income, they moved on to new companies. So they were leaving people behind. When an editor left for a new company, she would leave her novelist back at the old publishing house.

"But I saw Elaine keeping clients for twenty years. She watched their lives grow, in addition to their careers."

Callamaro brings that same care and dedication into her business. Why do some agents value that kind of personal concern more than others?

"It's personality or style," Callamaro said. "Who trained you? How were you trained? How much time does an agent have in a day? I have fewer clients, so I have more time to devote to each of them every day by sheer mathematics. Some days I'll have more time with one of them than the others.

"I talk to all of my clients as often as I can, but some of them need me to read as they write, or to commiserate with them, and some of them just call to say, 'How are you?' I think my clients are more comfortable with a boutique, while others might be better off at a big packaging agency.

"Personal investment for agents is more common than people think, but there are a lot of agents who are not in a position to give that sort of care. They're a lot of people who would like to have more time to devote to each of their clients, but because of their work environment or other demands, they're just not able to do so for all the people on their list. Still, some of the best people I know in this business are agents. They go out of their way to make certain their clients are protected."

So she regrets the stereotypical image of the cigar-smoking, hustler agent who rips off anybody in range.

WHAT DO YOU CALL 100 DEAD AGENTS?

"We're the butt of all the jokes. There's always that moment at the dinner party when people discover I'm an agent and I expect everyone to start throwing food at me because they've had such bad experiences. Agents might have a better position in the publishing business because it's more gentle, but in the film business, we're seen as leeches. Somewhere along the line, a few bad apples earned us that reputation."

She hinted that an agent can often feel like the last kid picked for the pick-up football team: "I've been in a lot of situations where I've been at a table with a lot of creative people like actors, writers, and directors, and they were involving me in the conversation of the evening— until they asked me what I do. When I tell them I'm an agent, this wall goes up. They don't think you're creative, or that you care about movies. Somehow, you lose all of your personality to them and become nothing but a suit. They never grasp that someone might choose to represent an artist rather than be one."

In many industry circles, the concept of managing a writer's professional life in addition to handling basic deals falls more into the arena of a manager than an agent. Managers are usually credited with building an overall career for the good of the artist, while agents are often assigned to the nuts and bolts of business.

Callamaro doesn't believe such dedication is the sole prerogative of the manager, though some of the bottom-line philosophies at the Big Houses might mean less personal attention for clients. She explained that, in the past, agents were more accustomed to giving their clients that same managerial attention:

"Managers now are what agents were," she explained. "Agents have become a conduit for deals now because of the sheer number of writers on their lists. Many agents, especially those at the Big Houses, are under a lot of pressure to make ends meet. If they don't bill the right amount, they'll lose their jobs. It doesn't mean that agents at those places don't care at all about their clients. But a particular writer might find his agent's time used elsewhere."

As to how writers should go about finding that agent who will care about their career and fight for them, Callamaro suggested that it all comes down to a question of personality.

That said, Callamaro was reluctant to claim that a boutique agency is superior to a Big House because of the personal attention factor. She indicated that every writer's career has different needs:

"I've always said there are great things about a packaging agency and there are great things about boutiques. They both have a lot to offer, but they're apples and oranges. There's not one thing that's good or bad about the other. It's all about whether the writer likes apples or oranges. It all depends on the type of person you are as a writer—how you interact with people. There are writers out there who are comfortable only talking to their agents twice a year as long as they're working and getting paid. Or they might be real self-generators who don't need their agents involved as often. So not every writer wants that personal contact."

TO BE AN AGENT OR NOT TO BE

Since Callamaro devotes more one-on-one attention to her clients, many of her peers question why she doesn't officially become a manager. In fact, management companies have approached her to join their ranks. She responds that she values her status as licensed literary agent in spite of the risks involved.

"You can sell a management company, but you can't sell an agency, so I have no assets," Callamaro explained. "I have money as long as I'm a licensed agent and can commission the deals I make. I can't deal in assets because I'm not a manager who produces and 'owns' the show or movie. So if my clients aren't working, I'm not eating.

"There's a certain breed of managers out there that I'm wary of," she said. "There are managers out there who work hard and really care about their clients. They put their clients first, and that's what is important to me. But there are also those managers who are only building their own producing careers on the backs of their clients. I have a big problem with that.

"There have been cases in my own career when a client has had a project, and I've gone out and found the cast, a producer, a director, and the financing. The client could come back to me and say, 'You produced this movie. Why can't I give you credit as a producer?' But, I was just looking to find a way to get the project made."

Callamaro is careful to keep her eye on that pie to make sure her writers get as big a slab as possible. She admits that that can prove difficult: "I represent writers, and I think that's a specific challenge. In the scheme of things, the writer will always make less than the director or the actor. The writer becomes a tool, rather than the focus of a project. So that's why I have a problem with some managers who take the producer's role, while their writer clients take a smaller cut."

When it comes down to watching their own careers and pocketbooks, she warns writers against managers who have not been in the business that long. Some of these younger professionals may hold just one development job, then go into business for themselves, saying they're managers.

"They try to make deals for people or try negotiating, and I just see disaster," Callamaro pointed out. "They're more interested in being producers than managers. They build a stable of writers mainly to get a first look at a pool of material. Unless the writer is strong enough to say I want another producer attached to us, that writer had better ask a lot of hard questions before they sign. Whom does a manager represent? What projects are they attached to? If they attach themselves as a producer, will they also commission the writer?"

Callamaro clearly sympathizes with aspiring writers' search for agents because of the myriad choices they face. Agent or manager? Motion picture literary agent or television representative? Big House or boutique? The agent business became so compartmentalized in recent years that Callamaro had to make a decision.

"I don't handle publishing anymore. I came to a fork in the road. As an agent, you have to know your specific buyers. I could no longer know my buyers on the West Coast unless I got out here among them. Once I got out here, I couldn't keep in touch with East Coast buyers anymore. It became too hard to keep on top of who would be interested in what project in both industries, and on both coasts.

"The business is about relationships and what you know someone would respond to," she said. "Now the market and what an audience wants is driving the industry in a different way, but it's still about relationships and who an agent feels comfortable working with. I didn't work in series television, and when someone asked me why, I'd say, 'Because it's a whole different lunch crowd.'"

A CHANGED PLAYING FIELD

"Now, as television comes over looking to hire feature writers for their series, I've done more television work this year than feature work because the markets are merging."

Callamaro added that the increased number of screenwriters means more agents gravitating toward specializing in the motion picture literary field. More writers are looking to write screenplays now instead of novels because of the proliferation of entertainment magazines and Hollywood news programs. America looks to the movies now, instead of the printed page.

"I think we have fewer buyers now for more material, so we see more agents working with that material," Callamaro explained. "An agent has to know the market. I think it would be really hard for any one agent to know all the film producers and TV producers and book editors, so agents specialize. I wouldn't know the first thing about who to sell an interactive piece to. I could do it, I'm sure, but I'd really have to take the time to research it. It would be better for a writer to take that project to someone who specializes in interactive."

So how do writers looking for an agent get to one as skillfully specialized as Lisa Callamaro? They cannot wait for Callamaro or any other agent to offer a card or telephone number. Like most representatives, she believes writers looking for an agent should be willing to research and find someone right for them. Then the writers should approach that agent professionally.

"It shows some initiative," she added. "But, before they even write a query letter or look up my phone number, they should be working on their craft. They should be writing and learning.

"They should also be realistic about the business. There are more individual writer stories than run on the front page of *Variety*. They need to familiarize themselves with other writers and discover what it's really like to be in the film business. Talk to professional writers already in the mix and see what the life is really all about."

Callamaro explained that she often sees writers who arrive at that moment when they get that coveted big break. They have three projects to juggle. Business is seemingly great. However, they realize they haven't been on vacation for two years. They haven't left their office because projects are overlapping. Producers are calling with pressures. Directors want to see their pages. Actors want specific changes. Reality falls like a coal mine cave-in.

"The glamour of the professional screenwriting life completely disappears," Callamaro warned. "Writers believe that, when they're successful, they're going to be writing on a beach in Tahiti. That's not true because this is a very tough job. There is a lot of pressure, and you're the only person in the process who really works alone. The actors, directors, and producers are never alone and have plenty of assistance. You're alone in a room, and it's all on you.

"If aspiring writers can balance that reality with the *Hollywood Reporter* headlines of 'Spec Sells for $1 Million,' they might think about another way to live their life—or another way to write. Those headlines don't tell you how long it took to get that break or how many incarnations a script had before it sold. I had a client who did eleven drafts on a project, and the sex of the main character changed five times. If you're not willing to make those kinds of changes with some sort of happiness or team spirit, maybe you should write novels."

Callamaro acknowledged that novel writing allows the product of a writer's labor to be more in his control. So scribes should do some research and decide what kind of work they want to do. Would they prefer the literary atmosphere and individual control of novels to the team influence of screenwriting? Might they like sitcom television writing more than penning movies of the week? Callamaro would rather a writer make those kind of creative choices before growing discouraged.

"I hate to discourage people from writing," she said. "Screenwriting is about getting a movie produced, so you're working to become part of that process. But writing on its own is a useful, therapeutic tool, whether it's a screenplay, stage play, or novel. Writers have something to say. Even if a project is not yet at a saleable level in this marketplace, that doesn't mean that its writer shouldn't keep working to express himself. I've never told someone, 'Go away! Don't quit your day job!' That's not my place.

"I run into writers I don't want to take on, but I have never come across someone who I thought was so bad that I felt a need to tell them to stop! I find a lot of the writers out there are too concerned about their work to allow that. So I try to encourage those writers to keep writing, even if I pass."

That said, Callamaro warned any prospective clients hoping to approach her to have their act together and their scripts in polished form:

"If I don't have vested interest in the material, I can't really take the time to help them along with their writing. If there's something that I see there, I might take a chance. But if I run across someone who doesn't have it on the page, I have to pass. That doesn't prevent another agent from feeling differently. There are scripts that sold and got produced out there that I know I passed on. So this remains a subjective business. There are projects that I see on screen that I never would have identified as a real movie. Then there are other times when I deserve 'agent of the year' for selling ideas that no one believed would go anywhere.

"There're plenty of agents in town who are gifted at selling concept," Callamaro added. "They know how to sell a script that really isn't all there. So the original writer will make a deal, but will end up off the project. Because I have a smaller business, I'm more concerned with the longer career path. I want to make sure my writer is not going to be removed from a project. Besides, those one-liner pitch concepts are not something I do particularly well. So I prefer to be approached with completed, developed ideas as completed scripts or books."

Callamaro urged nonrepresented writers to use common sense and honor polite protocol when approaching her or any other agent. A party or other social gathering is not a good time to hit someone up to look at your material. Get her number and call or write her at the office in a proper, businesslike manner. If you don't make an agent's personal acquaintance (but would still like to request consideration), the standard industry practice of submitting a query letter and an SASE still stands as the best and most widely accepted method.

"Still, the best way to get to me is to get to a producer, studio, or production company I work with and get a referral," Callamaro urged. She then pointed to a stack of scripts piled from floor to desktop that all came in based solely on referrals. Blind queries didn't stand a chance that week. Only writers who got into the market ahead of any agent and opened some doors for themselves earned Callamaro's valuable consideration.

"It's important for writers to know that they have to champion their own careers. An agent is not an employment agency. It's all about building a career. The best and most successful relationships I have with my clients are those in which we view each other as team members. They don't sit at home every day and ask me to tell them what's going on in their lives. They get out there. They tell me about opportunities they find. We work on those together. I can put them in the right rooms, but they have to close the deal and get the job. It's a matter of teamwork, and it'd be deadly for my clients to sit at home believing it was up to me to make their careers happen. A writer and an agent need to work together to maximize opportunities."

CHAPTER REVIEW

- Whether the medium is books, movies, or TV, the sales principles involved in agenting remain largely the same. It's simply a question of knowing the individual markets and the players within them.
- A good agent tells clients the truth—not merely what they want to hear. That can prove difficult on occasion, since writing is as much a business as it is an art form.
- The best agents have a real passion for their work, just as writers do.
- A truly dedicated agent should really like working with and befriending writers.
- Give me an R . . . E . . . F . . . E . . . R . . . R . . . A . . . L . . . S. What does that spell?

8

THE
MANAGER

If you have talent, we'll find you . . . we'll send a car for you!

Many writers struggle with the dilemma of whether they need an agent or a manager. You should have a clear idea of what an agent does by now. But what can a manager do for you?

As explained in the introduction, a personal manager advises and counsels talent and personalities in the entertainment industry. For a writer, the manager oversees and advises on all facets of that individual's career. Whereas agents usually focus on only one market, managers must stay on top of all their clients' interests and potentials for income.

If a scribe writes screenplays *and* novels, he will most likely have separate agents handling either market. Sometimes a writer will have two agents from the same agency working together with producers or publishers (especially at the Big Houses), but a different multi-disciplined writer could use totally separate boutiques—potentially on opposite coasts.

A manager supervises that entire situation, often helping a writer find the right agent to whom to submit material. Once a client secures agency representation, the manager helps the writer work with that agent to find open markets and interested parties.

Since they act as personal, often nonlegal counsel, managers do not require licenses to operate their businesses, as agents do. Also, managers often take a higher cut of a deal for their services, usually 15 percent as compared to an agent's 10 percent. If a manager works with an agent to cut a deal, he will often reduce that 15 percent down to 10 percent. That prevents any client from paying out a whopping 25 percent in commissions on sold written work.

A good manager takes advantage of every opportunity to promote his clients. That practice operates in the best interests of both manager and client because the representative in the equation gains maximum benefits when artists he represents gain the rewards or acceptance in different areas of the entertainment field.

For a writer's purposes, a manager needs to have experience and knowledge of the many facets of the entertainment field. He should know the feature market, the TV business and, ideally, some aspects of publishing. That kind of representative can use this specialized knowledge to guide, advance, and promote the careers of clients who retain his services.

A manager can provide advantages to a younger or less established writer that an agent often cannot. Good managers find and develop new talent and create opportunities for the writers they represent. Since a manager oversees all aspects of a writer's career, he remains in a good position to build and expand on that career. Agents don't often find themselves in the business of grooming new talent. Any good agent tries to maintain at least a couple baby writers on her client lists, but she needs to make money to maintain the boutique or her position within a Big House. So the profitable or hot clients often come first. Still, a manager more often tries to nurture a fledgling career.

However, if you choose to focus on a single market for your work, a manager is probably not for you. Agents specializing in that market would be a better bet, as they would have more extensive contacts than a manager with fingers in many pies.

A code of ethics applies to manager's, just as it does to agents. Managers should always deal honestly and fairly with their clients. Ideally, managers should not derive personal (that is, non–business related) gains at the expense of their clients. Obviously, a client should expect all interactions to remain confidential.

It is also an unwritten (and, sadly, often broken) rule that no manager should encourage or induce an artist to breach an existing personal management contract, nor represent an artist while the artist is under a valid contract to another manager. Put bluntly, reps aren't supposed to steal clients from one another. But, as you've seen elsewhere in this text, it happens sometimes anyway.

Michele Wallerstein, Wallerstein Management

For insight into the mind of a devoted literary manager, we turn to Michele Wallerstein of Wallerstein Management. Wallerstein represents established, working clients as well as up-and-coming writers. We met her earlier in the introductory section. She formerly managed The Wallerstein Company, a boutique agency handling fewer clients than a Big House like William Morris.

Before opening her own boutique, Wallerstein worked at the Big Houses, representing both film and television writers. She made the switch to managing in 1999 in hopes of offering a smaller pool of writers more personal advice and attention.

I spoke with Wallerstein over breakfast at Hugo's, a homey little eatery in West Hollywood.

Since Wallerstein started out as an agent and moved to managing later in her career, she has had hundreds of writers approach her for representation over the years. She stressed that one of the main mistakes writers make is sending out their material too soon. If writers can't get access to a producer or a professional writer to critique their material, she suggested going to any one of several professional screenwriting consultants.

"I'm friendly with some of the consultants, even though I was not initially in favor of the entire business. Now I think they're a terrific idea.

"There are so many people who want to be screenwriters. So they write one or two screenplays. They give them to their friends and family in Wisconsin or Ohio and get friendly feedback. Then they send them to an agent. My job is not to read new writers' material and critique it. My job is to look for talent that I can market, sell, and make into a writing entity in the Hollywood professional community.

"If someone sends me a new script that's never been read by a professional, then either I'm stuck reading some novice's material, or I have to pay someone to read it for me. I should not need to do that. It's not my job.

"You should see the number of cover letters that come to me. I kept one for years that began, 'I have *wrote* a screenplay.' I couldn't wait to read that one, right? So I don't want to see a virgin script."

Wallerstein stressed that if writers spend money and go to a qualified consultant, they will receive protection from an early rejection:

"I know that somebody who's been in the industry and knows their job looked at the script. I know that somebody saw talent, a spark, or some level of ability there. That writer has good story sense or good character development ability."

However, screenwriters should make sure that they find the right person to offer a referral to any agent or manager. Sometimes, if a referral comes from someone with a bad reputation, that can cost a writer dearly.

"I find that there are two kinds of people who read scripts and refer them for the wrong reasons. One kind is an entertainment lawyer. Entertainment lawyers do not know how to read a script. Why would they know how to read a screenplay? Lawyers don't know how stories work. They don't know the details of marketing and what's happening in the business creatively. I was married to a lawyer! I know! Now, some entertainment lawyers might get mad at me, but they have a law degree. What does that teach them about narrative?"

People who are not development professionals, such as film school teachers, can also refer scripts and cause similar problems.

Wallerstein explained that she once visited one of the lesser-known LA-area film schools to address a class. During a break, she visited the bookstore and checked out the section for theatre arts. The books the school offered for sale dated back to the 1980s. Since the film business is changing moment to moment, such older texts become dated very quickly.

"These are people teaching screenwriting who are not professional screenwriters, and they're using old books. I'd rather read a script that's been looked at by a professional producer or consultant. There are very few rules in this business, but the ones that exist, you must pay attention to at all costs. One of them is have a professional read and comment on your work before you hand it over to an agent or manager."

Finally, writers should be careful how they handle their current representation. If a screenwriter is fortunate enough to have an agent and wants to add a manager, or visa versa, he could inadvertently send out a negative message.

Wallerstein explained, "I don't mind receiving a script from an agent, but if another manager sends me a script, I wonder why that manager isn't representing the writer.

"Writers need to learn what a contact is and how useful such a person can be as a referral," she said. "They often don't know the connections they have. They can't see the forest for the trees and realize that they have people around them who could give them a referral to an agent who only then would agree to read their material.

"If they see a great producer like Gale Anne Hurd speak at a conference or in a class, they could write her a letter. They could explain that they enjoyed her talk and polished their screenplay afterward, according to her comments. I bet they can send it to her . . . and I bet it gets read! It won't be read by her, but if it shows talent, it will get to her."

Wallerstein continued, "As for agents and managers, screenwriters can meet them at writing conferences and other events. If a writer meets me at such a gathering, I know that person. I am now a 'contact.'

"Every professional you meet is a contact. Call them up. Write them a letter. Send them your script. The fact that we put ourselves out there at events as agents and managers, even though we might possibly say *no* to your material, means that writers should be making use of those contacts.

"If you are a writer and I meet you at a conference or another such event, *I will* read your material. Why? I speak at conferences all over the country, and very few writers follow up. Those who do will get a response."

Wallerstein is surprised by how few writers follow up on their contacts: "I receive very little response from the writers I meet. Maybe I scare them. But it's the writer's job to follow up. The writer needs to overcome the fear of making that call or sending that letter and hearing *no*."

Wallerstein offers very simple, but absolute rules for writers to follow before submitting material:

- Do not send your first script. Send your third or your fourth.
- Do not send a treatment or a pitch.
- Unless you meet Wallerstein at a conference, she will not read your material if you write from outside Southern California. Why does she make the conference exception for out-of-state talent? "They made sacrifices. They spent their money. They have high expectations. They followed through up to this point. They must be fairly serious."

Wallerstein urges all writers to listen to and learn those rules. They should apply them no matter what agent or manager they contact.

That advice also applies to writers of any experience or any age. So much is made of Hollywood as a youth-obsessed environment. Wallerstein conceded that the industry does prefer attracting a youthful audience with disposable income. But that fact need not deter any writer beyond thirty years of age.

"Age can be a huge problem, especially for first-time writers, but not in the way everyone believes," Wallerstein said. "Often I meet first-time writers who recently retired from whatever their careers were. Someone told them they had an interesting life, and they should turn their lives into a screenplay.

"That doesn't often work, and I don't want to read those stories. Almost all people think their lives are interesting, especially when their friends tell them so. Unfortunately, interesting lives don't always make good movies. So age can trick a would-be writer in that case.

"As for new writers who are starting so late, I ask, Why did they wait this long? If they had talent, why didn't they begin writing sooner?"

Wallerstein quickly added that the doors of Hollywood are not always closed to older talent: "Executives and producers never ask me the age of the writer. If I send them a really good script, they don't care. In that case, age doesn't matter. Unfortunately, you hardly get a wonderful screenplay from anyone, let along just older writers.

"Writing a great script is more difficult than most people imagine. It's not just about telling a story. It's about real talent. It's about maintaining momentum, developing characters that the viewers care about, giving them interesting things to struggle through, etc."

Wallerstein admitted that she could occasionally crush the dreams of a few writers who simply did not have the knack, but, "I'm not their mother. It's not my job to tell them what to do.

"I know people who gave up their careers to begin writing. When I read their stuff, it was horrifying. It's a difficult situation then whether or not to tell them how bad the work is. My feeling is that it's not my job to tell someone to continue as a waiter or to go back to waiting tables or being a lawyer."

She added, "I might tell someone to keep writing, but maybe change genres or forms. I argued with one woman writer who published a couple of novels and now wanted to sell her next piece as a screenplay. Unfortunately, the story was more appropriate for a book. I told her that, but she wouldn't believe it. If one marketplace won't accept a piece, another might.

"Also, you don't know if you're reading someone's second script or their tenth, so why would you want to tell someone not to write?"

That memory gave Wallerstein a moment to vent over her huevos rancheros: "It drives me nuts when people insist that they have a great story just because it's a 'great story.' I can't deal with just that issue. I also deal with marketing."

She added, "The role of marketing can be frustrating for me, as well as for a writer. I will invariably read an intimate, emotional, beautiful screenplay . . . and realize I could never sell it to the studios. I wouldn't know where to set it up. It won't get foreign distribution or appeal to a young audience. It's a very hard sell. You hope someone might raise their own money and make it independently, but it rarely happens."

On the bright side, Wallerstein points out that such a script can serve as a writing sample, opening the doors for later scripts: "I'd be thrilled to read that writer's next script. We're always looking for that kind of talent."

When Wallerstein does reject material, she uses a standard form letter. While some writers might think that's an insult or an effort on her part to show them no individual respect, Wallerstein is really testing their resolve. A generic form letter should encourage a writer to call the agent in question for more feedback on the script. It shows openness to criticism and a commitment to their work.

"Writers often don't ask, 'What was the problem?' or 'What did you think?' They don't want to know, and they don't want to push."

If a given screenwriter produces a piece that does not warrant a quick pass letter, that does not guarantee immediate success or acceptance. There is still the difficulty of getting it through the Hollywood maze. The script must reach an agent or manager like Wallerstein. That rep needs to steer the work to interested producers. It can all seem like a mountain too high to climb.

Wallerstein said, "So often I hear frustrated writers say, 'How do I break in?' I say that talent will be found. If you have talent, we'll find you. We'll send a car for you!"

Wallerstein quickly pointed out that talent isn't always enough: "I've had clients very strong on the talent side who blew their careers right out of the water by making mistakes on the business side.

"For example, ego can always be a trap, especially too much ego too soon. You might see some major screenwriters throwing their egos around, but they have something in their pockets. They have a right to their opinion. But younger writers don't have that kind of authority, even if they want it."

Even though some of her clients can upset or frustrate her, just as some producers can mystify her with a pass on slam-dunk script, Wallerstein said she keeps her spirits high.

"This is a hard, cynical town, but I don't think that I'm cynical," she said. "I like the idea that I can take someone new and make them a success. I like that I can make spec sales. I like that I can manage my clients' careers.

"The last time I sold a young writer's first spec script, that writer had written fifteen scripts up to that point. When I read that spec, I was so excited that I went through the roof.

"If I was cynical, I wouldn't come to the conferences to talk to young writers. Any professional who speaks at writers' conferences is doing it with a lot of openness and optimism, and with a very positive attitude. We're not doing it for any other reason. The chance of finding the next up-and-coming star is very slim, and those discoveries are very rare. Any manager or agent not looking for that talent is not doing his or her job."

Glenn Sobel, Glenn Sobel Management

Glenn Sobel is a twenty-year entertainment industry veteran who runs his own boutique management firm out of Sherman Oaks, CA. As he branches his business out into the Internet and other new media, Sobel is not seeking new clients. But since he helped to build the careers of successful screenwriters like Dan O'Bannon (*Alien*, *Total Recall*), he can offer some genuine insight into the role of a manager in place of an agent.

After a stint in the army, Sobel began his career in the mailroom of Columbia Pictures in 1969. Afterward, he worked with his uncle, Carl Foreman, developing projects. After earning his law degree, he became head of business affairs for Mark Harris Management and head of business affairs for Anthony Quinn's production company. Finally, he worked for a small entertainment law firm in Beverly Hills before starting a management firm with Jim Rogers and Richard Berman in 1982.

Now operating his own boutique, Sobel decided that he didn't want to be an entertainment attorney because he preferred to manage and produce. His partnership with Jim Rogers led him to full-time managing:

"I wanted to do less drudgery kind of tasks and more creative work. There's a horrible amount of paperwork in the legal world. A lot of research and relatively boring work. I wanted to be more involved in the creative side of the business. Even when my uncle convinced me to go to law school, it was only because every big producer and exec was a lawyer. But law school gave me a lot of skills that you can use a producer and manager."

Sobel chose managing over agenting for the opportunity to produce:

"That's the biggest advantage that managers have over agents for a beginning or established client—they can produce, while an agent can't. I'm not saying it's fair, but that is the way it is. That gives a manager options to do things for a client that an agent isn't allowed to do."

The potential for personal attention is also another strong point for managers, according to Sobel.

"A manager tends to spend more time with the client creatively, while an agent feels her job is to sell a finished project. An agent doesn't have a lot of time to spend with a writer/client. She wants to see a finished product to go out and sell. It's more a matter of time than anything else. If you're working at a big agency, and you're paid on commission, you're paid to sell, not to develop material. That's where they have to put their time.

"If you're a successful agency and your choice of clients comes from the cream and not the milk," he said, "you expect the client to deliver something more polished. Agents in that situation shouldn't expect to spend as much time developing material. They're in the sales business. Any agent *can* spend additional time with a client. It depends on their schedule and their philosophy. If they care about how much money they can make, they're going to spend all of their time selling."

Sobel explained that, at one time, agents did what managers do now. Managers evolved out of a need, as the marketplace put more pressure on agents to sell instead of develop material.

"The agents' work level grew to a point where they could do nothing else but sell," he said. "Why should they sell your script with that limited time if the bigger writer's script is easier to sell? It's a funnel—eventually, all of your time narrows down to selling. Giving notes to develop a script is a service. The time crunch grew to the point where agents could no longer offer that service in every case.

"Managers evolved into the business because they were more willing to invest time and work with less accomplished clients and managed to build careers there. So it got to a point where the clients realized, 'What do I need an agent for if my manager is doing everything an agent does in addition to helping me to develop my material?'"

"There's no conspiracy here," Sobel stressed. "Agents didn't get together and decide to stop helping their clients while taking their money. They had to focus on selling with the limited time they had."

Sobel identified packaging as part of the problem because "Where does most of the attention go? To the money. If you have a director who makes $2 million and a writer who makes $250,000, whose deal will the agency work hardest to make? The director's! So, in that case, who's protecting the writer? Writers started to look for managers to look after their best interests."

When working with an agent, Sobel sees his role as a manager as a delicate road. Sometimes agencies try to position him as an outsider because they don't want him looking over their shoulder:

"I urge all of my clients to get the manager or attorney first and have them bring them to the agent. If you go to an agent and say you hired a manager, you just told the agent that you don't trust them and you need someone else to look over their shoulder. They don't like that."

When the agent/manager communication works well, it's as good as any other partnership, Sobel said.

"Both parties have access to certain information. If they pool it, both parties have more information and can accomplish more. A smart agent/manager team can also play good cop/bad cop when making deals. When it comes to negotiating, it's nice to point the finger elsewhere and say, 'Sorry. The other guy is making me ask for this.' You never want to position the client as the bad guy—or as the reason why a deal didn't come together."

When working with a manager, Sobel urged the writer/client never to pit an agent and manager against each other. Also, a writer should never do anything that's inconsistent with whatever the agent or manager is doing for the writer. If you tell a manager one thing, stick to that statement. Don't change your minimums or what you're willing to do without the manager's knowledge. Essentially, a writer must never negotiate behind the manager's back.

"I've seen it happen, and it is always disastrous," Sobel said. "There are buyers out there who will pull that trick. They'll put clients in a position where they are afraid to say *no*, and they jump.

"You shouldn't have an agent or manager that you don't trust. You need to trust them to do their job for you. If you can't, move on. You need an unemotional, objective, third party to negotiate because you will bring too much personal investment into the deal. A good manager won't panic during a negotiation.

"Negotiation is a sport. If you do it a lot, you're going to be better at it. It's not a fair fight for a writer to negotiate on his own behalf because it's not his skill. A manager provides the barrier against that. Let someone else do the fighting for you."

Richard Berman, Berman Management

According to Sobel's one-time partner, Richard Berman of Berman Management and Lancaster Gate Productions, being a manager allows him to give a few clients individual attention instead of trying to serve multiple ranks of clients. Also, it gives him more freedom creatively to create and produce projects.

"My reasons for producing are a lot different than many managers," Berman said, "Most of them produce because it's just another way of generating more revenue. We produce because we want to make a genuine creative contribution to the project. In most cases, we originate the project and bring it to the forefront. It's not so much about riding on the coattails of a writer/client. It's created here, originated here, and developed here."

According to Berman, managers can offer a much more personalized, one-on-one kind of relationship. They are much better able to work with clients to grow and nurture their careers. It's more than just sending clients from one job to another. It's about creating a path, a specialty, or a niche. That's very difficult to do when you're representing a lot of clients.

Berman now reps about twenty writers and directors. While he was a founding member of The Agency, the firm handled more than 100 professionals among its different agents.

He agreed with Sobel that, in a client-agent-manager relationship, the agent doesn't have as much time for the client as the manager does:

"They don't have the time these days, unless the client is very hot. If the client is not hot, they're not going to put that kind of time into it. So, often, it falls on the manager to get the heat going again. When a client loses the momentum, the agency moves on to another client. The manager needs to get the momentum going again.

"Maybe it's a growing, up-and-coming client. Maybe it's someone with a hot and cold running career. Maybe someone is in a cold period and needs to be jump-started again. At the large agencies, the reality is that those clients without the heat will die until they realize they're not getting any kind of attention at all.

"By the time they realize they are neglected, the damage to their career is done. That's why managers are so important in those situations—to figure out how best to move someone's career forward."

In some cases, managers can help to decide if a client stays at a large agency. Sometimes, a manager might urge a client to move to a small agency.

Berman said, "Sometimes the big agency makes the decision for us and tells us a client is not hot enough. A big agency will let them go as a result. A good manager will usually see that coming, however, and make the moves to answer the problem."

For a young writer, Berman said one of the toughest decisions to make is whether or not to work with a manager or a boutique agency.

"It depends on the manager. If he is a hands-on individual who can lay groundwork, it's a good fit. If it's just a manager who interacts with an agent to do most of the submitting, it might be better to go with a boutique agency."

A good manager looks to build a career, and whatever the agent brings to the table is a bonus. Unless there's some real genuine heat, Berman doesn't expect the agent to move mountains and break down doors for the client initially.

"It's nothing against the agent. It's just the way the business positions them. If everyone is excited about a client the agent has, the agent will also get excited. Agents are rarely looking for the new and upcoming. They're looking for the already hot."

Berman added, "Some smaller agencies will work with you. But everyone is looking for something where the phone is already ringing. Nobody wants to get in and start from ground zero. Managers are more willing to lay some of that groundwork. They're the ones who do most of the schlepping.

"That's the way the business is now. When I was an agent, I started from ground zero. These days, agents don't do that. I don't call ground zero finding someone who won Sundance. That person already has people flocking all over him. Maybe he doesn't have a major feature, but he won a major award. I'm talking about some guy who directed a little independent film with no distribution—or a writer with a bunch of good specs who hasn't made a sale yet. That's what managers look to build."

BONUS SECTION

The Agent/Manager Wars: Mike Ovitz Versus CAA

We already discussed the differences between agents and managers. On the heels of Wallerstein's insights, it's important to point out that those differences can turn into conflicts at times.

Agents are regulated by the State of California, subject to antitrust statutes, other bylaws, standards, and practices. For example, agents cannot produce films because they would then control both sides of the talent-hiring process. They would originate projects and hire their own clients, restricting competition. That's a sort of monopoly.

Managers have no such restrictions. They can produce projects written by their clients. They can even cast those in-house movies or TV shows with actors repped by the same management firm. Some managers do this. Some don't. The vast majority of managers do business by the same standards as agents, often making the distinction between the two camps irrelevant.

However, in the past year, mega-agent and CAA cofounder Mike Ovitz opened his own management company, AMG (Artists Management Group). Some felt the management company was doing business like an agency and luring clients away from CAA and other Big Houses. That led to a full-blown war as the agent/manager gap widened and became a battleground.

To understand the conflict, we turn to a Reuter's News Service /*Daily Variety* news article, dated January 26, 1999. Reporters Dan Cox, Chris Petrikin, Nick Madigan, and Mike Fleming contributed to the article. It not only describes the specific antagonism between CAA and AMG, it also illustrates the occasionally tense interactions between agencies and management companies:

Creative Artists Agency Draws a Line in Sand for Ovitz

Creative Artists Agency fired a warning shot across the bow of Michael Ovitz's new artist management group Monday, declaring it would no longer represent any client who signed with Ovitz.

The agency, which Ovitz and his original partners founded more than two decades ago, also called the clients who have already signed with AMG and issued an ultimatum, him or us.

"He is a competitor, not a collaborator. His work cannot be trusted," Creative Artists Agency president Richard Lovett said. "We're not going to be sharing any clients."

Creative Artists Agency placed the ultimatum calls Monday morning to director Sidney Pollack, Martin Scorsese, actors Claire Danes, Mimi Rogers, Marisa Tomei, Lauren Holly, and Minnie Driver, all of whom have signed with Ovitz under the assumption that they would be shared with Creative Artists Agency.

CAA said it would continue to work with other managers on an amicable basis. Insiders fear the clash may exacerbate the rising tensions between agents and managers in Hollywood.

Ovitz's recently announced AMG has systematically gone after high caliber clients like Scorsese, Pollack, Barry Levinson, and Penny Marshall.

"What Michael is building looks like an agency but calls itself a management company," Lovett said. "He is aggressively raiding the agencies."

Though Ovitz has maintained that he wants to work in tandem with the agencies, Lovett and CAA managing partner Brian Lourd claimed Ovitz's actions have proven just the opposite.

The final straw for CAA came with the defection of client Robin Williams and agent Mike Menchell to AMG. But the pair alluded to several other instances of clandestine behavior on Ovitz's part.

"We know Ovitz," Lovett said. "He has proven himself untrustworthy. He has betrayed the people closest to him."

"We don't have to live like this," added Lourd. "We don't have to participate in this lie."

Sources with CAA said Ovitz had been meeting with Robin and Marsha Williams for months before they joined AMG. And that came just after CAA and AMG had worked out an informal agreement whereby Ovitz and AMG would not poach any CAA clients without at least notifying CAA of their intentions.

Ovitz, meanwhile, had no comment on the development.

Within the industry, the CAA proclamation had telephone lines and fax machines burning up.

"CAA is a powerhouse," said manager Brad Grey of Brillstein Grey Entertainment. "They enjoyed great success. CAA has the privilege of deciding who they will and won't do business with."

"It's a full-scale war," said one former agent turned producer. "This was the first shot."

The CAA toppers called Universal Studios President Ron Meyer over the weekend to inform him of their intentions. Meyer did not advise them on their decision. Insiders say Meyer remains close to the CAA leaders and they regularly consult with him.

Meyer and Ovitz are also landlords for the CAA building, which they partially own.

Lovett and Lourd confirmed that CAA would continue to work closely with the other major management firms in Hollywood.

In fact, one high-profile manager said the move would probably solidify the working relationship between other managers and CAA.

"CAA is going to be a little more user-friendly with management," said the manager.

Legislation that may be brewing in Sacramento could prove problematic for Ovitz and for virtually all managers.

Sources said the bill is being drawn up in the California Legislature to regulate managers in much the same way agents are regulated; though no details could be confirmed.

It was unclear whether the bill would be an amendment to the Talent Agency Act or a separate act.

The announcement by CAA came just a short time after a meeting Monday morning of the Association of Talent Agents, the industry trade group that reps talent agents.

At that meeting it's understood that CAA reps told their peers that they would be making the announcement later that day.

While ATA executive director Karen Stewart declined to speak about the meeting, it's understood the primary topic discussed was the unregulated business practices of managers.

While many agents outside CAA said it was a gutsy move, most added that they weren't likely to enact the same type of restrictions any time soon.

One agent at the meeting said Ovitz's activities have highlighted the management business' lack of guild or state regulation.

"He certainly appears to be going in the direction of a non-regulated agency, but the situation will take care of itself," said the agent.

"The guilds are going to have to enforce their restrictions on managers soliciting employment for their clients or perhaps you'll just start seeing agencies surrendering their franchise agreements and becoming management companies."

Others warn that if the situation is not addressed by the guilds and/or by the state, then many agencies might go out of business altogether, unable to compete with managers who can produce and, despite restrictions, solicit employment for their clients.

So while an aspiring writer is unlikely to flirt with the massive monoliths of CAA and AMG, he may wish to consider the issues at hand when choosing between an agency and a management company.

BONUS SECTION

Screenwriting Conferences

Since Michele Wallerstein went out of her way to mention the value of screenwriting conferences, I thought this was a good time to take a moment to look at a few of the gatherings across the country where you could meet agents and managers. Since Wallerstein encouraged all writers to meet and develop contacts to act as potential referrals, you should know where the conferences are and what they offer. You'll recall that

Angela Cheng did not share Wallerstein's enthusiasm for these gatherings and I leave it to you to decide which, if any, of these conferences to attend.

Be forewarned that new conferences crop up every now and then, so I choose to offer notes on a few of the more established and accessible conferences. I personally attended each of the following and recommend them all. Any of them will give you an opportunity to meet and interact with agents or other professionals who could refer you to agents:

Indiefest: The Telluride Independent Film and Video Festival
Winter, Telluride, Colorado

A handful of filmmakers and screenwriters come to a mountain resort to enjoy a weekend in the thin, fresh air while discussing their work in supportive environments. As the weekend winds down and the artists gather around the ski lodge fireplaces, all that is missing is the marshmallows on sticks.

Independent filmmakers and screenwriters come from across the United States and gather in "picture-postcard perfect" Telluride, Colorado, to enjoy the view—out on the slopes and in the screening room. After a weekend spent examining and discussing each other's work in this old mining-town-turned-ski-resort hideaway, most of the artists agree on one thing: There are worse ways to spend a weekend.

The Telluride Indiefest promises to be an enjoyable and productive festival on the national scene for years to come. The festival's intimate atmosphere gives serious, dedicated filmmakers and screenwriters a chance to show their work to an audience before unleashing it on Hollywood.

Indiefest is to the larger, more widely attended Telluride Film Festival as Slamdance is to the now world-famous Sundance Film Festival. Sundance was originally conceived to give the aspiring visionary an environment in which to share and improve his work away from LA's rat race. When this Utah festival began attracting overwhelming (yet welcome) industry attention, independent filmmakers developed their own subfestival (Slamdance) to serve the original Sundance's purpose.

Every August, the Telluride Film Festival invites top young directors and their work so top industry executives and producers can sample the new meat among the sun-soaked peaks of the San Juan Mountains.

Telluride Indiefest takes place during the peak ski season (late January or early February) and gives less established filmmakers and screenwriters an opportunity to show off their efforts in small group sessions and larger public screenings.

While the larger, summer festival focuses exclusively on filmmakers, Indiefest welcomes selected screenwriters to present their best scripts in interactive, staged readings.

While the end result of these readings in no way truly resembles the movies these scripts will become, the presentations give the writers an invaluable opportunity to hear the product of their imaginations performed by others. The read-throughs prove very valuable in some cases as writers can see and hear the strengths and weaknesses of their scripts vibrantly demonstrated.

Also, after the readings, the actors, audience members, and fellow writers join together to discuss the fine points of each script. These lively discussions often spill over into after-hour sessions at the resort's bars and restaurants.

Meanwhile, Telluride's old Sheridan Opera House becomes a movie theater for the festival's duration, as screenings of independent features, fictional short films, and short- and long-form documentaries run day and night.

Festival entrants pay an application fee of $30 for an opportunity to attend the festival. The creators of the films and scripts selected by the Indiefest judges for exhibition win a free four-day pass to the festival, along with comped accommodations at various hotels, inns, and ski lodges around the resort. An entrant who accepts an invitation to Indiefest is responsible for transportation to and from the event (and for meals).

Finally, all the accepted entrants enjoy one complimentary recreational activity during the festival. They can enjoy a horseback ride, a snowmobile excursion, a sleigh ride, or a day flying down any one the of resort's world-class ski runs.

For more information, visit the festival Web site at *http://telluridemm.com/indifest.html.*

Selling to Hollywood, Summer, Glendale, California

The Annual Selling to Hollywood screenwriting conference attracts a bumper crop of aspiring scribes and industry professionals. Every year's list of attendees includes agents and managers open to reading your material.

Every year, writers from around the world fill the banquet halls and meeting rooms of a sophisticated Glendale hotel. Silver screen scribblers of different ages, experience levels, and abilities attend a series of lectures and interactive presentations aimed at improving their writing and professional presentation skills.

The topics for writers to select from often include: "Writing Treatments That Sell"; "Breaking the Ice, The Art and Power of Creating Relationships"; "The Reality of Options"; and "Hands-On Pitching." Guests can also sign up for opportunities to speak one on one to agents or producers in ten-minute individual consultation sessions.

Fortunately for Selling to Hollywood attendees, legitimate Hollywood agents attend the conference and share their views and advice.

Christine Foster is a literary agent with Shapiro-Lichtman Talent Agency. She represents writers, directors, producers, cinematographers, and editors. Foster attended the most recent Selling to Hollywood and said she enjoyed speaking to people new to the industry. She considers it a chance to give something back to the entertainment community.

"I think the people who come to Selling to Hollywood enjoy interacting with professionals in the industry," Foster said. "The featured guests deserve credit because they are frank about whatever topic they're talking about. The professionals really speak very honestly because there's no sense in misleading people."

While impressed with the featured guests and the attending writers at the conference, Foster had a couple of constructive suggestions for scribes heading to Selling to Hollywood.

"I think any writer who would like to pitch at the conference should have a one-page synopsis they can present. They should come prepared with a professional document created at home."

Foster added, "The conference should then explain the criteria by which agents and producers choose the best pitches at the conference. It would help the writers make the most of their time before and after their pitch."

Karen Wakefield, an agent with Epstein-Wyckoff & Associates, attended Selling to Hollywood because she knew many of the people who were attending the conference or who had attended the gathering in the past.

"It made sense for me to attend because I knew this was a conference that was for real," she said.

Wakefield represents screenwriters, directors, book authors, producers, and playwrights. She has also worked in development and production.

"I think Selling to Hollywood is intended more for beginner or intermediate writers," Wakefield said. "A featured guest needs to know this up front and be willing to explain a lot of the realities to the writers."

Wakefield said she supported the screenwriters trying to educate themselves and further their goals at the gathering, but she also emphasized the good sense of bringing the struggles of an aspiring writer to the fore.

"What some people don't understand is that many writers who might once have written books are now writing screenplays for the glamour," she said. "The competition is fierce. A writer might have a nicely structured screenplay, but there has to be something more than that on the page. At conferences like Selling to Hollywood, a writer has an opportunity to gain some insight into how to push their script to the next level."

For more information, visit *www.sellingtohollywood.com*

The IFP/West Screenwriting Conference, Spring, Los Angeles, California

The Independent Features Project/West actively supports the production and presentation of indie films. It also lends a helping hand to aspiring filmmakers trying to turn their visions into reality outside the cookie-cutter studio system.

Throughout the year, IFP/West sponsors special events and screenings to educate, inspire, and fund hard-working indie moviemakers. Its annual Independent Spirits Awards, honoring the best nonstudio films of the year, have become a popular, star-studded predecessor to the Oscars every spring.

Every spring the IFP/West opens its arms to aspiring screenwriters at its IFP/West Screenwriters Conference. Held in the meeting rooms at the Writers Guild of America, West's headquarters on Los Angeles' west side, the intimate setting gives writers in attendance an opportunity to learn from the industry's best working scribes and some of the most writer-friendly producers and agents working today.

This members-only conference presents a series of seminars to screenwriters in the IFP/West. Much like other successful conferences, industry experts take center stage while eager writers in the audience offer questions and take notes.

The highlight of the 1999 staging of the conference was a presentation on "The Business of Writing" by Adam Shulman, vice president of the Motion Picture Literary Department of LA's prestigious literary agency, APA. An agent for some of the most successful indie screenwriters in Hollywood, Shulman was recently named one of the top ten "independent friendly" agents by *Filmmaker Magazine*.

Before starting his agenting career in the mailroom at United Talent Agency, Shulman practiced corporate law and litigation in New York and Boston. A member of the California, New York, and Massachusetts bars, he is a graduate of Harvard College and the University of Pennsylvania. Finally, Shulman serves on the board of directors for OUTFEST, the Los Angeles Gay and Lesbian Film Festival.

Shulman shared some of his thoughts on the IFP/West Screenwriting Conference.

"I was approached by the IFP to participate in the conference, and I was happy to do so," Shulman said. "They run superb programs, and I saw a good list of people assembled for this conference.

"There's a slim chance for me to add to my client base at such a gathering because I need to remain loyal to the clients I have, but I pass along whatever bits of wisdom I have."

Shulman explained that he enjoys taking advantage of opportunities like this to help writers, and he learns a great deal himself while trying to impart some insider's advice.

"I learn what's on people's minds," Shulman said. "It gives me a chance to talk through issues affecting writers and think about issues I haven't thought of before."

Other topics for discussion during the conference include comedy writing theory, story structure, period piece scripts, and modern film noir stories.

In general, the conference is well-run and offers a very solid array of industry professionals.

For more information, visit *www.ifp.org*.

"Cinestory Scriptsessions," Spring, Chicago, Illinois, or San Francisco, California

Attended by scores of aspiring writers from the far-flung corners of the English-speaking world, Cinestory gives screenwriters access to some of the most talented and writer-friendly minds in the movie game. Big screen scribes get a chance to listen in on educational seminars, practice their pitches, receive notes on treatments or their script's opening pages, and commiserate with other writers on the rigors of breaking into the industry.

By day, guests attend lectures, pitch sessions, and screenings. By night, they venture into the city for social events.

In addition to its regular list of seminars, Cinestory provides a central hall or lounge—an all-purpose, casual meeting place for attendees and featured guests alike. Some of the most enjoyable and informative chats of the weekend happen here over bottomless cups of tea and coffee.

The rest of the weekend is dedicated to the business of writing. A series of seminars scheduled throughout Saturday and Sunday give all writers in attendance something to think about—regardless of their favorite genre or individual career goal.

Some of the conference's popular events include "Comedy Shop Talk—A Comedy Coffee Klatsch," "The Art—and the Heart—of the Pitch," "Script Coverage and Analysis," and, of course, "Getting an Agent."

By combining real professional insight with creative encouragement and a new sense of realistic expectations, the Cinestory Script Sessions promise an outstanding weekend every year.

For more information, visit *www.cinestory.com*.

Austin Heart of Film Screenwriters Conference, Spring, Austin, Texas

Atmospheric, historic, and intellectual Austin plays host to this popular conference.

The Austin Film Festival is dedicated to the writer as the heart of the creative process of filmmaking. The AFF uncovers outstanding, emerging writers, and fosters their development through panels, workshops, and master classes conducted by professionals (including agents and managers).

The conference recognizes, encourages, and challenges the talents of the young and provides outreach opportunities to Austin school children.

For more information, visit *www.austinfilmfestival.org*.

CHAPTER REVIEW

- A manager oversees all aspects of a writer's career, often focusing not just on one medium or market.
- A manager can often work with an individual client more closely than an agent can, building a career in ways an agent cannot.
- A manager can work with an agent to develop a client's career.

- As managers reach the highest levels of the industry, they encounter occasional conflict with agents over clients and the role of representation.
- Writing conferences can prove a useful tool in meeting representatives or professionals than refer you to them.
- Referrals. OK. I said it again.

9

THE ENTERTAINMENT ATTORNEY

I'm not here to be another obstacle to someone's career.

The entertainment attorney offers expertise that some agents and managers cannot. Obviously, attorneys know intellectual property and copyright law and can protect a client from any contractual conflict or related rip-off. They can represent writers in negotiations and submit their material to producers or executives. However, they usually do not work on a commission basis. While an agent or manager will take a 10–15 percent cut of a completed deal, a lawyer charges by the billable hour. Therefore, writers don't usually turn to entertainment attorneys until they have action already under way.

Dinah Perez

Dinah Perez is a California bar–registered attorney specializing in entertainment, intellectual property, and copyright. She represents writers, producers, directors, actors, below-the-line talent, talent agencies, management companies, and record labels. She bills in a variety of ways—hourly rates, expenses, flat fees, and, only occasionally, commissions (only for clients with an established track record). She does not work on a contingency basis. Her average hourly rate comes in at more than $200 per hour.

During an interview in her office high over Century City, we spoke at length about the different roles of a lawyer in Hollywood.

After completing her undergraduate education, Dinah became an investment banker. She wasn't happy in that line of work, discovering that she was more of a creative soul. She headed to LA, hoping to break into producing.

"I thought that, if I had good business acumen, I should be employable anywhere," Perez said. "I came to realize that there is a mindset in the entertainment industry that, whatever you know, if you didn't learn it in the business, you don't really know it. So people would interview me and couldn't make me entry level because I was over qualified, and they couldn't hire me for management because they didn't think I really knew anything.

"For whatever reason, they didn't look at me as someone they could insert into middle management and build into something more. Therefore, I went from a high-paying career to not being employable. I decided that I needed to go back to school. If I went to film school, I could end up unemployed for the rest of my life. If I went to law school, I'd always be working."

During her legal studies, Perez researched all of the entertainment-related courses. After earning her JD, she opened her own practice and has practiced entertainment law ever since.

Comparing her job to the role of an agent, Perez focused on the specific advantages that attorneys can offer clients, due to their distinct, professional qualifications:

"I negotiate deals like agents. Sometimes, I will shop projects around. However, unlike most agents, I can look at an agreement and make sure the language actually reflects the client's desires and what he agreed upon originally. Sometimes, a contract can turn on a word.

"Recently, I had a client come to see me with an option agreement. Usually, a writer gets 5 percent of net profits from a motion picture and anything that gets created as a result of that motion picture—be it a sequel, a remake, a TV series, whatever. But this agreement said she only got 5 percent of the producer's net profits from the original film only, which obviously limited what the client could make off the deal. If a sequel or series were to be produced, she was never going to see any net profits from that.

"Unlike an agent, I'm trained to look for that kind of language," she explained. "Also, I will put clients in touch with banks once they have presales on their picture. I will introduce them to sales agents and distributors, which some agents don't do or don't have time to do. If you're at a big agency, they'll help you to package your script because they're getting a big fee and are happy about it. But, at a mid-size or smaller agency, they're not going to do that for a writer or producer. You have to make your own opportunities."

Perez considers agents and managers generally interchangeable, filling largely the same roles for writers.

"I know they don't like to hear that, but I believe it's true. The only real difference between them is that a manager can work with a conflict of interest. Managers can go out and produce projects that their clients created—even if it might prove better for the client if the manager shopped the project for the best possible opportunity."

As an attorney, Perez earns the automatic certification of California bar membership and must abide by the related ethics, standards, and practices. Agents must be state licensed and registered with the Writers Guild. However, managers have no such requirements.

Perez said most of her clients come from referrals. On the day we spoke, she met with her latest customer, a writer referred to her by another client.

"I get a lot of business that way. I also write articles for a Web site, (*www.surfview.com*), so I get a lot of calls from that. Also, I have another entertainment attorney who refers business to me. He writes entertainment law books now, but no longer practices. He sends that business to me."

The entertainment attorney offers writers a way out of the familiar Catch-22 of no agent without action, no action without agent:

"You can always hire an attorney. You may not be able to get an agent or manager, but as long as I have good chemistry with someone coming in to see me, and I think that I can help him, I will represent anybody. I'm not here to be another obstacle to someone's career.

"For example, a recent client came to me because he has a script that he had queried to production companies. They responded and wanted to read it, but they wouldn't unless it was sent in by an agent, a manager, or an attorney. I'm not going to read the script. Frankly, what I think about the script doesn't matter. I'm not here to be just another person judging his work. Who am I? I can tell you that 90 percent of the movies that get made are projects I wouldn't have green-lit if I had been in that position. I'm not here to judge the quality of the script or whether it's worthy of being read.

"I'm here to open a door for that writer. That's what I do. I help them make the submission. Then, the work must speak for itself."

Perez encourages prospective clients to call her directly or e-mail her (that contact information is included later in this chapter). She cites as her biggest pet peeve prospective clients who call repeatedly, thus failing to wait patiently for her to get back to them.

"I'm good about returning phone calls. If you call me in the morning, don't call back fifteen times that day because that makes me not want to deal with you. Have some respect that I'm a professional. I will return your call."

Perez offers new clients a thirty-minute consultation at no cost to judge chemistry and whether or not her services will work for that individual artist.

"I don't want to represent people that I can't help. I don't want to work with people who have an unrealistic expectation of what a lawyer can do for them. People come to me looking for a guarantee that I will make their movie happen. They don't understand that I'm a facilitator, not a decision maker. I don't want to work with people who are mentally unstable—and you can usually tell that in the first half-hour."

She added, "I don't want to do business with people who can't afford an attorney. I know there are people out there who think they can do business without an attorney. They write their own agreements, and they turn into big disputes later on because it didn't say what it needed to say. I've had prospective clients come in here with the audacity to ask me for my boilerplates (standard template contracts). They say, 'Give me your boilerplates and I'll do it myself.' I don't want to work with someone like that. I want to sit down with people who have an appreciation for the work that I do. It's a valuable service."

"Quite frankly," Perez confessed, "People who can't afford attorneys need to think twice about how they're doing business. Whether you're a screenwriter, an actor, or a producer, you are creating a business. You need working capital. You need an attorney and a CPA when the time comes."

Perez wouldn't say if there's an outright advantage to working with an attorney instead of an agent or manager, but points out, "I can provide an important service that not every agent or manager can provide. I am in the business of negotiating deals and making deals happen. An agent is in the business of knowing what's out in the marketplace and what's being purchased.

"I think it helps if a client has an agent and an attorney. The agent will have her hand on the pulse of the industry. She's going to be submitting that writer's work to the appropriate production companies and studios that she knows will be looking for the appropriate product. I'm not up-to-date on that every day because that's not what I do exclusively."

Perez said she has a good working relationship with Writers & Artists. The minute that someone gets involved with their common clients, both agent and attorney are on board:

"We talk about what it is we're going to ask for in that client's case and how we're going to negotiate that deal together. Ultimately, the agent negotiates the deal, but I'm involved every step of the way. I review all the documents and I serve as a sounding board for the agent."

Perez proudly pointed out that that she rarely has a problem working with an agent on a deal:

"I always approach every negotiation as, 'Let's make the deal happen.' I have had an occasional situation in which I felt the agent got in the way of that happening because they were asking for things that a producer couldn't afford. So they were making it more difficult."

She went out of her way to urge writers working with a partner to have a collaboration agreement in place before embarking on a new script:

"It's really important that no one puts their hand on a keyboard to write word one until there's an agreement on the collaborating writers. Invariably, there's always a fight when that happens. One writer thinks he did more work than the partner did, and maybe now 50 percent should be 75 percent, or his name should come first. If that agreement is in place first, you know the terms and they're won't be any fighting over it."

Perez represents clients out of state, offering those outsiders a useful path into the industry. She uses the same grounds to determine whether she wants to work with them. Obviously, it helps if a client brings some action to the table. Her biggest client comes from Spain (Perez speaks fluent Spanish). If you have something Perez can handle and can afford her rate, she'll work for you.

Occasionally, a writer might encounter the attitude shared by agents and managers that entertainment attorneys are less creative individuals than other professionals in the industry are:

"I don't think an agent or a manager is necessarily a creative person, either. If they were, they'd be doing something creative. Agents and managers are essentially sales people. That's really what they are. They're in the business of selling. I know as much about a good script as any agent or manager because I go to the movies, I know what I like, and I have fairly mainstream tastes."

Before contacting her, Perez urges writers to register a copyright on their material. The forms are downloadable off of the Internet, and the registration costs $30. In the Bonus Section of this chapter, Perez shares more detailed information on copyright.

"I also suggest that writers avoid pitching their idea to everybody. They need to pitch in a formal setting, such as a meeting. Don't pitch an idea at a party or in a restaurant because whoever hears the pitch didn't consent to the pitch and can use the idea. The writer has no recourse in those circumstances.

"When you schedule a meeting, they know what you're there for and you create an implied contract if they choose to use the idea. You should write a letter requesting or confirming the meeting and another letter thanking them for their time. Whatever the purpose of the meeting is, reiterate it in the letter."

There is no set amount of material or number of scripts a writer needs to compile before approaching Perez:

"If a writer calls me because they have a producer looking to option a property of theirs, they're there already. If someone wants to make submissions, they need to know how to write a screenplay. I can't tell you how many people contact me who never took a class or read a book, but they wrote a screenplay and believe it will be the next Oscar winner. They need to understand that this is a craft the requires education and hard work.

"I take what writers do very seriously, and I understand the amount of hard work it takes to produce a really fantastic, producible screenplay. It's really important that writers know the mechanics of reading a screenplay. They need to use the appropriate format and make certain there is not a single typo in the script. It's a reflection of who they are. Writers are wasting their time and money if they have me send a screenplay out that isn't ready."

Perez added, "You only get one chance with some people. If that person reads a really bad screenplay, they're going to remember that name, or they're going to check the coverage on file. They're going to remember and you're not going to get anywhere."

BONUS SECTION

The Legal Perspective

Following my interview with Perez, she graciously offered to share her wisdom and expertise by allowing me to reprint two of her essays on doing business in Hollywood.

Before we begin, I wanted to include a basic overview of copyright. Perez will go into superior detail in her pieces. Although the Copyright Act affords you protection for creating your work in a tangible form, many writers wonder how to register works with the U.S. Copyright Office.

The registration process is straightforward. Copyright protection attaches immediately and automatically upon fixation (reduction to a tangible form) of the work in question. You simply need to include a date, your name, and the all-powerful © symbol. So why bother to file a federal copyright registration? Two reasons:

- Ability to sue
- Statutory damages

Although copyright attaches upon fixation, you cannot sue someone for infringing your copyright until you registered your work with the Copyright Office.

If you register your work within three months of the date of first publication, or at least prior to the date of infringement, you can collect statutory damages from the infringer. Otherwise, you only get actual damages, which could prove very small.

According to federal government documents, copyright protects expression. The Copyright Act of 1976 states that the items of expression can include literary, dramatic, and musical works; pantomimes and choreography; pictorial, graphic, and sculptural works; audio-visual works; sound recordings; and architectural works. An original expression is eligible for copyright protection as soon as it is fixed in a tangible form.

Consequently, almost any original expression that is fixed in a tangible form is protected as soon as it is expressed. For example, an original script, outline, treatment, book, or article is protected as soon as the file is completed and saved to disk. This book was protected as soon as I stopped typing and saved the file.

Most of the items any writer is likely to create are eligible for copyright protection, including multimedia material, letters, the text of Web pages, contents of e-mail messages, graphics files, etc.

However, not everything is eligible for copyright. The following are items that, by their very nature, are not eligible for copyright protection:

- Ideas
- Facts
- Titles
- Names
- Short phrases
- Blank forms

So, as we move on now to Perez's essays, I don't think I need to remind you that she holds the copyright on the following articles. She gave me specific permission to use them. I wouldn't be stupid enough to steal intellectual property from an intellectual property attorney!

PROTECTING YOUR IDEAS, TREATMENTS AND SCREENPLAYS
by Dinah Perez, Esq.

Just about every writer and producer I know or represent is concerned that their ideas will be stolen by some unethical and unscrupulous producer, production company, studio executive, or competitor. As such, this article is meant to educate writers and producers regarding the protection of their ideas, treatments, and screenplays.

The U. S. Copyright Act (the "Act") protects literary works, literary characters, music, movies, videos . . . when these are original works of authorship, which are fixed in a tangible medium.

By fixed, the Act means that the work is embodied in a manner which is "sufficiently permanent or stable to permit it to be perceived, reproduced or otherwise communicated for a period of more than transitory duration," i.e., a treatment, screenplay, video, film, etc.

The Act does not protect ideas, concepts, principles, and discoveries. Therefore, writers and producers should never blurt out an idea to anyone who has not agreed previously to purchase the idea from them, or to attach them to whatever is produced based upon the idea. It is necessary to ask for permission and to condition disclosure on purchase of the idea because contract law can afford protection where copyright law falls short. An agreement in this regard creates a confidential relationship, which obliges the pitchee to pay for use of the idea.

Therefore, the writer should refrain from pitching an idea if the potential pitchee refuses to agree to the terms for the disclosure. If the pitchee agrees and the writer pitches the idea, then the writer should follow up the pitch meeting with a letter thanking the pitchee for his time, reiterating the purpose of the pitch meeting, and how the pitchee agreed to pay, or attach the writer, should the pitchee decide to use the writer's idea.

Sending the letter will remind the pitchee of the agreement, and it will provide the writer with proof of an agreement should the pitchee use the idea without the agreed upon compensation. Again, since ideas are not protected by copyright, the writer should ask the pitchee not to disclose the idea without the writer's permission, and the writer should include request in his letter, as well.

In 1976, the Act required that the writer of the work register the work with the U.S. Register of Copyright and that the writer post a copyright notice on the work. These formalities are no longer necessary for copyright protection. Today, copyrights are automatic as of the moment of creation. Nonetheless, it is recommend that the writer of the work adhere to the formality of registration, since it affords the writer certain valuable benefits not otherwise available.

For example, if the writer of the work discovers that someone has infringed his copyright, the writer can have a court order an injunction against the infringer and win a suit, assuming there was an infringement, where damages are awarded by the court. The writer may secure an injunction whether or not the writer registered with the U.S. Register of Copyrights, but damages are only available if the work was registered.

It is also wise for writers to place the copyright symbol and year of copyright on their works; this formality is no longer necessary, but it does serve to deter potential infringes.

Writers must file a copyright registration form with the U.S. Register of Copyrights, in order to register a copyright for their original work. A registration form may be secured by calling (202) 707-9100, or by sending a self-addressed and stamped envelope to the author of this article at 1888 Century Park East, Suite 1100, Los Angeles, CA 90067.

The completed form is mailed to the address provided on the form, along with a copy of the work, and a $20 check made payable to the U.S. Register of Copyrights. Proof of registration is usually forthcoming within eight to twelve weeks.

Self-mailing has been referred to as the "poor man's copyright." This entails the writer placing the work in an envelope, mailing it to himself via registered mail, and not opening it upon receipt. The reasoning behind this is the unopened envelope, which is postmarked, can be used as evidence in a court proceeding to provide verification as to the date of existence of the work. The poor man's copyright provides no more protection than the unregistered copyright. It is best to register original works with the U.S. Register of Copyright.

Many writers and producers mistakenly believe that WGA registration protects their idea, treatment, or screenplay. The WGA does not provide protection against infringement since only the Act is capable of such protection. As such, WGA registration only serves to provide evidence at trial.

The WGA may be called as a witness for testimony regarding the date of WGA registration if someone infringes the WGA registered writers' work. The WGA cannot testify as to the originality of the writer's work, or the validity of the infringement claim. The cost of WGA registration is $20 for nonmembers and $10 for members.

Writers are very often asked to sign a release when making submissions to production companies and studios. This occurs when the writer is unrepresented by an agent or attorney. If the writer takes the time to read the release, then he will notice that the release more likely than not gives the release's beneficiary carte blanche to use the writer's idea without compensation. As such, it is highly unlikely that the writer will be attached to whatever project is developed from his idea. Since copyright law does not protect the idea, the writer is admitting via the release that the idea is in the public domain, and the release establishes that there is no contract for payment.

Obviously, writers should avoid signing releases. If a writer is underrepresented by an agent, then it is best for the writer to hire an attorney to make submissions. The legal fees for a submission range between $30 and $100.

The best protection for a writer's idea, treatment, or screenplay is non-disclosure, but that approach is impractical if the writer intends to have a writing career in the film industry. The next best alternative is registration of the work with the U.S. Register of Copyrights and the creation of oral contracts, as detailed above, to protect the writer's ideas during the pitching and submission process. The aforementioned procedures for protection are not a guarantee against theft, but they are a deterrent with legal punch.

This article is not a complete review of the subject matter and, as such, the reader should not make decisions on the basis of the above without consulting with an attorney.

THE NINE GOLDEN RULES FOR CREATING GOOD ENTERTAINMENT INDUSTRY KARMA
By Dinah Perez, Esq.

Every day, I counsel people who have dug the proverbial grave for themselves because of the manner in which they have comported themselves or conducted business. I have written this article in order to impart what my years in the worlds of law, business, and metaphysics have taught me. These "Nine Golden Rules" are simply tools for creating a more positive and productive professional life. I hope you find them helpful.

1. Do Not Lie.

Your word and reputation are priceless commodities in an industry riddled with hype and lying wannabes. Be truthful no matter the consequences and you will stand out as a person of integrity.

For example, do not tell sales agents you have an actor attached, when you do not. The truth eventually catches up with you and you may face: losing your credibility, being permanently shunned by the actor and/or her agent, and/or you may have a legal claim filed against you for having made the misrepresentation.

2. Do Not Steal.

If it is not yours, then do not take it, be it an idea, an equity contact, a piece of equipment, or otherwise.

For example, someone shares an idea for a screenplay with you, which you usurp, rationalizing that it happens all the time or, in fact, has happened to you. If you are completely passionate about the idea and you cannot get it out of your system, then ask the disclosing party if he would mind partnering up with you. If the disclosing party declines, despite your passion for the project, move on knowing that the Universe is full of ideas ready for the picking. If you go on and steal the idea, you may not be able to warrant and represent that the idea is wholly original to you, when called upon to do so. Furthermore, the disclosing party may file a legal claim against you for breach of an implied contract.

3. Be Fair/Do Not Be Greedy.

People tend to assert their power in a deal when they are in the power position. Avoid the temptation to squeeze the last penny, or deal term, out of a negotiation if the aforementioned does not affect you negatively, and if it is going to result in someone being treated unfairly. Remember, everyone has to work together when the deal is done. Resentment is going to permeate your relationship with the unfairly treated party; it is virtually impossible to have a positive working relationship with someone who resents you.

4. Do Not Gossip.

Gossip can ruin a person's career, business relationships, and personal life. Do not succumb to the temptation to gossip, even if the information is based in fact, because everyone (you included) has done, or will do, something regretful. If you decide to proceed, remember that the gossiper rarely makes a good impression: the person with whom you share the gossip will wonder if you will ever do the same to her, and you may be perceived as a liar, back stabber, and petty person.

5. Treat People the Way You Want to Be Treated.

You need as many people in your corner as possible when you are on the rise. Treat everyone from the assistant to the studio executive with respect, kindness, and honesty. People may put up with arrogance and attitude from a director whose movies gross over $100 million dollars at the box office, but they do not have to tolerate the same from a nobody. In other words, be the kind of person people want to know and with whom they want to work.

Also, the assistants and the junior agents are the gatekeepers for the people to whom you need access. Make allies of the gatekeepers by being pleasant and sensitive to the stresses of their job. They will be more apt to assist you if you are friendly and respectful to them.

It is also important for you to note that the assistant to whom you are speaking today may be the studio executive with the ability to greenlight your picture tomorrow.

7. Lend a Helping Hand.

Function as if opportunity is abundant and it will be so. Share information and contacts when called to do so. It is perfectly acceptable to decline this request if this referral is going to be detrimental to you, i.e., the referral will reflect badly on you.

8. Keep Your Commitments.

People tend to make commitments they do not honor for a myriad of selfish reasons. You need to be able to depend on people just as much as they need to depend on you. Keep your word unless the object of your promise is illegal, immoral, or likely to harm someone other than yourself. If you decide that you cannot keep your commitment, then be mature and up front about it so that the other party can make other arrangements.

9. Give Back.

The Universe is like a saving account—you have to make deposits if you want to make withdrawals. Share your accomplishments with others: be a mentor, make referrals, executive produce a film for an up-and-coming filmmaker, give to charity, be a speaker at your child's school career day, etc.

Working in the film industry is full of complications and stress. Why complicate matters further by being dishonest, undignified, and unfair, and creating potentially explosive legal situations? Approach your business dealings from a positive place and you are more likely to succeed and enjoy your success.

This article is not a complete review of the subject matter and, as such, the reader should not make decisions on the basis of the above without consulting with an attorney.

Dinah Perez, the author of the article, is available for consultation. She may be reached by phone at (310) 553-1155, fax at (310) 553-2510 and e-mail at *Entlaw@msn.com*.

BONUS SECTION
Standard Contracts

As a supplement to Dinah Perez's outstanding commentary on legal issues, protection, and professional practices, we take a moment here and include the sample legal contracts the Writers Guild offers free of charge for features and television projects:

THE WRITERS GUILD STANDARD WRITING SERVICES CONTRACT

The WGAw created a standard writing services contract that can be tailored to reflect the negotiated terms of any writing services contract. Using this contract can and will make your life easier both at the time the deal is negotiated and in those unfortunate instances when a dispute arises at a later time. This contract can help get writers paid sooner, reduce disputes over contract language, and eliminate the inclusion of unexpected and unwelcome provisions that too often are discovered after a contract is signed. Currently, the Guild's standard form contract is for employment on theatrical motion pictures, but other forms will be available in the future.

According to the Guild, this contract is not intended to constitute legal advice, but is offered by the Guild as an aid to ensure the timely delivery of contracts and, therefore, timely payment to the writer. The WGA Minimum Basic Agreement (MBA) requires companies to deliver contracts within specific time frames following agreement on major deal points and/or commencement of services (generally within two to three weeks.) In the event the company fails to deliver a contract within the MBA time limits after negotiation of the major deal points, this form contract may be used to confirm the deal with the company, in the same manner as a deal memo is used.

The contract is intended to facilitate the negotiating process between a writer or his representative and a company employing that writer. Companies, writers, and their representatives may use these forms to memorialize employment agreements before the submission of a "long-form" agreement.

The form contains blanks to be filled in and boxes to be checked to reflect the individual agreement, as negotiated. Please ensure that all relevant spaces are filled in. When subject to the MBA, the terms of the MBA supersede any provisions in the form that are less favorable. This form also contains provisions not required in the MBA, but which the WGAw recognizes as either "standard" or important to negotiate in an individual writer's contract. Please call the WGAw Contracts Department at (323) 782-4501 if you have questions.

WRITERS THEATRICAL SHORT-FORM CONTRACT

DATE : _____

1. NAME OF PROJECT: _____
   ("PROJECT")

2. NAME/ADDRESS OF COMPANY:
   _____ ("COMPANY")
   _____
   _____

3. NAME OF WRITER: _____ ("WRITER")
   SOCIAL SECURITY NUMBER _____

4. WRITER'S REPRESENTATIVE: _____

5. CONDITIONS PRECEDENT:
   ❏ W-4   ❏ I-9   ❏ OTHER, IF ANY

6. COMPENSATION:
   A. GUARANTEED COMPENSATION (SEE 11, BELOW): $_____
   B. CONTINGENT COMPENSATION (SEE 11, BELOW): $_____
   C. PROFIT PARTICIPATION: IF SOLE WRITING CREDIT, _____% OF
      (NET/GROSS) PROCEEDS; REDUCIBLE FOR SHARED CREDIT TO
      _____% (SEE 27, BELOW)

7. SPECIFIC MATERIAL UPON WHICH SERVICES ARE TO BE BASED, IF ANY
   (A COPY WILL BE SENT TO WRITER UNDER SEPARATE COVER):

8. OTHER WRITERS EMPLOYED ON SAME PROJECT OR FROM WHOM
   MATERIAL HAS BEEN OPTIONED/ACQUIRED, AND DATES OF MATERIAL,
   IF ANY:

9. COMPANY REPRESENTATIVE AUTHORIZED TO REQUEST REVISIONS:

10. COMPANY REPRESENTATIVE TO WHOM/PLACE WHERE MATERIAL IS TO BE DELIVERED:

11. SERVICES TO BE PERFORMED, INCLUDING NUMBER OF STEPS *(e.g., story and first draft, two rewrites, and a polish):*

      A. FOR STEP 1:   ❏ GUARANTEED
                                  ❏ OPTIONAL
      WRITING PERIOD: _____ WEEKS
      READING PERIOD: _____ WEEKS
      PAYMENT DUE: $_____
      (50% DUE ON COMMENCEMENT, 50% ON DELIVERY)

      B. FOR STEP 2 (IF APPLICABLE): ❏ GUARANTEED
                                    ❏ OPTIONAL
      WRITING PERIOD: _____ WEEKS
      READING PERIOD: _____ WEEKS
      PAYMENT DUE: $_____
      (50% DUE ON COMMENCEMENT, 50% ON DELIVERY)

      C. FOR STEP 3 (IF APPLICABLE): ❏ GUARANTEED
                                  ❏ OPTIONAL
      WRITING PERIOD: _____ WEEKS
      READING PERIOD: _____ WEEKS
      PAYMENT DUE: $_____
      (50% DUE ON COMMENCEMENT, 50% ON DELIVERY)

      D. FOR STEP 4 (IF APPLICABLE): ❏ GUARANTEED
                                  ❏ OPTIONAL
      WRITING PERIOD: _____ WEEKS
      READING PERIOD: _____ WEEKS
      PAYMENT DUE: $_____
      (50% DUE ON COMMENCEMENT, 50% ON DELIVERY)

E. FOR STEP 5 (IF APPLICABLE): ❏ GUARANTEED
                                 ❏ OPTIONAL

WRITING PERIOD: _____ WEEKS

READING PERIOD: _____ WEEKS

PAYMENT DUE: $_____

(50% DUE ON COMMENCEMENT, 50% ON DELIVERY)

F. ADDITIONAL STEPS (IF APPLICABLE):

_____

_____

12. COMPANY SHALL PAY THE ABOVE GUARANTEED AMOUNTS DUE IF READING PERIODS PASS AND COMPANY DOES NOT REQUEST SERVICES; HOWEVER, IF THERE HAS BEEN NO INTERVENING WRITER(S), SERVICES SHALL BE DUE, SUBJECT TO WRITER'S PROFESSIONAL AVAILABILITY, FOR A PERIOD NOT TO EXCEED _____ MONTHS.

13. BONUS:
    A. For sole writing credit: $_____
    B. For shared writing credit: $_____
    Shared credit bonus will be paid on commencement of principal photography if no other writer has been engaged; balance to be paid on determination of writing credit.
    C. For "green light" or engagement of an "element": $_____
    If Writer is writer of record or is most recent writer on the Project at the time the Project is given a "green light" by a studio or an element is attached on a pay-or-play basis, Writer shall be given a bonus of _____ Dollars ($_____) which may ❏ may not ❏ be applied against the bonus in A. or B., above.

14. CREDITS AND SEPARATED RIGHTS:
    Per WGA MBA.

15. EXISTING CREDIT OBLIGATIONS REGARDING ASSIGNED MATERIAL, IF ANY (SUBJECT TO WGA MBA):

16. VIEWING CUT:
    Per WGA MBA: Writer shall be invited to view a cut of the film in time sufficient such that any editing suggestions, if accepted, could be reasonably and effectively implemented. Writer shall also be invited to [_____] other screenings.

17. PREMIERES:

If writer receives writing credit, Company shall ❑ shall not ❑ provide Writer and one (1) guest with an invitation to the initial celebrity premiere, if held, with travel and accommodations at a level not less than the director or producer of the project.

18. VIDEOCASSETTE:

Per WGA MBA.

19. TRANSPORTATION AND EXPENSES:

If Company requires Writer to perform services hereunder at a location more than ____ miles from Writer's principal place of residence, which is _____, Writer shall be given first class (if available) transportation to and from such location and a weekly sum of $_____ ($_____ per week in a high cost urban area).

20. SEQUELS/REMAKES:

If separated rights,

- Theatrical sequels = 50% initial compensation and bonus; remakes = 33%.
- Series Payments: $_____ per ½ hour episode; $_____ per 1 hour episode; $_____ per MOW (in network primetime or on pay television, otherwise $_____ per MOW); $_____ per sequel produced directly for the videocassette/videodisc market; $_____ per product produced for the interactive market based on the Project; _____
  [other, e.g., theme park attractions based on the Project].
- Spin-offs: Generic—½ of above payments
              Planted—¼ of above payments
- If Writer is accorded sole "Written by" or "Screenplay by" credit, Writer shall have the right of first negotiation on all audio-visual exploitation, including, but not limited to remakes and sequels and MOWs, mini-series and TV pilots (or first episode if no pilot) for a period of seven (7) years following release.

21. NOTICES:

All notices shall be sent as follows:

TO WRITER: TO COMPANY:

22. MINIMUM BASIC AGREEMENT:

The parties acknowledge that this contract is subject to all of the terms and provisions of the Basic Agreement and to the extent that the terms and provisions of said Basic Agreement are more advantageous to Writer than the terms hereof, the terms of said Basic Agreement shall supersede and replace the less advantageous terms of this agreement. Writer is an employee as defined by said Basic Agreement and Company has the right to control and direct the services to be performed.

23. GUILD MEMBERSHIP:

To the extent that it may be lawful for the Company to require the Writer to do so, Writer agrees to become and/or remain a member of Writers Guild of America in good standing as required by the provisions of said Basic Agreement. If Writer fails or refuses to become or remain a member of said Guild in good standing, as required in the preceding sentence, the Company shall have the right at any time thereafter to terminate this agreement with the Writer.

24. RESULTS AND PROCEEDS:

Work-Made-For-Hire: Writer acknowledges that all results, product, and proceeds of Writer's services (including all original ideas in connection therewith) are being specially ordered by Producer for use as part of a Motion Picture and shall be considered a "work made for hire" for Producer as specially commissioned for use as a part of a motion picture in accordance with Sections 101 and 201 of Title 17 of the U.S. Copyright Act. Therefore, Producer shall be the author and copyright owner thereof for all purposes throughout the universe without limitation of any kind or nature. In consideration of the monies paid to Lender hereunder, Producer shall solely and exclusively own throughout the universe in perpetuity all rights of every kind and nature whether now or hereafter known or created in and in connection with such results, product and proceeds, in whatever stage of completion as may exist from time to time, including: (i) the copyright and all rights of copyright; (ii) all neighboring rights, trademarks, and any and all other ownership and exploitation rights now or hereafter recognized in any Territory, including all rental, lending, fixation, reproduction, broadcasting (including satellite transmission), distribution and all other rights of communication by any and all means, media, devices, processes and technology; (iii) the rights to adapt, rearrange, and make changes in, deletions from and additions to such results, product, and proceeds, and to use all or any part thereof in new versions, adaptations, and other Motion Pictures including Remakes and

Sequels; (iv) the right to use the title of the Work in connection therewith or otherwise and to change such title; and (v) all rights generally known as the "moral rights of authors."

25. WARRANTY AND INDEMNIFICATION:
  A. Subject to Article 28 of the WGA Basic Agreement, Writer hereby represents and warrants as follows:

  1. Writer is free to enter into this Agreement and no rights of any third parties are or will be violated by Writer entering into or performing this Agreement. Writer is not subject to any conflicting obligation or any disability, and Writer has not made and shall not hereafter make any agreement with any third party, which could interfere with the rights granted to Company hereunder or the full performance of Writer's obligation and services hereunder.
  2. All of the Work (and the Property, if any) shall be wholly original with Writer and none of the same has been or shall be copied from or based upon any other work unless assigned in this contract. The reproduction, exhibition, or any use thereof or any of the rights herein granted shall not defame any person or entity nor violate any copyright or right of privacy or publicity, or any other right of any person or entity. The warranty in this subparagraph shall not apply to any material as furnished to Writer by Company (unless such furnished material was written or created by Writer or originally furnished to Company by Writer) or material inserted in the Work by Company, but shall apply to all material which Writer may add thereto.
  3. Writer is sole owner of the Property together with the title thereof and all rights granted (or purported to be granted) to Company hereunder, and no rights in the Property have been granted to others or impaired by Writer, except as specified, if at all, in this Agreement. No part of the property has been registered for copyright, published, or otherwise exploited or agreed to be published or otherwise exploited with the knowledge or consent of Writer, or is in the public domain. Writer does not know of any pending or threatened claim or litigation in connection with the Property or the rights herein granted.
  4. Writer shall indemnify and hold harmless Company (and its affiliated companies, successors, assigns, and the directors, officers, employees, agents, and representatives of the foregoing) from any damage, loss, liability, cost, penalty, guild fee or award, or expense of any kind (including attorney's fees hereinafter "Liability") arising out of, resulting from, based upon or incurred because of a breach by Writer of any agreement, representation, or warranty made by Writer hereunder. The party receiving

notice of such claim, demand or action shall promptly notify the other party thereof. The pendency of such claim, demand, or action shall not release Company of its obligation to pay Writer sums due hereunder.

B. Company agrees to indemnify Writer and hold Writer harmless from and against any and all damages and expenses (other than with respect to any settlement entered into without Company's written consent) arising out of any third party claim against Writer resulting from Company's development, production, distribution, and/or exploitation of the Project.

26. NO INJUNCTIVE RELIEF:

The sole right of Writer as to any breach or alleged breach hereunder by Company shall be the recovery of money damages, if any, and the rights herein granted by Writer shall not terminate by reason of such breach. In no event may Writer terminate this Agreement or obtain injunctive relief or other equitable relief with respect to any breach of Company's obligations hereunder.

27. PROFIT PARTICIPATION:

Terms to be negotiated in good faith. If the parties fail to reach agreement within [ ] months after execution hereof, either party, upon 30 days notice to the other, may submit the matter to what is known as a "baseball arbitration," in which each party presents one profit proposal and the arbitrator is required to adopt one of the two proposals. The arbitrator shall be selected and the arbitration conducted pursuant to the Voluntary Labor Arbitration Rules of the AAA.

28. AGREEMENT OF THE PARTIES:

This document [including Attachment 1, if any] shall constitute the agreement between the parties until modified or amended by a subsequent writing.

BY: _____   BY: _____
            [NAME OF WRITER]   TITLE

CC: WGA CONTRACTS DEPARTMENT

ATTACHMENT 1

ADDITIONAL PROVISIONS, IF ANY:

_____

_____

_____

_____

_____

_____

_____

_____

_____

THE SHORT-FORM CONTRACT FOR LONG-FORM TELEVISION

As a companion to the WGA Standard Contract for Theatrical Motion Pictures, there's now a WGA Standard Contract created specifically for movies of the week, movies made for television, and miniseries.

This short-form contract can help with the following:

- Streamline the drafting process.
- Ensure inclusion of provisions of particular importance to Television Long-Form writers (especially regarding "Producer's Drafts").
- Assist in assuring timely payment.

This contract can be tailored to reflect the negotiated terms of any writing services contract you negotiate. Use it in place of deal memos or those quickly jotted notes you write to confirm the terms just negotiated. Using this contract can and will make your life easier, both at the time the deal is negotiated and in those unfortunate instances when a dispute arises at a later time. The WGA believes this contract can help get writers paid sooner, reduce disputes over contract language, and eliminate the inclusion of unexpected and unwelcome provisions that too often are discovered only after a contract is signed.

This contract is not intended to constitute legal advice, but is offered by the Guild as an aid to ensure prompt written confirmation of agreed-upon terms, the timely delivery of contracts, and, therefore, timely payment to the writer. The WGA Basic Agreement requires companies to deliver contracts within specific time frames following agreement on major deal points and/or commencement of services (generally within two to three weeks.) In the event the company fails to deliver a contract within the MBA time limits after agreement on the major deal points, this form contract may be used to confirm the deal with the company. If you have any questions, call the WGAw Contracts Department at (323) 782-4501.

WRITERS TELEVISION SHORT-FORM CONTRACT
(For Movies of the week and Mini-Series)

DATE: _____

1. NAME OF PROJECT: _____
   ("PROJECT")

2. LENGTH OF PROGRAM: _____ MINUTES (OVER _____ BROADCAST
   PERIODS/NIGHTS)

3. NAME/ADDRESS OF COMPANY:
   _____ ("COMPANY")
   _____
   _____

4. NAME OF WRITER: _____ ("WRITER")
   SOCIAL SECURITY NUMBER _____

5. WRITER'S REPRESENTATIVE: _____

6. CONDITIONS PRECEDENT:
   ❑ W-4   ❑ I-9   ❑ OTHER, IF ANY

7. COMPENSATION:
   A. GUARANTEED COMPENSATION (SEE 15, BELOW): $_____
   B. CONTINGENT COMPENSATION (SEE 15, BELOW): $_____
   C. PROFIT PARTICIPATION: IF SOLE WRITING CREDIT, _____% OF
      (NET/GROSS) PROCEEDS; REDUCIBLE FOR SHARED CREDIT TO
      _____% (SEE 33, BELOW)

8. SPECIFIC MATERIAL UPON WHICH SERVICES ARE TO BE BASED, IF ANY
   (A COPY WILL BE SENT TO WRITER UNDER SEPARATE COVER):

9. OTHER WRITERS EMPLOYED ON SAME PROJECT OR FROM WHOM
   MATERIAL HAS BEEN OPTIONED/ACQUIRED, AND DATES OF MATERIAL,
   IF ANY:

10. COMPANY REPRESENTATIVE AUTHORIZED TO REQUEST REVISIONS:

11. COMPANY REPRESENTATIVE TO WHOM/PLACE WHERE MATERIAL IS TO BE DELIVERED:

12. ANNOTATIONS WILL ❑ WILL NOT ❑ BE REQUIRED (IF YES, COMPANY'S ANNOTATION GUIDE WILL BE PROVIDED TO WRITER IMMEDIATELY)

13. PRODUCER IS ❑ IS NOT ❑ AUTHORIZED BY THE NETWORK/LICENSEE TO REQUEST ADDITIONAL REVISIONS BEFORE SUBMITTING DRAFTS TO THE NETWORK/LICENSEE.

14. PRODUCER IS ❑ IS NOT ❑ A SIGNATORY TO THE NETWORK WGA MBA (WHICH REQUIRES THE COMPANY TO NOTIFY THE NETWORK/LICENSEE IN WRITING WHEN WRITER HAS DELIVERED TO THE COMPANY).

15. SERVICES TO BE PERFORMED, INCLUDING NUMBER OF STEPS *(e.g., story and first draft, two rewrites and a polish)*

[*Note:* Not less than 10% of agreed compensation for the first delivered material is due upon commencement, not less than 30% of agreed compensation is due on delivery of story, not less than 40% of agreed compensation on delivery of first draft teleplay, not less than 90% of WGA minimum shall be paid by delivery of first draft teleplay. The balance is due on delivery of final draft teleplay. In addition, if the writer is employed for story and teleplay, not more than 14 days shall elapse between the first submission of the story and the commencement of the preparation of the teleplay. For teleplay, the applicable time limits for teleplay in Article 13.B.8. shall control.]

A. FOR STEP 1: _____ (*EXAMPLE:* STORY/TELEPLAY/REWRITE)
❑ GUARANTEED
❑ OPTIONAL

WRITING PERIOD: _____ WEEKS
READING PERIOD: _____ WEEKS
PAYMENT DUE: $_____
(50% DUE ON COMMENCEMENT, 50% WITHIN SEVEN (7) DAYS OF DELIVERY)

B. FOR STEP 2 (IF APPLICABLE): _____

❑ GUARANTEED

❑ OPTIONAL

WRITING PERIOD: _____ WEEKS

READING PERIOD: _____ WEEKS

PAYMENT DUE: $_____

(50% DUE ON COMMENCEMENT, 50% WITHIN SEVEN (7) DAYS OF DELIVERY)

C. FOR STEP 3 (IF APPLICABLE): _____

❑ GUARANTEED

❑ OPTIONAL

WRITING PERIOD: _____ WEEKS

READING PERIOD: _____ WEEKS

PAYMENT DUE: $_____

(50% DUE ON COMMENCEMENT, 50% WITHIN SEVEN (7) DAYS OF DELIVERY)

D. FOR STEP 4 (IF APPLICABLE): _____

❑ GUARANTEED

❑ OPTIONAL

WRITING PERIOD: _____ WEEKS

READING PERIOD: _____ WEEKS

PAYMENT DUE: $_____

(50% DUE ON COMMENCEMENT, 50% WITHIN SEVEN (7) DAYS OF DELIVERY)

E. FOR STEP 5 (IF APPLICABLE): _____

❑ GUARANTEED

❑ OPTIONAL

WRITING PERIOD: _____ WEEKS

READING PERIOD: _____ WEEKS

PAYMENT DUE: $_____

(50% DUE ON COMMENCEMENT, 50% WITHIN SEVEN (7) DAYS OF DELIVERY)

F. ADDITIONAL STEPS (IF APPLICABLE):

_____

_____

16. COMPANY SHALL PAY THE ABOVE GUARANTEED AMOUNTS DUE IF READING PERIODS PASS AND COMPANY DOES NOT REQUEST SER-VICES. THE READING PERIOD FOR A POLISH SHALL NOT IN ANY EVENT EXCEED THIRTY (30) DAYS. IF THERE HAS BEEN NO INTERVENING WRITER(S), HOWEVER, SERVICES SHALL BE DUE, SUBJECT TO WRITER'S PROFESSIONAL AVAILABILITY, FOR A PERIOD NOT TO EXCEED _____ MONTHS. IF COMPANY AT ANY TIME GIVES WRITER NOTICE THAT NO FURTHER SERVICES ARE REQUIRED, THEN ANY REMAINING UNPAID INSTALLMENTS OF THE ABOVE FIXED COMPENSATION SHALL BE PAYABLE AT SUCH TIME AS COMPANY NOTIFIES IN WRITING THAT NO FURTHER SERVICES ARE REQUIRED.

17. BONUS:
    A. For sole writing credit: $_____
    B. For shared writing credit: $_____
    Shared credit bonus will be paid on commencement of principal photog-raphy if no other writer has been engaged; balance to be paid on deter-mination of writing credit.
    C. For "green light" or engagement of an "element": $_____
    If Writer is writer of record or is most recent writer on the Project at the time the Project is given a "green light" by a network or an element is attached on a pay-or-play basis, Writer shall be given a bonus of _____ Dollars ($_____) which may ❑ may not ❑ be applied against the bonus in A. or B., above.

18. CREDITS AND SEPARATED RIGHTS:
    Per WGA MBA. It is understood that Writer has not sold any reserved rights by virtue of this agreement. If Company wishes to acquire any reserved rights, or the compensation above is equal to or in excess of the "upset price," Writer and Company will negotiate separately regarding such reserved rights, subject to the WGA MBA.

19. EXISTING CREDIT OBLIGATIONS REGARDING ASSIGNED MATERIAL, IF ANY (SUBJECT TO WGA MBA):

20. VIEWING CUT:
    Per WGA MBA: Company shall invite Writer to view the "Director's Cut" with-in forty-eight (48) hours after the Company's viewing. If, in lieu of a viewing,

the Company is provided with a videocassette copy of the cut, the Company shall simultaneously provide the Writer with a videocassette copy of the cut. Writer shall also be invited to [_____] other screenings.

21. PREMIERES:

If Writer receives writing credit, Company shall ❑ shall not ❑ provide Writer and one (1) guest with an invitation to the initial celebrity premiere, if held, with travel and accommodations at a level not less than the director or producer of the project.

22. VIDEOCASSETTE:

Per WGA MBA.

23. TRANSPORTATION AND EXPENSES:

If Company requires Writer to perform services hereunder at a location more than _____ miles from Writer's principal place of residence, which is _____, Writer shall be given first class (if available) transportation to and from such location and a weekly sum of $_____ ($_____ per week in a high cost urban area). If Company requires Writer to perform services at such location for two (2) weeks or more, Writer shall be given one (1) additional first class round trip transportation for Writer's companion.

24. SEQUELS/REMAKES:

If separated rights,

- Series Payments: $_____ per ½ hour episode; $_____ per 1 hour episode; $_____ per MOW (in network primetime or on pay television, otherwise $_____ per MOW); $_____ per sequel produced directly for the videocassette/videodisc market; $_____ per product produced for the interactive market based on the Project; _____ [other, e.g., theme park attractions based on the Project].
- Spin-offs: Generic—½ of above payments
  Planted—¼ of above payments
- Sequel Movies for Television: If Project is ninety (90) minutes or longer, Writer shall be offered the opportunity to write any sequel Project ninety (90) minutes or longer, at not less than the Writer was paid to write the Project.
- Other Sequels: If Writer is accorded sole "Written by" or "Screenplay by" credit, Writer shall have the right of first negotiation on all audio-visual exploitation, including, but not limited to remakes and sequels and MOWs, mini-series, and TV pilots (or first episode if no pilot) for a period of seven (7) years following release.

25. THEATRICAL EXHIBITION: 100/50/50 (BUT NOT LESS THAN WGA MINIMUMS): If the Project, or any edited version thereof, either in whole or in part, is released theatrically, then Company will pay Writer the following compensation in addition to all other compensation provided for in this Agreement.

(a) If the Project, or any edited version thereof, either in whole or in part, is released theatrically anywhere in the world prior to its initial telecast in the United States, then Writer will receive the greater of: (i) an amount equal to 100% of Writer's compensation specified in Paragraphs 15 and 17 of this Agreement, or (ii) WGA minimum for such theatrical release.

(b) If the Project, or any edited version thereof, either in whole or in part, is released theatrically subsequent to its initial telecast in the United States, then: (i) upon such theatrical release in the Domestic Territory, Writer will receive an amount equal to 50% of Writer's compensation specified in Paragraphs 15 and 17 of this Agreement, or WGA minimum for such theatrical release, whichever is greater; and (ii) upon such theatrical release in the Foreign Territory, Writer will receive an amount equal to 50% of Writer's compensation specified in Paragraphs 15 and 17 of this Agreement, or WGA minimum for such theatrical release, whichever is greater. For purposes hereof, the "Domestic Territory" means the United States and/or Canada; the "Foreign Territory" means any area(s) of the world outside the Domestic Territory.

(c) It is understood that regardless of the number or sequence of theatrical releases of the Picture, Company will not be required to pay Writer a grand total of theatrical release payments under subparagraphs 25(a) and 25(b) in excess of 100% of Writer's compensation specified in Paragraphs 15 and 17 of this Agreement, or the aggregate WGA minimum for all theatrical releases, whichever is greater.

(d) All theatrical release payments will be made within 30 days following the applicable theatrical release to which the payment relates.

26. NOTICES:
All notices shall be sent as follows:
TO WRITER: TO COMPANY:

27. MINIMUM BASIC AGREEMENT:
The parties acknowledge that this contract is subject to all of the terms and provisions of the Basic Agreement and to the extent that the terms and pro-

visions of said Basic Agreement are more advantageous to Writer than the terms hereof, the terms of said Basic Agreement shall supersede and replace the less advantageous terms of this agreement. Writer is an employee as defined by said Basic Agreement and Company has the right to control and direct the services to be performed.

28. GUILD MEMBERSHIP:

To the extent that it may be lawful for the Company to require the Writer to do so, Writer agrees to become and/or remain a member of Writers Guild of America in good standing as required by the provisions of said Basic Agreement. If Writer fails or refuses to become or remain a member of said Guild in good standing, as required in the preceding sentence, the Company shall have the right at any time thereafter to terminate this agreement with the Writer.

29. PLUGOLA AND PAYOLA:

Writer acknowledges that it is a crime to accept or pay any money, service, or other valuable consideration for the inclusion of any plug, reference, product identification or other matter as a part of a television program unless there is a full disclosure as required by the applicable sections of the Federal Communications Act. Writer will not accept or pay any such consideration or agree to do so, and any breach of such undertaking will be considered a breach of this Agreement.

30. RESULTS AND PROCEEDS:

Work-Made-For-Hire: Writer acknowledges that all results, product, and proceeds of Writer's services (including all original ideas in connection therewith) are being specially ordered by Producer for use as part of a Motion Picture and shall be considered a "work made for hire" for Producer as specially commissioned for use as a part of a motion picture in accordance with Sections 101 and 201 of Title 17 of the U.S. Copyright Act. Therefore, Producer shall be the author and copyright owner thereof for all purposes throughout the universe without limitation of any kind or nature. In consideration of the monies paid to Writer hereunder, Producer shall solely and exclusively own throughout the universe in perpetuity all rights of every kind and nature whether now or hereafter known or created in and in connection with such results, product, and proceeds, in whatever stage of completion as may exist from time to time, including: (i) the copyright and all rights of copyright; (ii) all neighboring rights, trademarks, and any and all other ownership and exploitation rights now or hereafter recognized in any Territory, including all rental, lending, fixation, reproduction, broadcasting (including satellite transmission), distribution, and all other rights of communication by any and all means, media, devices, processes, and technology; (iii) the rights to adapt, rearrange, and make changes in, deletions from and additions to such results, product and proceeds, and to use all or any part thereof in new versions, adaptations, and other Motion Pictures including Remakes and Sequels; (iv) the right to use the title of the Work in connection therewith or otherwise and to change such title; and (v) all rights generally known as the "moral rights of authors."

31. WARRANTY AND INDEMNIFICATION:
   A. Subject to Article 28 of the WGA Basic Agreement, Writer hereby represents and warrants as follows:

   1. Writer is free to enter into this Agreement and no rights of any third parties are or will be violated by Writer entering into or performing this Agreement. Writer is not subject to any conflicting obligation or any disability, and Writer has not made and shall not hereafter make any agreement with any third party, which could interfere with the rights granted to Company hereunder or the full performance of Writer's obligation and services hereunder.
   2. All of the Work (and the Property, if any) shall be wholly original with Writer and none of the same has been or shall be copied from or based upon any other work unless assigned in this contract or in the public domain. The reproduction, exhibition, or any use thereof or any of the rights herein granted shall not defame any person or entity nor violate any copyright or right of privacy or publicity, or any other right of any person or entity. The warranty in this subparagraph shall not apply to any material as furnished to Writer by Company (unless such furnished material was written or created by Writer or originally furnished to Company by Writer) or material inserted in the Work by Company, but shall apply to all material which Writer may add thereto.
   3. Writer is sole owner of the Property together with the title thereof and all rights granted (or purported to be granted) to Company hereunder, and no rights in the Property have been granted to others or impaired by Writer, except as specified, if at all, in this Agreement. No part of the property has been registered for copyright, published, or otherwise exploited or agreed to be published or otherwise exploited with the knowledge or consent of Writer, or is in the public domain. Writer does not know of any pending or threatened claim or litigation in connection with the Property or the rights herein granted.

4. Writer shall indemnify and hold harmless Company (and its affiliated companies, successors, assigns, and the directors, officers, employees, agents, and representatives of the foregoing) from any damage, loss, liability, cost, penalty, guild fee or award, or expense of any kind, including outside attorney's fees (hereinafter "Liability") arising out of, resulting from, based upon or incurred because of a breach by Writer of any agreement, representation, or warranty made by Writer hereunder. The party receiving notice of such claim, demand, or action shall promptly notify the other party thereof. The pendency of such claim, demand, or action shall not release Company of its obligation to pay Writer sums due hereunder.

B. Company agrees to indemnify Writer and hold Writer harmless from and against any and all damages and expenses (other than with respect to any settlement entered into without Company's written consent) arising out of any third party claim against Writer resulting from Company's development, production, distribution and/or exploitation of the Project.

32. NO INJUNCTIVE RELIEF:

The sole right of Writer as to any breach or alleged breach hereunder by Company shall be the recovery of money damages, if any, and the rights herein granted by Writer shall not terminate by reason of such breach. In no event may Writer terminate this Agreement or obtain injunctive relief or other equitable relief with respect to any breach of Company's obligations hereunder.

33. PROFIT PARTICIPATION:

Terms to be negotiated in good faith. If the parties fail to reach agreement within [ ] months after execution hereof, either party, upon 30 days notice to the other, may submit the matter to what is known as a "baseball arbitration," in which each party presents one profit proposal and the arbitrator is required to adopt one of the two proposals. The arbitrator shall be selected and the arbitration conducted pursuant to the Voluntary Labor Arbitration Rules of the AAA.

34. WRITING TEAMS:

In the event two (2) or more writers are named as parties hereto, the word "Writer" whenever used herein shall be deemed to mean "Writers," and such writers shall be treated as a unit for purposes of compensation hereunder, and the compensation payable hereunder shall be payable to them in equal shares unless they otherwise direct Company in writing signed by both such writers or unless otherwise required by the WGA MBA, The writers signatory hereto represent and warrant that they agree with the other in good faith (and without suggestion or direction by Company) prior to offering themselves for employment hereunder to collaborate as a team and that they have obtained or will obtain any necessary WGA waivers with respect to their employment hereunder as a team.

35. AGREEMENT OF THE PARTIES:
This document [including Attachment 1, if any] shall constitute the agreement between the parties until modified or amended by a subsequent writing.

BY: _____   BY: _____
        [NAME OF WRITER]   TITLE

CC: WGA CONTRACTS DEPARTMENT

ATTACHMENT 1

ADDITIONAL PROVISIONS, IF ANY:

_____

_____

_____

_____

_____

_____

_____

_____

CHAPTER REVIEW

- Entertainment attorneys can offer the underrepresented writer protection because they work on billable hours, on demand, instead of on a commission basis. If a writer can afford the rate, he will be able to obtain representation.
- An entertainment lawyer can help a writer protect his work on the page or in formal pitch meetings.
- The entertainment attorney can work with an agent and manager during the negotiation process to review and approve contracts, etc.
- An entertainment attorney pays special attention to both the legal and ethical issues of doing business.
- Even an attorney relies on the dreaded "R" word—referral—to find clients.

10

THE NEW MEDIA AGENT

If it's good, it'll find its way to an agent.

Stefanie Henning, ICM

Stefanie Henning is one of the best interactive agents in Hollywood. She calls the prestigious Beverly Hills agency, ICM (International Creative Management) home and heads the New Media Department there. With experience at the highest levels of interactive entertainment, Henning represents writers, designers, and artists.

At one time, she worked in the movie and TV side of the agenting business, but her heart remained with games and interactive entertainment. A die-hard gamer who enjoys dealing and working with the people creating cutting-edge technologies and interactive games, Henning lives in Los Angeles with her husband (a writer himself) and their two children.

Top software developers make sure to call her when they need a reliable, skilled professional to help them create their games. When she links up a company with one of her clients, she negotiates the best deal available. She keeps her clients hopping, often rolling one job into the next. While some companies admittedly shy away from agents and the negotiation process as "too Hollywood," many strong, established companies turn to Henning to save them headaches and valuable time in finding the right person for the job. Most companies simply have better things to do than sift through résumés, so Henning is more than willing to pitch her clients' services.

So Henning's task is essentially the same as that of any other agent working in the film or television fields. The only differences are the professional people she deals with and the tasks they perform. Rather than match a screenwriter with a producer, she matches a game writer with a game developer. Rather than introduce a director to a studio, she introduces a game designer to a software company. Once the introduction is made and the employment negotiations under way, she works out the terms and work periods the same way any other agent devises those details.

While a film agent must keep on top of what development people are with which companies, or what TV producers are looking for in spec scripts in a given production season, Henning stays abreast of the game industry, online entertainment, educational multimedia, and other interactive new media. She knows what developers and companies need and what they look to do as new technology develops. To meet those needs, she maintains a stable of writers, artists, programmers, and game designers.

But she only represents established industry professionals. So interested writers need to pay their dues and log some legit experience before contacting her for potential representation. We already discussed ways writers can keep their ears to the ground and sense opportunities coming. By jumping on these openings when they show themselves, writers can log some good bylines and compile some decent interactive writing samples so an industry professional like Henning can take them seriously.

I met with Henning in her ICM corner office and we discussed her role in the interactive entertainment business. First, Henning tackled the age-old writers' Catch-22: "You can't succeed in a creative writing field without an agent, and you can't get an agent unless you have some success in the creative writing field." This dilemma cuts across all genres—from publishing to scriptwriting to interactive writing—and Henning acknowledged the problems involved:

"That is difficult. There's no way around it. But every successful writer had to fight through that. It can be done. I have a dual role because I represent my clients and I work for ICM. So while I have a duty to make the best deals I can for my clients, I also have to make money for the firm. So it does help if a writer has a track record before they approach me.

"It was easier when the industry was brand new, maybe six years ago or so. You didn't even need to have game experience. Companies were looking to hire writers who had experience in comedy, action, adventure, or horror, and writers just needed to have samples to show they could write. Now you have to have experience writing games. So, to get a start, a writer needs to leave it all out there and get something down on paper. If it's good, it'll find it's way to an agent."

BUILDING A CAREER

Once a writer gains some experience and becomes fortunate enough to enlist the support of a top-shelf rep such as Henning, the agent can help build and guide that writer's career.

"An agent helps you to expand what you're doing and make a career out of your work," Henning said.

But she added that good writers make the agent's job easier by drumming up work and attention wherever they can:

"You have to put yourself out there. You've got to get into the trenches and meet people and try to build relationships for yourself. In addition to the work itself, that's the way to create a positive reputation for you and your work that will keep you in the business and keep you on people's minds."

Henning offered a stark dose of reality for some writers when she explained how *ageism* impacts the new media industry. The topic came up earlier in this book, with regard to other parts of the entertainment industry: In the television industry, if a writer hasn't had some measure of success by the age of thirty, it's probably time to pack it in. Screenwriters may get a little more time, and the publishing industry may "forgive" the middle-aged writer more than most, but interactive new media is not so understanding. Obviously, ageism makes little sense, since writers supposedly become more skillful and experienced as they age. After all, pro writers aren't pro athletes, who have to retire in their mid-thirties. But, in the entertainment business, youth carries clout.

"Interactive entertainment is a young industry," Henning said. "Not only has it not been around that long, but it's product is aimed at a younger audience. It's a young person's medium. The truth is, you're not going to have a fifty-five-year-old man with no new media experience walk into a room and understand interactivity and game levels. A twenty-two-year-old kid who's an avid game player is the one who's going to know that kind of material."

Also, Henning pointed out that awkward situations can develop, even if that fifty-five-year-old does get hired, because he could end up working for a twenty-two-year-old who happens to be the producer on the project.

"Basically, if a writer already has a great deal of experience at an older age, he can continue to work in the business indefinitely. But an interactive writer is not going to break into the business at that age."

Henning also discussed the differences between writing for interactive media and writing for traditional Hollywood entertainment such as film and television. In fact, she pointed out that Hollywood itself is still learning the differences. Early on in the development of the interactive entertainment industry, many Hollywood studios got into the business of making CD-ROMs and other entertainment products based on their film and TV series. But not all knew what they were getting into, Henning explained.

"Many studios didn't take it seriously and hired less qualified people to create interactive business. At the end of the day, not all of those people were qualified to create that business. Hollywood also needed to learn that interactive products require an eighteen-month development process (roughly five times longer than the average motion picture), and the studios are used to getting everything they need yesterday."

A CHANGING NEW MEDIA LANDSCAPE

So many studios got out of the interactive business, taking some big money with them. Still, Henning was quick to point out that interactive writers and designers should never give up because the players in the interactive industry these days are people and companies who truly want to be there for the long haul:

"Writers and designers in the interactive business should be there because they're passionate about it. They get games and they like games, etc. The people who get into this business because they couldn't get into any other business should go home."

But how do those writers who want to work in the interactive business contact an agent like Henning? What shouldn't they do?

"Well, there's a right way to do it," Henning explained. "It's not a question of just calling constantly and getting on the phone sheet."

Henning suggested making friendly contact initially and following up from time to time by simply dropping lines and keeping the agent informed about your movements. By staying in touch, you stay on that agent's mind. When opportunities arise that might fit your skills and interest, that agent just might call and give you a shot.

This interactive writer can speak from experience, because that's exactly what happened to me. I stayed on good terms with my interactive agent for more than a year before an opportunity arose. When a company called my agent looking for writers, every one in the agent's stable was busy on other projects. I was brought in during that time of need and got a shot at a good gig.

Play your cards right, and the same could happen to you.

CHAPTER REVIEW

- As new media and interactive entertainment emerge and synergize with more established media, there's a need for agents to move in and represent talent looking for work in the groundbreaking fields.

- More agencies and more professionals are moving into the Internet and new media worlds, increasing the opportunities for writers and their need for representation.

- The role of an agent and the practices of doing business don't change, even within the cutting-edge industries like interactive entertainment.

- Referrals can . . . Oh, never mind. You figured it out by now.

11

IN THE MEANTIME . . .

Don't look at me!

You wrote your scripts. You revised and edited your work. You attended conferences and made industry contacts. You wrote your strong query letter and sent it out. You even managed to tackle a hallowed referral or two. Finally, you read this book and absorbed its wisdom, gaining a well-rounded picture of the agent/manager/client relationship and how such representation can (and can't) help you.

But you still don't have an agent. What went wrong? Is it your fault? The industry's fault? My fault? This book's fault? Is every single working man and woman in Hollywood so blind to the quality of your work that they can't see a solid opportunity when it falls in their lap?

Don't look at me! I don't have all the answers. It's safe to say that all the experts interviewed for this book would make the same admission. But while you struggle to find the agent and manager who will push your career to the next level, there are steps you can take right now to bring you closer to finding representation.

First of all, we'll assume you actually wrote your script. An idea is useless and legal to steal. Write the script! The sooner it's written, the sooner it can be registered and protected. Never pitch or openly share an idea. No matter how tempting it is to share, the safest bet is to keep quiet until it's on paper and registered.

The next question you need to ask is as simple in nature as it is difficult to face. "Is your work good enough?" This query does not question your innate ability as an artist. It doesn't ask, "Can you write a good story?" It asks, "Did you write one, or are you simply on the way to writing one?" Is your script ready to face the scrutiny of the marketplace? More than one agent profiled on these pages warned against approaching an agent or manager with a script too early. Did you fail to heed that advice?

For writers, a story becomes a child to develop and nurture. If it's any good at all, they should fall in love with the work on the page. As a result, intense revision and editing can seem like dangerous surgery. No writer wants to hear that his script is deficient, any more than a mother longs to learn that her child has a learning disability. But if you want to make sure that your script is good enough to warrant an agent's attention, you must revise, revise, revise.

Decide to get some feedback on your work. Start reading other spec scripts, too. There are a lot of talented writers out there. They can be your competition—or your teachers. Then, rewrite obsessively, hacking out every unnecessary word, every self-indulgent phrase, every cheat or cliché. Get more feedback. And get some more feedback. Rewrite some more. You get the idea. It's nothing to be ashamed of or to fear.

In all professions—from professional athletics to accountancy—mistakes are not tolerated. The pro must get it right the first time. Screenwriters catch a break in this department. While screenwriting is just as demanding and competitive as any other profession on Earth, movie and TV wordsmiths get to make initial mistakes. If they bang the right noun against the wrong verb once or twice, they have the opportunity to repair the mishap before anyone else sees the fruits of their labor.

Writing is rewriting. This is perhaps the most overused cliché in all of professional wordsmithing. However, no cliché rings with more truth. How well screenwriters revises their own work greatly determines how well a story is told. More important, the revision drafts determine how the screenplay is received by producers, executives, actors, and agents.

All script writers worth their weight in brass fasteners know that the first draft does not make the script. The first go-around can produce inspired images, sensitive characters, and entertaining plot twists. Odds are, though, that it will also produce wordy dialogue, flabby description, and a handful of spelling errors and assorted typos.

Now the real work starts.

Revision is a chore. That's why amateur writers don't handle this creative stage as well as professionals. No one cites the presence of a muse when they're poring over pages with a highlighter. Nobody ever claimed to be "in the flow" of the writing experience with a red pen in hand. While three hours may seem like ten minutes when a writer is really cooking, those same three hours may feel like three days when nothing seems to be going right. Every distraction calls out a little louder. When it's time to revise, a screenwriter will take a longer lunch or become hopelessly absorbed in every bad TV show.

Fortunately, we can briefly turn to three Hollywood professionals and learn their revision tips and techniques to make every scriptor's job a little easier. To provide the best possible insights, we consult an A-list feature writer, a successful television scribe and columnist, and a screenwriting educator and author.

Steven E. de Souza: Bulletproof the Script

Steven E. de Souza began his career in television as a writer, director, and producer on such shows as *Knight Rider, V, Tales from the Crypt,* and the animated *Cadillacs and Dinosaurs.* His feature career took off in the 1980s with credits including *48 Hours, Die Hard, Commando,* and *The Running Man.* He has become one of Hollywood's top action writers.

His recent credits include serving as writer and director on *Streetfighter* and co-credit on *The Flintstones.* De Souza said he usually completes a script before beginning revision. He may begin with the beginning or the end; or he may write specific action sequences he envisions for the story and flesh out the entire tale using those scenes as a framework.

He writes with a personal computer and edits his work on paper with the aid of a writer's assistant. An aspiring screenwriter may not be able to afford an assistant, but the editing and revision process work the same with or without an extra set of hands to handle the pages. When a draft is finished, de Souza will print out the entire script and edit line by line with a red pen. While he still looks for any typos, stray grammatical errors, or odd spelling mistakes that the word processor program didn't catch; de Souza uses the editing time to eliminate every last unnecessary sequence, paragraph, sentence, or word.

Apropos of his reputation as an action master, he refers to the process as making the script "bulletproof."

"No one should ever submit a first draft," de Souza said. "You should submit a fourth or fifth draft and call it your first."

De Souza used words like "wordy" and "flabby" when describing the work of many young writers. He was quick to point out that screenwriters with genuine talent can sabotage themselves by not being ruthless enough on their own work. He stressed that too many writers take a soft attitude when presenting their work—hoping the story catches a reader's eye as a product and not as entertainment on the written page.

"You have to realize that the reader is your first audience," de Souza said. "You have to entertain the reader first before it goes any further."

Larry DiTillio: Analyze First

If an A-List feature writer isn't enough to convince you to hunker down and start editing that wordy dialogue, maybe a top-shelf TV writer's encouragement will push you over the edge. Larry DiTillio specializes in writing science fiction, fantasy, and children's animation for television. Currently the head writer on the children's action cartoon *Beast Wars*, DiTillio has most recently served as story editor and writer for the science fiction series, *Babylon 5*. He has written for sci-fi and animated series on multiple networks.

DiTillio said that the reputation writers have in Hollywood can often work against them:

"One of the problems writers have is that they can be their own worst enemies," DiTillio said. "They can get a reputation as a loose cannon very easily when it comes time to revise their work according to what a producer or executive says. They resist or resent the notes they get."

When writing for television, you will probably want to avoid long lists of knit-picky notes from TV executives. To keep your TV script as free from such outside influence as possible, DiTillio urges screenwriters to get their work in the best shape possible before submitting it up the line.

DiTillio added that TV writers often face very tight rewrite deadlines—much more severe than those a feature film writer might face. So not only do TV scribes have to face input from multiple nonwriting sources, but they also have to implement that input in a very short time.

"The best way to avoid that situation," DiTillio said, "is to turn in a first draft that's mainly all there."

Again, DiTillio put the responsibility of revising solely on the writers' back. If they can soundly construct their script on their own desks, it'll pass over the desks of others much faster and with much less call for rewriting.

"The key to all this is not just knocking off a first draft quickly and turning it in," DiTillio explained. "It's spending time with the first draft and rewriting it four or five times before you hand it in and call it a first draft. That way you cut way down on your rewrite time."

DiTillio explained that he uses this technique to ensure that, when he finishes a teleplay, he knows it's all there: "When I turn in a script, I know the structure is right," he said. "I know just from reading it that the pacing is right. I can read the script on my own and know that the pace is not right. Then I can go in there and start cutting away."

Maybe the story beats are in the wrong places. Maybe the dialogue is too wordy. Whatever the problems might be, DiTillio's revision techniques make certain he catches and fixes them on his time before anyone else reads the end product. He stressed that by spending so much time on the beginning of a project, a screenwriter needn't worry so much about subsequent drafts beyond a few line changes here and there.

Finally, he urged aspiring TV writers to analyze their story ideas and outlines before they even begin writing. This way, a writer can see areas where the plot might slow down or simply not work at all. By looking for areas that present story problems before they're even written, a screenwriter would avoid having to cut or rewrite those sections later.

With two professional writers already calling on us to polish our work to a brilliant shine before letting anyone else see it, we turn to a professional educator, playwright, and author who specializes in teaching aspiring screenwriters how to make their work jump off the page.

Richard Krevolin: Checkpoints for Revision

Richard Krevolin is a professor at the USC Film School. This playwright, screenwriter, poet, and author holds a BA from Yale and a master's degree in screenwriting from UCLA. He also completed a master's in playwriting and fiction from USC before teaching for the institution. A finalist in multiple national writers' competitions, including the Nicholl Fellowship in Screenwriting, Krevolin optioned three screenplays. He also wrote the plays, *Stuck, Trotsky's Garden,* and *Yahrzeit.* In addition to his USC lectures, he appears at screenwriting conferences across the country speaking on, among other topics, screenplay revision.

Krevolin came right out and said what a professional screenwriter must be prepared to do in Hollywood: "The joke about the process of revision for a screenwriter is that he will revise whatever the studio says to revise as long as he gets paid. While that is part of the business, the truth is a little more artistic than that!"

Krevolin repeatedly stressed that screenwriters must have the ability to face and evaluate themselves and admit that not every word set down on the page is perfect:

"There comes that moment when you have to admit it's not perfect. And that's hard to do. You might get angry, or you might think the person criticizing the work is an idiot, but eventually, you realize that the criticism is right. Then you have to get back in there and revise."

While Oscar Wilde said, "A work of art is never finished; it is abandoned," Krevolin added that the truth of that statement really rests on how much of a perfectionist an individual writer is.

"I think all projects have a certain point where you have to let go," Krevolin said. "A writer needs to develop that sense of when it's time to complete this project and move on to the next one. At some point in the screenwriting process, you're going to release it to an agent or a director to interpret your script anyway. So letting it go is something a writer needs to accept. Just as mother's are reluctant to let go of their children, so writers can be reluctant to let go of their favorite scene or to make changes."

That said, Krevolin stressed that writers have control over the project before it reaches those stages. They can shape the story into an original vision before anyone else gets to it—if they are self-critical and can admit shortcomings in the work. Krevolin recommended that writers consider every rewrite a focal point for an individual problem area within a script. Perhaps one rewrite deals only with a certain character's development. Maybe the next focuses on dialogue . . . the next on plotting. By tackling problems one at a time, a screenwriter can remain much more focused on the story as a whole and avoid getting intimidated or overwhelmed by the rewrite process.

"If writers thought beforehand of all the revisions they'd need to do to complete a project," Krevolin joked, "we'd be crippled before we started!"

Krevolin offered a list of useful checkpoints a script should pass before it leaves the writer's hands. Each checkpoint on this list could be the focus of a revision draft. Consider this list of ten examples:

- Never have two characters agree on anything. Did you release the tension from your tires before you got off the road?
- Don't split your heavy into two or more people. A good heavy = a good heavy.
- Have at least one strong, castable leading role.
- Have I ever seen *anything* like this before? Always be original and full of surprises.
- End with one final. Not four quarterfinals.
- In every scene, come in late and get out early.
- Every scene must end in a different place than it began.
- Your main character must have arc/growth/epiphany.

- In dialogue, brevity is the filet of soul.
- With your characters, did you scab the wound?

These points will change from script to script or writer to writer. However, the spirit behind them remains the same. Writers need to examine their script on level after level, scene by scene, word after word. They need to have the script in the best possible shape imaginable because screenwriters tend to lose control of their work once it ventures into the marketplace.

Is Your Script Ripe Yet?

Remember, you only get one chance to make a good impression. As Ann Zald said, many writers make the mistake of being far too anxious to hurry their work to the industry. Few have the patience to learn the craft or to bury beloved early drafts. Most aspiring writers jump the gun and query before a script is ripe.

In addition to Krevolin's checkpoints, there are any number of questions you need to ask about your script to confirm that it's solid enough for submission. The analysis standard can vary depending on your source, book, or teacher. Syd Field might have different criteria than Robert McKee. Michael Halperin might advise you differently than Linda Sega. Paramount will want something different than Fox Searchlight. Imagine the trailer. Is the concept marketable? Is there a three-act structure? What are the obstacles?

Consider any of the following:

- Is the concept original?
- What is the screenplay trying to say? What's the theme?
- Is the premise intriguing?
- What is the inciting incident?
- Does the screenplay generate questions?
- Has a strong need-to-know hook been built into the story?
- Is there a goal?
- Is the story funny or thrilling?
- Can it be both?
- Is the screenplay predictable?
- What does the story have that the audience can't get from real life?

- What's at stake?
- Action and humor should come from the characters.
- Avoid cheap laughs—even though those seem to sell these days.
- Audiences want to see characters who care about something.
- Does the concept create the potential for the characters' lives to be changed?
- Does the story transport the audience to someplace life can't take them?
- Lead characters must be sympathetic.
- Are the characters complex or one-dimensional?
- What does the audience want for the characters?
- Is there a scene where the conflict of the main character comes to a head?
- What are the characters' wants and needs?
- Character traits should be independent of the character's role in the story.
- Avoid stereotypes.
- Avoid clichés.
- Character conflicts should be both internal and external for leads and supporting players.
- Is the lead involved with the story throughout?
- Distinguish characters by their speech, background, and intelligence.
- Each character needs to have a point of view to act, not just react.
- Does the hero control the outcome of the story?
- Characters should struggle with themselves, and with others.
- Characters should not all think the same way.
- The audience should know more about the story than the main character until the end.
- Run each character through as many emotions as possible.
- Characters must change. What is each character's arc?
- Does the film have characters that actors will want to play?
- Is there a sufficient challenge for the heroes?
- Who is the target audience?
- Is there a decisive, inevitable ending?

- Is the ending believable, yet unpredictable?
- Is there strong emotion at the center of the story?
- Are all descriptions just what can be seen?
- Begin the screenplay as deep into the story as possible.
- Avoid fancy or obtuse plotting.
- Use short scenes sometimes. Sequences build pace.
- Is the subject matter thoroughly researched?
- Is every line necessary?
- Establish your plot points. No cheating.
- Tell your story with pictures.
- Every scene must have a purpose. If not, cut it.
- Every scene must have conflict. If not, add tension or cut it.
- Every scene must organically flow from the previous scene and into the following scene. If not, rewrite or rework your scenes to make the flow logical and smooth.
- In each scene, do you consistently show not tell?
- Are scenes in the right order? Would it be more interesting if a scene were moved or information in it were held until later on in the story?
- Rewrite or cut any scenes, characters, dialogue, exposition, or prose that are clichéd or "on the nose."
- Your first ten pages must set the story in motion with the inciting incident.
- Your first ten pages must establish your main characters and their motivations.
- Your first ten pages must state the premise.
- Your first ten pages must tie into the ending.
- Are the outcomes of scenes, situations, sequences, or story predictable?
- Are the stakes high enough?
- Does your screenplay ask questions for which the audience must find out the answers?
- Every plot and subplot must have a beginning, a middle, and an end. Be sure to leave no loose ends, unless you want to inject some mystery to your story, a la *The Blair Witch Project*.
- Every story element introduced at the beginning of the script must pay off.

- Does the tempo and pacing of the story build relentlessly to the climax?
- Are your main characters likeable? Do we care what happens to them?
- Do the main characters have strong enough conflict to carry the weight of the story?
- Have you externalized the inner lives of your characters? Audiences can read neither your scene descriptions nor the minds of your characters.
- Is the villain as smart as the hero?
- Every major character arc must have a beginning, a middle, and an end. No sudden character shifts. Remember, no cheating.
- Every character has to have a purpose in the scene.
- Could the script be funnier?
- Could the script be scarier?
- Could the drama seem more dramatic?
- Are all your scenes shootable?
- Avoid exposition, lengthy stage description, camera direction, flashbacks, dream sequences, and falling-in-love montages.
- Don't number the scenes.
- MOREs and CONTINUEDs are also usually unnecessary.

As you work your way through this barrage of questions and suggestions, you will soon realize that both self-criticism and patience are crucial. You can't hurry love, and you can't hurry the learning process. If your first script doesn't make it through the gauntlet of self-critiquing without being mortally wounded, don't worry. Just write the next story and the next script. You don't want to shop a first script that won't stand up to objective scrutiny; rejections can cripple your spirit. It's human nature. On the other hand, if you have the patience to wait for the right story idea and the perseverance to shape it into a truly marketable script, you'll have a better chance of finding representation, and ultimately, working as a professional writer.

More Tips and Tricks for Revision

I shouldn't need to say this, but be sure your script is properly formatted and thoroughly proofread. Improper format, typos, misspellings, and poor grammar are the marks of an amateur. Present yourself as a professional. Believe you have something they want. Take the extra time to ensure that your script is worthy of their effort.

There are some common tricks to revising a good script to make it better. First of all, after you finish it, set the script down and leave it alone for a week. Don't look at it. Don't think about it. Don't touch it.

After that waiting period, pick it up and give it a blistering read. As one expert put it, sit down, with coffee, a snack, a notepad, and a red pen. Take the phone off the hook. This will take a while. Begin by writing down your premise, a short log line, a synopsis of your story, and your theme and conflict. Do the same for your subplot.

On another page, work with your characters. List your main characters, hero, heroine, love interest, villain, henchman, and so on. Include each character's goal and character arc. Throughout this process, you should be reading your script coldly, dispassionately, and objectively. The further you can manage to get outside yourself and your ego, the better your end results. When in doubt, cut it. If the story works without an element or line, it's not needed. Read from page one to the end. Read straight through, only pausing to make notes. Pretend that you didn't write it. Your worst enemy did. Don't pull any punches. Be too cruel to be kind. When you're finished reading and noting, set the script down. Leave it alone. You'll be upset and discouraged anyway. Go live your life until your anger fades.

Now that the proofread and notes stage is completed, you must obviously attempt another draft to repair the damage. Examine your notes and ask why the script elicited such a complaint. Consider the possible structural, story, character, or development errors at fault. Remain cutthroat and don't try to come up with excuses. It's for the best.

Perhaps, you would choose at this point to re-evaluate your character arcs or the narrative as a whole. These new opinions of your work will be based entirely on your most recent reading of the screenplay and should provide new insights into the structure. Also, in some cases, you will come up with an amazing twist or improved ending that never occurred to you while you were actually working through any earlier draft. Reconsider your premise, log line, synopsis, theme, and story as before, and see if they still feel right.

You can read your first analysis and your most recent coverage. Contrast and compare. As time-consuming as this might seem, it actually saves you revision time. Instead of this system of multiple note passes on your script, imagine the potential drudgery of three complete page-one rewrites! By thoroughly analyzing your work before you settle down to a revision, you are guaranteed an easier writing job when it comes time to fix the script.

While revising, some writers use 3×5 index cards and a corkboard to arrange and shuffle scenes and characters. Number the scenes in your script and assign each scene to a card. Also, write brief bios about your major characters on the cards. You can copy any notes or concerns you have on the scene cards as well. Now you can arrange your cards for structure, story, character, dialogue, or subplot. While arranging the cards on the bulletin board, if you can't decide on a category for a card or don't know where a scene fits, lose it! Again, if a story works without something, that something doesn't need to be there. That's the primary purpose of editing and revising!

This generic revision process should make it fairly clear what's wrong with the script. It should also help you to realize precisely where you need to tweak, cut, or rewrite during revision. For each script you write, start at the beginning and work persistently through to the end. Hard work during the revision process saves a script. Laziness dooms it to the shredder.

Registering Your Work

Once you feel confident that your script is in the best possible shape, you can consider sending it out to producers yourself to generate some heat before tracking to agents or managers. However, you need to watch your back before stepping into the jungle.

As mentioned in Dinah Perez's chapter on the legal aspects of screenwriting and the role of registering one's work, you should take whatever you have on paper and protect it. Perez already provided an outstanding overview of the copyright process. However, you can also turn to the Writers Guild for some protection.

THE WRITERS GUILD REGISTRATION SERVICE

The Writers Guild's Registration Service (or Intellectual Property Registry) registers over 30,000 pieces of literary material each year, and is available to members and nonmembers alike. The Guild invites writers to submit material to be archived by the Writers Guild to protect their work.

According to Guild records, the WGA Registration Service was set up to assist writers in establishing the completion dates of particular pieces of their literary property written for the fields of radio, theatrical and television motion pictures, videocassettes/discs, and interactive media. Registration provides a dated record of the writer's claim to authorship of a particular literary work. If necessary a WGA employee may produce the material as evidence, if legal or official Guild action is initiated. The Registration Office does not make comparisons of registration deposits, nor does it give legal opinions, advice, or confer any statutory protections. Registration with the Guild does not protect titles.

Materials may be submitted for registration in person or by mail. The Registration Office must receive:

- One unbound, looseleaf copy of material on standard, 8½-by-11-inch paper.
- A cover sheet listing title of material and all writers' full legal names.
- The social security number (or foreign equivalent), return address, and phone numbers of authors.
- Registration fee: WGAw and WGAE members, $10; nonmembers, $20.

When the material is received, it is sealed in an envelope and the date and time are recorded. A numbered receipt is returned, serving as the official documentation of registration and should be kept in a safe place.

Registrable material includes scripts, treatments, synopses, outlines, written ideas specifically intended for radio, television, and theatrical motion pictures, videocassettes/discs, and interactive media. The WGA Registration Office also accepts stage plays, novels and other books, short stories, poems, commercials, lyrics, and drawings.

Registration is valid for a term of five years and may be renewed for an additional five years at the current registration rate. Renewals will be accepted up to three months prior to the expiration of the original registration. A grace period will be extended allowing renewals as late as three months following the expiration of the original registration. At the time of registration, or renewal, you authorize the WGA to destroy the material without further notice to you on the expiration of the first term of registration or any renewal period. Only the writers listed on the registration receipt may request confirmation of registration, the registration number, date of deposit, or any other information.

According to the Guild, the WGA will honor such written requests from writers regarding the registration of their own work(s) only if accompanied by photo identification. All verification or confirmation requests from a writer should contain as much specific information as possible, such as registration number, title of material, effective date, and social security number of writer, and may be submitted by facsimile, mail, or in person. The fax number for the Registration Service is (323) 782-4803.

Because the deposited material cannot be returned to the writer without defeating the purpose of registration, registered material may not be withdrawn. It is therefore important to retain a separate copy of the material being registered. If a writer finds it necessary to obtain a copy of deposited material, duplicates may be purchased for the price of registration upon written request by one or more of the listed authors, identified by photo identification. In the event that an author is deceased, proof of death and consent of the representative of the heirs and/or estate must be presented in order to obtain a copy of the material.

There are also online services that will provide a certifiable, if unofficial, registration and protection process. For decades, when writers finished their scripts and wanted to protect them from Hollywood hustlers more than willing to steal their work, they would turn to Federal Copyright or the Writers Guild of America's registration service for protection and peace of mind. However, with the coming of the information age, a new service is available for writers to protect their work and have constant, immediate access to proof of their ownership.

WWW.PROTECTRITE.COM

The ProtectRite Web site, *www.protectrite.com*, a service of the National Creative Registry, calls itself "the creator and pioneer of online intellectual property registration." Founded by writers and attorneys in 1994, the Registry's ProtectRite service processes thousands of online registrations each year from writers, screenwriters, attorneys, songwriters, advertising agencies, Internet and software developers, inventors, scientists, and corporations.

Through secure online servers, ProtectRite provides confidential, timed and dated registration of original creative works and intellectual property. ProtectRite legally establishes the completion date of registered materials and offers the security of long-term storage in the event that an original data copy crashes.

Any original or creative work is registerable through the service. Once a document is saved on the Registry's servers, only the creator has access to the registration data. ProtectRite offers three separate redundant storage systems to ensure that every file is secure and protected.

Following registration, the creator can print a certificate immediately as hard copy proof of protection. The registrant also receives an e-mailed receipt with a confidential registration confirmation number. Requests for access to registered materials can only be made by the original registrant, accompanied by registration number and a notarized letter.

The service costs $18.95 for a ten-year registration. The site accepts MasterCard, Visa, and American Express and uses secure servers to protect account privacy. At any time, up to one month prior to expiration, a user can renew for an additional ten-year term by paying the same fee. At the time of registration, you authorize ProtectRite to destroy your file without further notice to you on the expiration date, in the event that you choose not to renew.

ProtectRite does not make comparisons of registration submissions, give any legal advice, or confer any statutory protections.

Adam Jacobs, National Creative Registry's chief, explained that his father was a novelist. Since he came from a family of writers, Jacobs said that he wanted to make writers' lives easier by offering them an alternative when protecting their work. Asked why a writer should consider his service over Copyright or Guild protection, Jacobs pointed out that writers need to understand what ProtectRite does in detail:

"First, I think it's important not to misrepresent what we do," he said. "We offer the same level of protection as the Writers Guild. But we offer more for less. We provide ten years of registration instead of the Guild's five. Our service is less expensive than Guild registration and more convenient since writers can verify their certificate twenty-four hours a day, on demand."

Original registrants can request an emergency copy of their registration file via e-mail, as long as registrants use the e-mail address specified at the time of registration. Upon approval, registration files will only be e-mailed to that address.

"Protecting intellectual property essentially comes down to two questions," Jacobs said. "'How do you prove it was yours?' and 'What date and time was it created?' So, ProtectRite provides a digital date and time stamp."

Jacobs urges writers to copyright their work in addition to using his registration service. During disputes of ownership, copyright verifications via mail can take months, while the Writers Guild might require a visit to their headquarters. Only the U.S. Copyright Office can issue a formal copyright; however, the law states that when a creator affixes his name and date to an original work, he is automatically entitled to copyright protection.

Since the copyright office takes an average of six months to process applications, Jacobs said many writers register with ProtectRite for instant peace of mind and as added protection so they can begin showing their work immediately.

"Writers want peace of mind now," Jacobs said. "Our service allows them to have that."

For information on this service, write: ProtectRite, National Creative Registry, 1106 Second Street, Encinitas, CA 92024 or visit *www.protectrite.com* or e-mail *info@protectrite.com.*

Rethinking Your Approach

After revision and protection, perhaps you need to consider how you're approaching your agency contacts. As stated elsewhere, there are professional protocols involved in contacting an agency. If you shortcut any of them, you're probably shooting yourself in the literary foot.

A few agencies are only open to referrals, rather than queries. It's a hard fact, but one you need to accept. Very few are either not open to submissions at a certain time or are not accepting any outside submissions at a particular time. Those facts are not intended to insult or betray you and your work. It simply means that the agency's client roster is full, and you need to move to another more open company.

Realize that many agencies are deluged with queries from writers all around the world. Remember that you want to make the agents' jobs as easy as possible. Give them no reason to say *no* immediately, or to approach your work with a negative attitude. That should give you the best possible chance of success.

For example, if you use the WGA agent list or any published list of agencies, read it carefully. Only submit to the companies taking submissions, and send samples of the genres requested. Submit to the addresses supplied. You only get one chance to make a first impression. Follow their rules. You won't stand out as being quirky or entertaining if you deliver your script via singing telegram. You'll look like an amateurish idiot. That's unfair to you because, if you've taken the time and made the commitment to write your work and do your research (including reading this little tome), you are not an idiot. You are an artist.

As stated earlier, always send a SASE. You must include a self-addressed, stamped envelope if you're sending a query or a script. Occasionally, an agent will suggest that you don't bother—as is becoming the case with online queries. Sometimes, agencies will toss your SASE into the recycle bin. (Nobody throws paper away in LA anymore.)

But as Angela Cheng explained earlier, if agencies paid their own postage on rejection letters, they'd go out of business. The classiest operations will at least take the time to send you a polite rejection on your 33 cents. So you must include an SASE.

Also, send a follow-up letter. If you choose to pitch an idea for whatever reason, send a follow-up letter that details what concepts were discussed. This is also a handy way to keep track of people and dates as well. Plus, it's polite and it helps to make a good impression.

Do's and Don't's of Query Letters

If you use a query letter, what does it look like? Do you even need to write a query letter? Perhaps you prefer phone calls and personal contacts. Then you send out the script with a simple cover letter. But perhaps you wish to try the letter route in addition to phone calls. If you do choose to use a query letter, make sure the letter is professional and effective.

If you decide to submit a query letter, avoid common mistakes made by first-time writers. Proofread your letter and make sure that it is, in and of itself, a writing sample. If you are a writer, you are a writer in everything you write. A weak letter, loaded with passive voice and grammatical errors, will kill your script before it gets read. Here are some additional pointers to keep in mind:

- Make sure you only pitch one story in the letter. Don't include a list of log-lines. It overloads the agent or manager and makes it seem as if you don't recognize your own best work.

- Avoid gimmicks to call attention to your letter. As Marcie Wright said, she received everything from a can of tuna to a urinary specimen cup with her letters. That serves no purpose and plants the idea that you are so insecure about the actual quality of your work that you need tricks to sell it. Don't use fancy paper, handwritten notes, or elaborate fonts. No drawings, fake advertisements, or photos. The letter must present the idea, and the idea must sell itself.

- Don't send gifts to agents or managers. It makes you look like a kiss-up and, again, suggests insecurity over the quality of the work. Gifts force a weird sense of responsibility by the receiver, and you don't want agents or managers to think you're trying to trick them.

- Don't lie in your query letter or rave so intensely about the quality of your work that you make yourself sound like a used-car pitchman. Most writers hope that their script is destined to become the biggest box office hit of all time. Only the naïve openly claim it in their letters.
- Even though you hear movies pitched this way all the time, you don't need to use that tired Hollywood practice of "Star Wars meets Wuthering Heights" or "There's Something About Mary" meets "Out of Africa." More often than not, the agent or manager will have no clue what you're trying to say and will wonder why you just don't say what the story is about!
- In your letter, be sure to sound professional and competent, but not hyper or pretentious. Don't write prose poems in your letter to highlight the drama of your pitch. Don't beg the reader to take a look, either. Again, a professional business letter with a good overview of an appealing story is the best route.

With a script in its best possible shape, properly protected, and well marketed with a top-flight, flawless query letter, your chances of gaining representation shoot up dramatically. But breaking into the film business is not a problem that resolves itself through a single answer or path. Don't become obsessive about it. Write your queries, send them out, and forget about them. Don't get caught up in thinking, "It's been four weeks since I wrote that letter. Why haven't they answered?" If a company or agency does respond with a request to look at your script, it isn't some sudden validation of your talent. Send them the script and forget about it. You don't have an agent to follow up, yet, and you don't want to make a pest out of yourself.

The important thing to keep in mind throughout this process is that just because the principles listed here didn't work on your first or second attempt, they remain sound and reliable and will work eventually. Listen to the experts presented on these pages and the professional practices described here, and you will find your way to an agent or manager who can push your career forward.

CHAPTER REVIEW

- Registering your screenplay can mean turning to the Copyright Office, the WGA, or online services.

- If your attempts to gain representation fail at first, reconsider the quality of your script and spend more time in the revision process.
- Always send your best script.
- Never pitch more than one idea in a query letter.
- If you still can't get representation, you simply need to write more scripts, better scripts, and better-marketed material. The same principles that failed the first time will succeed the next time.

Conclusion

If you learn anything from reading this book, I hope it's the simple fact that agents are people. No more, no less.

I spent all this time telling you what agents are. Maybe I should spend a moment telling you what they are not. They are not mere means to an end. They are not tools to be used and discarded while you chase your career goals. They are not unapproachable professional machines that you need to fear. They are not a receptacle for your disappointments and frustrations. They are not your parents. They are not your therapists. But, in a perfect world, they can become your partners.

You do not need to go overboard to impress them. You do not need to trick them. You do not need to lie to them. You do not need to change who you are to earn their attention. You do not need to angle your material to suit their tastes. You need to drive your career yourself, and hope they can provide guidance and opportunities beyond your reach.

Remember: They are people doing a job. You need to interact with them as a professional. Have your homework done before you write or call. If you want them to respect you and your stories, show your work that same respect before they see it.

Finally, approach agents or managers with the firm belief that you have something they want and need—because you do. You create the material they sell. They need your voice, your stories, and your artistic spirit.

Please remember that agents are people. In your eagerness to drive your career forward, don't forget to treat them with the same common courtesy you might show your neighborhood grocer or mail carrier.

I don't know what else to tell you. You heard it from the experts themselves—the very professionals slugging it out in the trenches representing writers as agents and managers. I digressed from time to time in the Bonus Sections to keep it all fresh, but I'm certain you sensed the threads weaving through this text. I hope it helps you understand and appreciate artists' representatives even before you approach them professionally.

Oh, by the way . . . be sure to get a referral.

Appendix A

Contacting Production Companies Directly

But what if, after minding your Ps and Qs and polishing your script to a T, you still find yourself agentless? How do you proceed? You can always bypass the agent route and contact producers directly. To that end, I include a quick list of production companies with their contact information:

ACME FILMWORKS
6161 Temple Hill Drive
Los Angeles, CA 90068
(323) 462-7124

AFRA FILM ENTERPRISES
137 S. Robertson Blvd., #254
Beverly Hills, CA 90211
(310) 785-6671
Fax: (310) 785-6683

ALCON ENTERTAINMENT
3000 W. Olympic Blvd.
Santa Monica, CA 90404
(310) 315-4725
Fax: (310) 315-4734

ALLIANCE ATLANTIS
PICTURES
808 Wilshire Blvd.
Santa Monica, CA 90401
(310) 899-8000
Fax: (310) 899-8100

ALLIED ENTERTAINMENT
GROUP
14930 Ventura Blvd.,
Suite 304
Sherman Oaks, CA 91403
(818) 728-9900
Fax: (818) 728-9904

AMERICAN WORLD
PICTURES
21700 Oxnard St., Suite 660
Woodland Hills, CA 91367
(818) 715-1480
Fax: (818) 715-1081

ARTISAN ENTERTAINMENT
2700 Colorado Ave.
Santa Monica, CA 90404
(310) 449-9200
Fax: (310) 255-3770

157 Chambers St., 12th floor
New York, NY 10007
(212) 577-2400
Fax: 212-577-2890

THE ARTISTS' COLONY
7421 Beverly Blvd., Suite 13
Los Angeles, CA 90036
(323) 930-7900
Fax: (323) 930-7919

THE ASYLUM
7560 Hollywood Blvd., Suite 401
Los Angeles, CA 90046
(323) 874-3670
Fax: (323) 874-6858

ATMOSPHERE
ENTERTAINMENT
1828 Broadway
Santa Monica, CA 90404
(310) 449-9220
Fax: (310) 449-9240

AXIOM FILMS LIMITED
12 D'Arblay Street
London, W1V 3FP, UK
(44 20) 7287-7720
Fax: (44 20) 7287-7740

BEHAVIOUR WORLDWIDE
1925 Century Park E.,
Suite 1700
Los Angeles, CA 90067
(310) 226-8300
Fax: (310) 226-8350

BERGMAN LUSTIG
PRODUCTIONS
3940 Laurel Canyon Blvd.
P.O. Box #356
Studio City, CA 91604
(818) 557-7490
Fax: (818) 557-7494

BLOW UP PICTURES
198 Avenue of the Americas
New York, NY 10013
(212) 625-9090
Fax: (212) 343-1849

CAPELLA FILMS
9242 Beverly Blvd., #280
Beverly Hills, CA 90210
(310) 247-4700
Fax: (310) 247-4701

CEO FILMS/AUGUST
ENTERTAINMENT
838 N. Fairfax Ave.
Los Angeles, CA 90046
(323) 658-8888
Fax.: (323) 658-7654

CINEVILLE INTERNATIONAL
225 Santa Monica Blvd.
Santa Monica, CA 90401
(310) 394-4699
Fax: (310) 394-3052

CLT/UFA
45 Boulevard Pierre Frieden
L-1543, Luxembourg
(352) 421-423-935
Fax: (352) 421-423-771

COSMOS FILM EQUITIES/
URBAN ARTS
MANAGEMENT
P.O. Box 7752
Beverly Hills, CA 90210
(310) 550-1121
Fax: (310) 550-7188

CURB ENTERTAINMENT
3907 W. Alameda Ave.
Burbank, CA 91505
(818) 843-8580
Fax: (818) 566-1719

CYPRESS FILMS, INC.
630 Ninth Avenue, Suite #415
New York, NY 10036
(212) 262-3900
Fax (212) 262-3925

DAVIS ENTERTAINMENT
CLASSICS
2121 Ave. of the Stars, 29th floor
Los Angeles, CA 90067
(310) 551-2266
Fax: (310) 556-3760

ECHO LAKE PRODUCTIONS
213 Rose Ave., 2nd floor
Venice, CA 90291
(310) 399-9164
Fax: (310) 399-9278

EMMETT/FURLA FILMS
Quixote Studios
1011 N. Fuller Ave., Suite D
Los Angeles, CA 90046
(323) 876-4823
Fax: (323) 851-0842

FILMTOWN INTERNATIONAL
SALES
5707 Melrose Ave.
Los Angeles, CA 90038
(323) 464-6644
Fax: (323) 464-6699

FINE LINE FEATURES
116 N. Robertson Blvd., Suite 509
Los Angeles, CA 90048
(310) 854-5811
Fax: (310) 854-1824

FORENSIC FILMS
180 Varick St., 11th Floor
New York, NY 10014
(212) 652-0140
Fax: (212) 652-0146

FOX SEARCHLIGHT
PICTURES
P.O. Box 900
Beverly Hills, CA 90213-0900
(310) 369-4402
Fax: (310) 369-2359

FURST FILMS
8954 W. Pico Blvd., 2nd floor
Los Angeles, CA 90035
(310) 278-6468
Fax: (310) 278-7401

GOOD MACHINE
417 Canal St., 4th floor
New York, NY 10013
(212) 343-9230
Fax: (212) 343-9645

GUN FOR HIRE
110 Leroy St.
New York, NY 10014
(212) 414-1557
Fax: (212) 741-6457

HELKON MEDIA
Bad Brunnthal 3
81675 Munich, Germany
(49 89) 9980-5100
Fax (49 89) 9980-5111

HIGHLAND CREST
PICTURES
7471 Melrose Ave., #7
Los Angeles, CA 90046
(323) 852-9848
Fax: (323) 658-7265

IFC FILMS
1111 Stewart Ave.
Bethpage, NY 11714
(516) 803-4511
Fax: (516) 803-4506

IFDC
1888 Century Park E., Suite 1900
Los Angeles, CA 90067
(310) 284-6858
Fax: (310) 552-1814

IFM FILM ASSOCIATES
1328 E. Palmer Ave.
Glendale, CA 91205
(818) 243-4976
Fax: (818) 550-9728

INDEPENDENT
INTERNATIONAL
PICTURES CORP.
400 Perrine Road
Old Bridge, NJ 08857
(732) 727-8500
Fax: (732) 727-8881

INITIAL ENTERTAINMENT
GROUP
6380 Wilshire Blvd., Suite 1600
Los Angeles, CA 90049
(323) 658-5603
Fax: (323) 658-5605

INTERLIGHT
8981 Sunset Blvd., Suite 101
Los Angeles, CA 90069
(310) 248-4477
Fax: (310) 248-4494

INTERNATIONAL KEYSTONE
ENTERTAINMENT
23410 Civic Center Way,
Suite E9
Malibu, CA 90265
(310) 317-4883
Fax: (310) 317-4903

IQ ENTERTAINMENT
3905 Via Dolce
Marina Del Rey, CA 90292
(310) 821-6780
Fax: (310) 821-5162

ITASCA PICTURES
345 N. Maple Drive, #278
Beverly Hills, CA 90210
(310) 273-6505

KINGMAN FILMS
9220 Sunset Blvd., Suite 210
Los Angeles, CA 90069
(310) 385-9199
Fax: (310) 385-0799

KUSHNER-LOCKE
11601 Wilshire Blvd., 21st floor
Los Angeles, CA 90025
(310) 481-2000
Fax: (310) 481-2101

LIONS GATE FILMS
561 Broadway, Suite 12B
New York, NY 10012
(212) 966-4670
Fax: (212) 966-2544

LUMIERE FILMS
8079 Selma Ave.
Los Angeles, CA 90046
(323) 650-6773
Fax: (323) 650-7339

MANIFESTO FILMS
USA:
73 Spring Street, Suite 408
New York, NY 10012
(212) 966-7686
Fax: (212) 966-4512
ITALY:
C.so Monte Grappa 18/9
16137 Genova, Italy
(39) 010-839-1660
Fax: (39) 010-837-2323
E-mail:
manifestofilms@hotmail.com

MILLENNIUM FILMS
9145 Sunset Blvd.
Los Angeles, CA 90069
(310) 246-0240
Fax: (310) 246-1655

MIRAMAX FILMS
375 Greenwich St.
New York, NY 10013
(212) 941-3800

7966 Beverly Blvd.
Los Angeles, CA 90048
(323) 951-4200
Fax: (323) 951-4213

MOONSTONE
ENTERTAINMENT
335 N. Maple Drive, Suite 222
Beverly Hills, CA 90210
(310) 247-6060
Fax: (310) 247-6061

MORGAN CREEK
PRODUCTIONS
4000 Warner Blvd., Building 76
Burbank, CA 91522
(818) 954-4000
Fax: (818) 954-4811

MSTRADING/ PARADISO
6 rue du Parc, BP 65
Bertrange, L 8005, Belgium
(32-2) 461-0555
Fax: (32-2) 461-0822

MUTUAL FILM CO.
Clinton Building
650 N. Bronson Ave.
Los Angeles, CA 90004

NEWWORLD MANAGEMENT
6255 Sunset Blvd.
Los Angeles, CA 90023
(323) 461-9803
Fax: (323) 461-9804

NEXT GENERATION
1501 Main St., Suite 201
Venice, CA 90291
(310) 450-5887
Fax: (310) 450-5877

NEXTWAVE FILMS
2510 7th St., #E
Santa Monica, CA 90405
(310) 392-1720
Fax: (310) 399-3455

NORTH BY NORTHWEST
ENTERTAINMENT
903 W. Broadway
Spokane, WA 99201

OVERSEAS FILMGROUP/
FIRST LOOK PICTURES
8800 Sunset Blvd.
Los Angeles, CA 90069
(310) 855-1199
Fax: (310) 855-0719

PALISADES PICTURES
235 Park Ave. South, 11th floor
New York, NY 10003
(212) 614-1335
Fax: (212) 460-9475

PALM PICTURES
4 Columbus Circle, 5th floor
New York, NY 10019
(212) 506-5800
Fax: (212) 506-5809

PANDORA
USA:
1620 Broadway
Santa Monica, CA 90404
FRANCE:
7 rue Keppler 75116
Paris, France
(33-1) 4070-9090
Fax: (33-1) 4070-9091

PEAKVIEWING
TRANSATLANTIC
8 Astridge Road
Witcombe, Gloucestershire
GL34SY, UK
(44-1452) 863-217
Fax: (44-1452) 863-908

PERSISTENT PICTURES
6565 Sunset Blvd., Suite 317
Hollywood, CA 90028
(323) 960-1444
Fax: (323) 960-1434

PORCHLIGHT
ENTERTAINMENT
11777 Mississippi Ave.
Los Angeles, CA 90025
(310) 477-8400
Fax: (310) 477-5555

PRAXIS ENTERTAINMENT
GROUP
8235 Douglas Ave., Suite 650,
LB-65
Dallas, TX 75225
(214) 691-2556
Fax: (214) 691-0682

PROMARK
ENTERTAINMENT
3599 Cahuenga Blvd. W.,
3rd floor
Los Angeles, CA 90068
(323) 878-0404
Fax: (323) 878-0468

REDEEMABLE FEATURES
381 Park Ave. South, Penthouse
New York, NY 10016
(212) 685-8585
Fax: (212) 685-1455

REDWOOD
COMMUNICATIONS
228 Main St., Studio 17
Venice, CA 90291
(310) 581-9090
Fax: (310) 581-9093

REGENT ENTERTAINMENT
1401 Ocean Ave., Suite 300
Santa Monica, CA 90401
(310) 260-3333
Fax: (310) 260-3343

RHINO FILMS
10635 Santa Monica Blvd., #115
Los Angeles, CA 90025
(310) 441-6557
Fax: (310) 441-6553

RIDINI ENTERTAINMENT
Raleigh Studios
650 N. Bronson Ave., Suite 649
Chaplin Building
Los Angeles, CA 90004
(323) 960-8071
Fax: (323) 960-8013

RJN PRODUCTIONS
2934½ Beverly Glen Circle
PMB 394
Bel Air, CA 90077
(310) 476-2770
Fax: (310) 476-5164

ROADSHOW PRODUCTIONS
6 Basil Mansions, Basil Street
London SW3 1AP, UK
(44-20) 7584-0542
Fax: (44-20) 7584-1549

SAMUEL GOLDWYN FILMS
9570 W. Pico Blvd.
Los Angeles, CA 90035
(310) 860-3100
Fax: (310) 860-3195

SCANBOX
11846 Ventura Blvd.
Studio City, CA 91604
(818) 762-8662
Fax: (818) 762-0094

SCENERIES ENTERTAINMENT
8624 Wilshire Blvd.
Los Angeles, CA
(310) 652-9900
Fax: (310) 652-9901

SCREEN GEMS
10202 W. Washington Blvd.
Culver City, CA 90232
Fax: (310) 244-2037

SERENDIPITY POINT FILMS
1303 Yonge St., #300
Toronto, M4T,249, Canada
(416) 960-0300
Fax: (416) 960-8656

SEVENTH ART RELEASING
7551 Sunset Blvd., #104
Los Angeles, CA 90046
(323) 845-1455
Fax: (323) 845-4717

THE SHOOTING GALLERY
145 Avenue of the Americas,
7th floor
New York, NY 10013
(212) 243-3042
Fax: (212) 647-1392

SHORELINE
ENTERTAINMENT
1901 Avenue of the Stars,
Suite 1800
Los Angeles, CA 90067
(310) 551-2060
Fax: (310) 201-0729

SHOWTIME NETWORKS
10880 Wilshire Blvd., #1600
Los Angeles, CA 90024
(310) 214-5200
Fax: (310) 234-5392

SIDEKICK ENTERTAINMENT
922 19th St., Suite D
Santa Monica, CA 90403
(310) 829-7979
Fax: (310) 829-7977

SILVERLINE PICTURES
11846 Ventura Blvd., Suite 100
Studio City, CA 91604
(818) 752-3730
Fax: (818) 752-3758

SKY PICTURES
BSkyB
Grant Way
Isleworth, Middlesex TW7 5QD,
UK
(44-171) 805-8164
Fax: (44-171) 805-8169

SONY PICTURES CLASSICS
550 Madison Ave., 8th floor
New York, NY 90232
(212) 833-8833
Fax: (212) 833-8844

SOUTH FORK PICTURES
1101 Montana Ave., Suite B
Santa Monica, CA 90403
(310) 395-7779
Fax: (310) 395-2575

STORM ENTERTAINMENT
225 Santa Monica Blvd.,
Suite 601
Santa Monica, CA 90401
(310) 656-2500
Fax: (310) 656-2510

STRAND RELEASING
1460 4th St., Suite 302
Santa Monica, CA 90401
(310) 395-5002
Fax: (310) 395-2502

STRATOSPHERE
ENTERTAINMENT
767 5th Ave., Suite 4700
New York, NY 10022
(212) 605-1010

TAPESTRY
11 Hanover Square, 14th floor
New York, NY 10005
(212) 505-2288
Fax: (212) 505-5059

TAURUS ENTERTAINMENT
1420 N. Beachwood Drive
Hollywood, CA 90028
(323) 993-7355
Fax: (323) 933-7316

TOMORROW FILM CORP.
1453 Third Street Promenade,
Suite 350
Santa Monica, CA 90401
(310) 656-6300
Fax: (310) 656-6304

TRIBE PICTURES
174 Hudson
New York, NY 10013
Fax: (212) 343-0904

TRIDENT RELEASING
8401 Melrose Place, 2nd floor
Los Angeles, CA
(323) 655-8818
Fax: 655-0515

UNAPIX FILMS
200 Madison Ave., 24th floor
New York, NY 10016
(212) 252-7711
Fax: (212) 252-7626
15910 Ventura Blvd., Suite 900
Encino, CA 91436
(818) 205-1290
Fax: (818) 205-1289

UNITED FILM
ORGANIZATION/UFO
20 W. Burbank Blvd.
Burbank, CA 91502
(818) 846-0465
Fax: (818) 846-0256

USA FILMS
9333 Wilshire Blvd.
Beverly Hills, CA 90210
(310) 385-4400
Fax: (310) 385-4408

VINE INTERNATIONAL
PICTURES
Astoria House
62 Shaftesbury Ave.
London W1 V 7DE, UK
(44-171) 437-1181
Fax: (44-171) 494-0634

WESTAR ENTERTAINMENT
1050 Venice Blvd.
Culver City, CA 90232
(310) 836-6790
Fax: (310) 836-6795

WINCHESTER FILMS
29130 Kingly St.
London W1R 5LB, UK
(44-171) 434-4374
Fax: (44-171) 287-4334

WINSTAR TV & VIDEO
419 Park Ave. South
New York, NY 10016
(212) 686-6777
Fax: (212) 687-7578

XENON ENTERTAINMENT
GROUP
1440 9th St.
Santa Monica, CA 90403
(310) 451-5510
Fax: (310) 395-4058

Appendix B

WGA Agent List

There is one certain resource for locating all the reputable agents and management firms. The Writers Guild of America publishes a list of agents that agreed to the Guild's business bylaws. The Guild publishes that list free of charge.

According to Writers Guild documents, the history of the Writers Guild of America can be traced back to 1912. At that time, the Authors Guild was first organized as a protective association for writers of books, short stories, articles, and the like. Subsequently, writers of drama formed a Dramatists Guild and joined forces with the Authors Guild, which then became the Authors League.

In 1921, the development of another medium of expression for writers—the motion picture industry—led to the formation of the Screen Writers Guild which also became a branch of the Authors League. In the period between 1921 and 1933, the Screen Writers Guild operated more as a club than a Guild. Members had a clubhouse for social activities, put on plays, and exchanged professional information. However, the need for some kind of action for the protection of writers' rights and economic conditions became apparent during this period.

So, in 1933, a group of ten writers gathered at the Roosevelt Hotel in Hollywood. The group began the process to seek protection for writers under the U.S. Labor Codes.

In 1937, the historic U.S. Supreme Court decision upholding the constitutionality of the National Labor Relations Act gave those working for unification of the Screen Writers Guild an opportunity to call for an election and eventually certified the reincorporated Screen Writers Guild as the collective bargaining agent of all writers in the motion picture industry.

In 1939, collective bargaining with the producers commenced. A deal was finalized in 1941, and the first contract was signed in 1942. However, most of the organizational efforts were postponed during the years of World War II. The Screen Writers Guild went through a period of internal political struggle from 1939 to 1947.

During this time, the Radio Writers Guild had been organized as another branch of the Authors League in response to the development of radio. Then television appeared on the scene in 1949.

In 1950, the Screen Writers Guild, which had helped to organize the Radio Writers Guild, began organizing a group of television writers under its auspices. The goal was to give TV writers protection for their work, with the thought that this group would eventually strike out on its own. A Television Writers Group was organized within the Authors League with the same purpose in mind. However, the practice of endless proliferation of branches became burdensome to the Authors League and, commencing in 1949, meetings took place in New York between representatives of the Authors Guild, the Dramatists Guild, the Radio Writers Guild, the Television Writers Group, and the Screen Writers Guild to try to devise a simpler but stronger form of unification.

Finally, in 1954, a revised organizational structure was set up and the Writers Guild of America west and East was born. The WGA today is a labor organization representing writers in the motion picture, broadcast, cable, interactive, and new media industries. It is made up of Writers Guild of America, west and East, with offices in Los Angeles and New York. The Mississippi River is used as the dividing line for administrative jurisdiction between the two Guilds.

As a result of the merger in 1954 between the Screen Writers Guild and the western branch of the Radio Writers Guild, the screen writers then became the Screen Branch of WGAw, the television and radio writers became the TV-Radio Branch of WGAw. On January 18, 1973, Guild membership approved the amalgamation of the branches, and the Screen and TV-Radio Branches were absorbed into the parent body. WGAw is run by a sixteen-member Board of Directors under a president, a vice president, and a secretary-treasurer. WGAE has a twenty-one–member Council under a president, a vice president, and a secretary-treasurer.

The administration of Writers Guild west and East is carried out under the supervision of an Executive Director for each organization.

The Writers Guild of America is the sole collective bargaining representative for writers in the motion picture, broadcast, cable, interactive, and new media industries. It has numerous affiliation agreements with other U.S. and international writing organizations, and is in the forefront of the debates concerning economic and creative rights for writers.

The WGAw does not offer assistance in finding or suggesting an agent. Each agency has its own submission policy. The WGAw recommends that writers initially telephone an agency or send a letter of inquiry, rather than submitting an unsolicited script. This letter should be concise, outlining the script writer's relevant credentials and briefly describing the nature of the work.

As a courtesy, most agents will return literary material if a self-addressed stamped envelope is included with the submission. However, agencies are under no obligation to return the submitted material, nor can the WGAw assist in the recovery of nonreturned material.

Guild policy prohibits an agency from appearing on this list if it charges reading fees or similar fees as a condition to read literary material. Such literary material includes but is not limited to screenplays, teleplays, telescripts, stories, treatments, bibles, formats, plot outlines, breakdowns, sketches, narration, noncommercial openings and closings, and long-form story projections and/or pilots—including all rewrites and polishes thereto.

Please contact the Guild at (323) 782-4502 if you find that any of the listed agencies charge reading fees or similar fees for this type of literary material. The WGAw "No Fees" policy also applies to agencies that refer writers to entities that charge reading fees or similar fees. NOTE: Some agencies on this list charge reading fees or similar fees for other forms of literary material (e.g., novels or plays).

If you believe an agency is a signatory and you do not see it listed here, contact the Guild's Agency Department at (323) 782-4502.

As a service to writers (WGAw members and nonmembers), we include the outstanding WGA Agency List. All writers should share their gratitude with the Guild for offering this service.

These agencies represent film, television, and interactive writers.

LEGEND

[*]   This agency indicated that it will consider new writers.

[**] This agency indicated that it will consider writers ONLY as a result of references from persons known to it.

[P] A packaging agency is one that represents several people associated with a film or television project, rather than just one client. It receives a commission from the producer for the group of clients it represents rather than the usual 10 percent from the individual clients.

[S] Society of Authors Representatives, signed through WGAE only.

[L] This agency indicated it will accept only a letter of inquiry. If there are no symbols next to the agency, this agency will not accept unsolicited material.

CALIFORNIA

[L] ABLAZE ENTERTAINMENT INC.
1040 N. LAS PALMAS AVE, BLDG. 30
LOS ANGELES, CA 90038
(323) 871-2202

[**] ABOVE THE LINE AGENCY
9200 SUNSET BLVD., #401
WEST HOLLYWOOD, CA 90069
(310) 859-6115

[**] ACME TALENT & LITERARY AGENCY
6310 SAN VICENTE BLVD., #520
LOS ANGELES, CA 90048
(323) 954-2263

[**,P] AGENCY FOR THE PERFORMING ARTS
9200 SUNSET BLVD., #900
LOS ANGELES, CA 90069
(310) 888-4200

[**,P] AGENCY, THE
1800 AVENUE OF THE STARS #400
LOS ANGELES, CA 90067
(310) 551-3000

ALLEN TALENT AGENCY
3832 WILSHIRE BLVD., 2ND FLOOR
LOS ANGELES, CA 90010-3221
(213) 896-9372

[L,P] ALPERN GROUP, THE
15645 ROYAL OAK ROAD
ENCINO, CA 91436
(818) 528-1111

[L] AMSEL, EISENSTADT & FRAZIER
5757 WILSHIRE BLVD., #510
LOS ANGELES, CA 90036
(323) 939-1188

[L] ANGEL CITY TALENT
1680 VINE ST., #716
LOS ANGELES, CA 90028
(323) 463-1680

[**] ARTHUR, IRVIN ASSOCIATES, LTD.
9363 WILSHIRE BLVD., #212
BEVERLY HILLS, CA 90210
(310) 278-5934

[P] ARTISTS AGENCY, THE
10000 SANTA MONICA BLVD., #305
LOS ANGELES, CA 90067
(310) 277-7779

ARTISTS GROUP, LTD., THE
10100 SANTA MONICA BLVD., #2490
LOS ANGELES, CA 90067
(310) 552-1100

[**] BECSEY, WISDOM, KALAJIAN
9200 SUNSET BLVD., #820
LOS ANGELES, CA 90069
(310) 550-0535

BENNETT AGENCY, THE
150 SOUTH BARRINGTON AVE., #1
LOS ANGELES, CA 90049
(310) 471-2251

[**] BLACK, BONNIE TALENT AGENCY
4660 CAHUENGA BLVD., #306
TOLUCA LAKE, CA 91602
(818) 753-5424

[L] BLISS, E. THOMAS AND ASSOCIATES
292 S. LA CIENEGA BLVD., #202
BEVERLY HILLS, CA 90211
(310) 657-4188

[**] BOHRMAN AGENCY, THE
8899 BEVERLY BLVD., #811
LOS ANGELES, CA 90048
(310) 550-5444

[**] BRANDON, PAUL & ASSOCIATES
1033 NORTH CAROL DR., #T-6
LOS ANGELES, CA 90069
(310) 273-6173

[**,P] BRANDT COMPANY, THE
15250 VENTURA BLVD., #720
SHERMAN OAKS, CA 91403
(818) 783-7747

[P] BRODER/KURLAND/WEBB/UFFNER
9242 BEVERLY BLVD., #200
BEVERLY HILLS, CA 90210
(310) 281-3400

[**,P] BROWN, BRUCE AGENCY
1033 GAYLEY AVE., #207
LOS ANGELES, CA 90024
(310) 208-1835

[**,L,P] BUCHWALD, DON & ASSOCIATES
6500 WILSHIRE BLVD., #2200
LOS ANGELES, CA 90048
(310) 655-7400

CAREER ARTISTS INTERNATIONAL
11030 VENTURA BLVD., #3
STUDIO CITY, CA 91604
(818) 980-1315

[**] CARROLL, WILLIAM AGENCY
139 NORTH SAN FERNANDO ROAD, #A
BURBANK, CA 91502
(818) 845-3791

[**] CAVALERI & ASSOCIATES
178 S. VICTORY BLVD., #205
BURBANK, CA 91502
(818) 955-9300

[**] CHASIN AGENCY, INC., THE
8899 BEVERLY BLVD., #716
LOS ANGELES, CA 90048
(323) 278-7505

[L] CNA & ASSOCIATES, INC.
1925 CENTURY PARK EAST, #750
LOS ANGELES, CA 90067
(310) 556-4343

[*] COAST TO COAST TALENT GROUP
3350 BARHAM BLVD.
LOS ANGELES, CA 90068
(323) 845-9200

[**] COPPAGE COMPANY, THE
3500 WEST OLIVE, #1420
BURBANK, CA 91505
(818) 953-4163

[**] CORALIE JR. THEATRICAL AGENCY
4789 VINELAND AVE., #100
NORTH HOLLYWOOD, CA 91602
(818) 766-9501

[L] DADE/SCHULTZ ASSOCIATES
6442 COLDWATER CANYON, #206
VALLEY GLEN, CA 91606
(818) 760-3100

[**,L] DOUROUX & CO.
445 SOUTH BEVERLY DR., #310
BEVERLY HILLS, CA 90212
(310) 552-0900

[**,P] DYTMAN & ASSOCIATES
9200 SUNSET BLVD., #809
LOS ANGELES, CA 90069
(310) 274-8844

[L] ELLECHANTE TALENT AGENCY
274 SPAZIER AVE.
BURBANK, CA 91502
(818) 557-3025

[**,L,P] ENDEAVOR AGENCY, THE
9701 WILSHIRE BLVD.
10TH FLOOR
BEVERLY HILLS, CA 90212
(310) 248-2000

EPSTEIN-WYCKOFF-CORSA-ROSS & ASSOCIATES
280 SOUTH BEVERLY DR., #400
BEVERLY HILLS, CA 90212
(310) 278-7222

[L] ES AGENCY, THE
777 DAVIS ST.
SAN FRANCISCO, CA 94111
(415) 421-6272

FAVORED ARTISTS AGENCY
122 SOUTH ROBERTSON BLVD., #202
LOS ANGELES, CA 90048
(310) 247-1040

[P] FIELD-CECH AGENCY, INC., THE
12725 VENTURA BLVD., #D
STUDIO CITY, CA 91604
(818) 980-2001

FILM ARTISTS ASSOCIATES
13563 1/2 VENTURA BLVD.
2ND FLOOR
SHERMAN OAKS, CA 91423
(818) 386-9669

[L] FILM-THEATER ACTORS EXCHANGE
582 MARKET ST., #306
SAN FRANCISCO, CA 94104
(415) 433-3920

FLATE, DAVID TALENT AGENCY
9300 WILSHIRE BLVD., #300
BEVERLY HILLS, CA 90212
(310) 828-6289

[L] FREED, BARRY COMPANY, INC., THE
2040 AVENUE OF THE STARS, #400
LOS ANGELES, CA 90067
(310) 277-1260

[**,L,P] FRIES, ALICE AGENCY, LTD.
1927 VISTA DEL MAR AVE.
LOS ANGELES, CA 90068
(323) 464-1404

GAGE GROUP, INC., THE
9255 SUNSET BLVD., #515
LOS ANGELES, CA 90069
(310) 859-8777

[**] GARRICK, DALE INTERNATIONAL
8831 SUNSET BLVD.
LOS ANGELES, CA 90069
(310) 657-2661

GEDDES AGENCY
8430 SANTA MONICA BLVD., #200
WEST HOLLYWOOD, CA 90069
(323) 848-2700

[**] GELFF, LAYA AGENCY
16133 VENTURA BLVD., #700
ENCINO, CA 91436
(818) 996-3100

[**] GERARD, PAUL TALENT AGENCY
11712 MOORPARK ST., #112
STUDIO CITY, CA 91604
(818) 769-7015

[P] GERSH AGENCY, INC., THE
232 NORTH CANON DR., #201
BEVERLY HILLS, CA 90210
(310) 274-6611

[**,L] GORDON, MICHELLE & ASSOCIATES
260 SOUTH BEVERLY DR., #308
BEVERLY HILLS, CA 90212
(310) 246-9930

[**] GREENE, HAROLD R. AGENCY
13900 MARQUESAS WAY
BLDG. C, #83
MARINA DEL REY, CA 90292
(310) 823-5393

[L] GUSAY, CHARLOTTE LITERARY
AGENT/ARTISTS REPRESENTATIVE
10532 BLYTHE AVE.
LOS ANGELES, CA 90064
(310) 559-0831

GROSSMAN, LARRY & ASSOCIATES
211 SOUTH BEVERLY DR., #206
BEVERLY HILLS, CA 90212
(310) 550-8127

[**,L] HAMILBURG, MITCHELL J. AGENCY
8671 WILSHIRE BLVD., #500
BEVERLY HILLS, CA 90211
(310) 657-1501

[**] HENDERSON/HOGAN AGENCY,INC.
247 SOUTH BEVERLY DR.
BEVERLY HILLS, CA 90212
(310) 274-7815

[*] HERMAN, RICHARD TALENT AGENCY
124 LASKY DR., 2ND FLOOR
BEVERLY HILLS, CA 90212
(310) 550-8913

[**] HOHMAN, MAYBANK, LIEB
9229 SUNSET BLVD., #700
LOS ANGELES, CA 90069
(310) 274-4600

[**] HWA TALENT REPRESENTATIVES, INC.
3500 WEST OLIVE AVE., #1400
BURBANK, CA 91505
(818) 972-4310

[P] INNOVATIVE ARTISTS
1999 AVENUE OF THE STARS, #2850
LOS ANGELES, CA 90067
(310) 553-5200

[P] INTERNATIONAL CREATIVE MANAGEMENT
8942 WILSHIRE BLVD.
BEVERLY HILLS, CA 90211
(310) 550-4000

[*,L] JOHNSON WARREN LITERARY AGENCY
115 W. CALIFORNIA BLVD., #173
PASADENA, CA 91105
(626) 583-8750

KALLEN, LESLIE B. AGENCY
15303 VENTURA BLVD., #900
SHERMAN OAKS, CA 91403
(818) 906-2785

[**,P] KAPLAN-STAHLER-GUMER AGENCY, THE
8383 WILSHIRE BLVD., #923
BEVERLY HILLS, CA 90211
(323) 653-4483

[**] KARG, MICHAEL & ASSOCIATES
12220 1/2 VENICE BLVD.
LOS ANGELES, CA 90066
(310) 205-0435

[**] KJAR, TYLER AGENCY, THE
5116 LANKERSHIM BLVD.
NORTH HOLLYWOOD, CA 91601-3717
(818) 760-0321

[**,L] KLANE, JON AGENCY
120 EL CAMINO DR., #112
BEVERLY HILLS, CA 90212
(310) 278-0178

[**,P] KOHNER, PAUL INC.
9300 WILSHIRE BLVD., #555
BEVERLY HILLS, CA 90212
(310) 550-1060

[L] KOZLOV, CARY LITERARY REPRESENTATION
11911 SAN VICENTE BLVD., #348
LOS ANGELES, CA 90049
(310) 843-2211

[L] L.A. PREMIERE ARTISTS AGENCY
8899 BEVERLY BLVD., #510
LOS ANGELES, CA 90048
(310) 271-1414

[**,P] LAKE, CANDACE AGENCY, INC., THE
9200 SUNSET BLVD., #820
LOS ANGELES, CA 90069
(310) 247-2115

[**,L] LARCHMONT LITERARY AGENCY
444 NORTH LARCHMONT BLVD., #200
LOS ANGELES, CA 90004
(323) 856-3070

[**]LENHOFF & LENHOFF
9200 SUNSET BLVD., #1201
LOS ANGELES, CA 90069
(310) 550-3900

LENNY, JACK ASSOCIATES
9454 WILSHIRE BLVD., #600
BEVERLY HILLS, CA 90212
(310) 271-2174

[**] LICHTMAN, TERRY CO., AGENCY
12216 MOORPARK ST.
STUDIO CITY, CA 91604
(818) 655-9898

LUKER, JANA TALENT AGENCY
1923 1/2 WESTWOOD BLVD., #3
LOS ANGELES, CA 90025
(310) 441-2822

LYNNE & REILLY AGENCY
10725 VANOWEN ST.
NORTH HOLLYWOOD, CA 91605-6402
(323) 850-1984

[P] MAJOR CLIENTS AGENCY
345 NORTH MAPLE DR., #395
BEVERLY HILLS, CA 90210
(310) 205-5000

MARIS AGENCY
17620 SHERMAN WAY #213
VAN NUYS, CA 91406
(818) 708-2493

[**] MARKWOOD COMPANY, THE
1813 VICTORY BLVD.
GLENDALE, CA 91201
(818) 401-3644

[L] MEDIA ARTISTS GROUP/CAPITAL ARTISTS
6404 WILSHIRE BLVD., #950
LOS ANGELES, CA 90048
(323) 658-7434

[**,P] METROPOLITAN TALENT AGENCY
4526 WILSHIRE BLVD.
LOS ANGELES, CA 90010
(323) 857-4500

[L] MILES, MARJORIE & HARVEY, MATT
LITERARY TALENT AGENCY
836 N. LA CIENEGA, #358
LOS ANGELES, CA 90069
(213) 673-3717

[**] MILLER, STUART M. CO., THE
11684 VENTURA BLVD., #225
STUDIO CITY, CA 91604
(818) 506-6067

[**] ORANGE GROVE GROUP, INC., THE
12178 VENTURA BLVD., #205
STUDIO CITY, CA 91604
(818) 762-7498

ORIGINAL ARTISTS
9465 WILSHIRE BLVD., #840
BEVERLY HILLS, CA 90212
(310) 277-1251

[**] OSTROFF, DANIEL AGENCY, THE
9200 SUNSET BLVD., #402
LOS ANGELES, CA 90069
(310) 278-2020

[*] PANDA TALENT AGENCY
3721 HOEN AVE.
SANTA ROSA, CA 95405
(707) 576-0711

[*] PANETTIERE & CO. TALENT AGENCY
1841 N. FULLER AVE., #206
LOS ANGELES, CA 90046
(323) 876-5984

[P] PARADIGM
10100 SANTA MONICA BLVD., #2500
LOS ANGELES, CA 90067
(310) 277-4400

[**,P] PERELMAN, BARRY AGENCY, THE
9200 SUNSET BLVD., #1201
LOS ANGELES, CA 90069
(310) 274-5999

[**,P] PLESHETTE, LYNN LITERARY AGENCY
2700 NORTH BEACHWOOD DR.
HOLLYWOOD, CA 90068
(323) 465-0428

[**,P] PREFERRED ARTISTS
16633 VENTURA BLVD., #1421
ENCINO, CA 91436
(818) 990-0305

[**,P] PREMINGER, JIM AGENCY, THE
1650 WESTWOOD BLVD., #201
LOS ANGELES, CA 90024
(310) 475-9491

PREMIER ARTISTS AGENCY
400 S. BEVERLY DR., #214
BEVERLY HILLS, CA 90212
(310) 284-4064

PRICE, FRED R. LITERARY AGENCY
14044 VENTURA BLVD., #201
SHERMAN OAKS, CA 91423
(818) 763-6365

[**] PRIVILEGE TALENT AGENCY
9229 SUNSET BLVD., #414
WEST HOLLYWOOD, CA 90069
(310) 858-5277

[**] PRODUCTION ARTS MANAGEMENT
1122 S. ROBERTSON BLVD., #9
LOS ANGELES, CA 90035
(310) 276-8536

[**,P] QUILLCO AGENCY
3104 WEST CUMBERLAND CT.
WESTLAKE VILLAGE, CA 91362
(805) 495-8436

[L,P] RAINE AGENCY, INC., THE
5225 WILSHIRE BLVD., #421
LOS ANGELES, CA 90036
(323) 932-0897

[**] RICHLAND AGENCY, THE
2828 DONALD DOUGLAS LOOP N.
SANTA MONICA, CA 90405
(310) 571-1833

[**] ROBERTS COMPANY, THE
10345 WEST OLYMPIC BLVD.
PENTHOUSE
LOS ANGELES, CA 90064
(310) 552-7800

[L] ROBINS, MICHAEL D. & ASSOCIATES
23241 VENTURA BLVD., #300
WOODLAND HILLS, CA 91364
(818) 343-1755

ROGERS, STEPHANIE & ASSOCIATES
3575 CAHUENGA BLVD., WEST #249
LOS ANGELES, CA 90068
(323) 851-5155

[*] ROMANO, CINDY MODELING & TALENT AGENCY
1555 S. PALM CYN DR., #D-102
PALM SPRINGS, CA 92264
(760) 323-3333

[**,P] ROTHMAN AGENCY, THE
9465 WILSHIRE BLVD., #840
BEVERLY HILLS, CA 90212
(310) 247-9898

[**] SANFORD-GROSS & ASSOCIATES
1015 GAYLEY AVE., #301
LOS ANGELES, CA 90024
(310) 208-2100

SARNOFF COMPANY, INC., THE
10 UNIVERSAL CITY PLAZA, #2000
UNIVERSAL CITY, CA 91608
(818) 754-3708

[**] SCAGNETTI, JACK
5118 VINELAND AVE., #102
NORTH HOLLYWOOD, CA 91601
(818) 762-3871

[**,P] SCHECHTER, IRV COMPANY, THE
9300 WILSHRE BLVD., #400
BEVERLY HILLS, CA 90212
(310) 278-8070

[**] SCHWARTZMAN, PAUL OFFICE, THE
3000 WEST OLYMPIC BLVD.
SANTA MONICA, CA 90404
(323) 651-5500

[**] SHAFER & ASSOCIATES
9000 SUNSET BLVD., #808
LOS ANGELES, CA 90069
(310) 888-1240

[P] SHAPIRA, DAVID & ASSOCIATES, INC.
15301 VENTURA BLVD., #345
SHERMAN OAKS, CA 91403
(818) 906-0322

[**,P] SHAPIRO-LICHTMAN-STEIN
8827 BEVELRY BLVD.
LOS ANGELES, CA 90048
(310) 859-8877

[**] SHERMAN, KEN & ASSOCIATES
9507 SANTA MONICA BLVD., #212
BEVERLY-HILLS, CA 90210
(310) 273-8840

SHUMAKER ARTISTS TALENT AGENCY
6533 HOLLYWOOD BLVD., #401
HOLLYWOOD, CA 90028
(323) 464-0745

SIEGEL, JEROME S. ASSOCIATES
1680 NORTH VINE ST., #617
HOLLYWOOD, CA 90028
(323) 466-0185

[**] SINDELL, RICHARD & ASSOCIATES
8271 MELROSE AVE., #202
LOS ANGELES, CA 90046
(323) 653-5051

SMITH, SUSAN & ASSOCIATES
121 N. SAN VICENTE BLVD.
BEVERLY HILLS, CA 90211
(323) 852-4777

[**] SOLOWAY, GRANT, KOPALOFF & ASSOCIATES
6399 WILSHIRE BLVD., #414
LOS ANGELES, CA 90048
(323) 782-1854

[L] SORICE, CAMILLE TALENT AGENCY
13412 MOORPARK ST., #C
SHERMAN OAKS, CA 91423
(818) 995-1775

[*] STARLING, CARYN TALENT AGENCY
4728 GREENBUSH AVE.
SHERMAN OAKS, CA 91423
(818) 766-0436

STARWILL PRODUCTIONS
433 N. CAMDEN DR., 4TH FLOOR
BEVERLY HILLS, CA 90210
(323) 874-1239

[**] STONE MANNERS AGENCY, THE
8436 W. THIRD ST., #740
LOS ANGELES, CA 90048
(323) 655-1313

[*] A TOTAL ACTING EXPERIENCE
20501 VENTURA BLVD., #399
WOODLAND HILLS, CA 91364-2350

[L] TRIUMPH LITERARY AGENCY
3000 W. OLYMPIC BLVD., #1362
SANTA MONICA, CA 90404
(310) 264-3959

[*] TURNING POINT MANAGEMENT SYSTEMS
6601 CENTER DR. WEST, #500
LOS ANGELES, CA 90045
(310) 348-8171

[**] TURTLE AGENCY, THE
955 S. CARRILLO DR., #103
LOS ANGELES, CA 90048
(323) 954-4068

[**] UFFNER, BETH & ASSOCIATES
9242 BEVERLY BLVD., #200
BEVERLY HILLS, CA 90210
(310) 281-3400

[L] UNITED ARTISTS TALENT AGENCY
14011 VENTURA BLVD., #213
SHERMAN OAKS, CA 91423
(818) 788-7305

[**,P] UNITED TALENT AGENCY
9560 WILSHIRE BLVD., 5TH FLOOR
BEVERLY HILLS, CA 90212
(310) 273-6700

[**] UNIVERSAL TALENT AGENCY
8306 WILSHIRE BLVD., #530
BEVERLY HILLS, CA 90211
(310) 273-7721

[**,P] VISION ART MANAGEMENT
9200 SUNSET BLVD.
PENTHOUSE 1
LOS ANGELES, CA 90069
(310) 888-3288

[**] WARDEN, WHITE & ASSOCIATES
8444 WILSHIRE BLVD., 4TH FLOOR
BEVERLY HILLS, CA 90211
(323) 852-1028

[**,L] WARDLOW & ASSOCIATES
1501 MAIN ST., #204
VENICE, CA 90291
(310) 452-1292

[**] WEBB, RUTH ENTERPRISES, INC.
10580 DES MOINES AVE.
NORTHRIDGE, CA 91326
(818) 363-1993

[**]WILSON, SHIRLEY & ASSOCIATES
5410 WILSHIRE BLVD., #227
LOS ANGELES, CA 90036
(323) 857-6977

WOLF AGENCY, THE
2045 ROYAL AVE., #109C
SIMI VALLEY, CA 93065
(805) 306-9769

[**] WORKING ARTISTS TALENT AGENCY
10914 RATHBURN AVE.
NORTHRIDGE, CA 91326
(818) 368-8222

[**] WRIGHT, MARION A AGENCY
4317 BLUEBELL AVE.
STUDIO CITY, CA 91604
(818) 766-7307

[P] WRITERS & ARTISTS AGENCY (LA)
8383 WILSHIRE BLVD., #550
BEVERLY HILLS, CA 90211
(323) 866-0900

ILLINOIS

[*] AGENCY CHICAGO
601 SOUTH LA SALLE ST., #600-A
CHICAGO, IL 60605

[L] ARIA MODEL & TALENT MANAGMENT LTD
1017 W. WASHINGTON, #2C
CHICAGO, IL 60607
(312) 243-9400

[*] BRYAN, MARCUS & ASSOCIATES
3308 COMMERCIAL AVE.
NORTHBROOK, IL 60062
(847) 579-0030

[*] BULGER, KELVIN C.ATTORNEY AT LAW
11 EAST ADAMS, #604
CHICAGO, IL 60603
(312) 280-2403

[**] FOR WRITERS ONLY
220 SOUTH STATE ST., #1320
CHICAGO, IL 60604
(773) 769-6350

[**] HAMILTON, SHIRLEY, INC.
333 EAST ONTARIO AVE., #302B
CHICAGO, IL 60611
(312) 787-4700

[L] JOHNSON, SUSANNE TALENT AGENCY, LTD.
108 WEST OAK ST.
CHICAGO, IL 60610
(312) 943-8315

[L] K.P. AGENCY
10 EAST ONTARIO
CHICAGO, IL 60611
(312) 787-9888

[**,L] ORENTAS, DALIA LITERARY AGENT
6128 NORTH DAMEN AVE.
CHICAGO, IL 60659
(312) 338-6392

[*] ROSENTHAL, JASON B., LAW OFFICES, P.C.
20 NORTH CLARK ST., #444
CHICAGO, IL 60622-4111
(312) 345-0420

[L] SIEGAN & WEISMAN, LTD.
29 S. LA SALLE ST. #450
CHICAGO, IL 60603
(312) 782-1212

[L] SILVER SCREEN PLACEMENTS INC.
602 65TH ST.
DOWNERS GROVE, IL 60516
(708) 963-2124

[*] STEWART TALENT MANAGEMENT CORP.
58 WEST HURON
CHICAGO, IL 60610
(312) 943-3131

UNIVERSAL CREATIVE ARTISTS
6829 NORTH LINCOLN, #135
LINCOLNWOOD, IL 60646
(847) 679-3916

[**] WHISKEY HILL ENTERTAINMENT
1000 SOUTH WILLIAMS ST.
P O BOX 606
WESTMONT, IL 60559-0606
(630) 852-5023

NEW YORK

ADAMS, BRET LTD.
448 WEST 44TH ST.
NEW YORK, NY 10036
(212) 765-5630

[*] AMATO, MICHAEL AGENCY
1650 BROADWAY, SUITE 307
NEW YORK, NY 10019
(212) 247-4456

[**,P] AGENCY FOR THE PERFORMING ARTS
888 SEVENTH AVE.
NEW YORK, NY 10106
(212) 582-1500

[L] AMRON DEVELOPMENT, INC.
77 HORTON PL.
SYOSSET, NY 11791
(516) 364-0238

[L] AMSTERDAM, MARCIA AGENCY
41 WEST 82ND ST.
NEW YORK, NY 10024-5613
(212) 873-4945

ARTISTS AGENCY, INC.
230 WEST 55TH ST., #29D
NEW YORK, NY 10019
(212) 245-6960

[**,L] BERMAN, BOALS & FLYNN, INC.
208 WEST 30TH ST., #401
NEW YORK, NY 10001
(212) 868-1068

[**] BORCHARDT, GEORGES INC.
136 EAST 57TH ST.
NEW YORK, NY 10022
(212) 753-5785

BROWN, CURTIS, LTD.
10 ASTOR PL.
NEW YORK, NY 10003
(212) 473-5400

[L] BROWNE, PEMA, LTD.
PINE RD, HCR BOX 104B
NEVERSINK, NY 12765
(914) 985-2936

BUCHWALD, DON & ASSOCIATES
10 EAST 44TH ST.
NEW YORK, NY 10017
(212) 867-1070

[**] CARASSO, JOSEPH MARTIN, ESQ.
225 LAFAYETTE ST., #708
NEW YORK, NY 10012
(212) 343-0700

[L] CARRY-WILLIAMS AGENCY
49 WEST 46TH ST.
NEW YORK, NY 10036
(212) 768-2793

CARVAINIS, MARIA AGENCY
235 WEST END AVE.
NEW YORK, NY 10023
(212) 580-1559

[L] CIRCLE OF CONFUSION LIMITED
666 FIFTH AVE., #303
NEW YORK, NY 10103
(212) 969-0653

[L] DEE MURA ENTERPRISES, INC.
269 WEST SHORE DR.
MASSAPEQUA, NY 11758
(516) 795-1616

DONADIO & ASHWORTH, INC.
121 WEST 27TH ST.
NEW YORK, NY 10001
(212) 691-8077

[**,L] EARTH TRACKS ARTISTS AGENCY
4809 AVE., NORTH #286
BROOKLYN, NY 11234

[S] FREEDMAN, ROBERT A. DRAMATIC AGENCY, INC.
1501 BROADWAY, #2310
NEW YORK, NY 10036
(212) 840-5760

GERSH AGENCY, INC., THE
130 WEST 42ND ST.
NEW YORK, NY 10036
(212) 997-1818

[**,L] GURMAN, SUSAN AGENCY, THE
865 WEST END AVE., #15A
NEW YORK, NY 10025
(212) 749-4618

[L] HASHAGEN, RICK & ASSOCIATES
157 WEST 57TH ST.
NEW YORK, NY 10019
(212) 315-3130

HOGENSON, BARBARA AGENCY, INC.
165 WEST END AVE., #19-C
NEW YORK, NY 10023
(212) 874-8084

[*,L] HUDSON AGENCY
3 TRAVIS LN.
MONTROSE, NY 10548
(914) 737-1475

[P] INTERNATIONAL CREATIVE MANAGEMENT
40 WEST 57TH ST.
NEW YORK, NY 10019
(212) 556-5600

[L] JANSON, MARILYN JUNE
LITERARY AGENCY
4 ALDER COURT
SELDEN, NY 11784
(516) 696-4661

[*] KALLIOPE ENTERPRISES, INC.
15 LARCH DR.
NEW HYDE, NY 11040
(516) 248-2963

[**,L] KERIN-GOLDBERG ASSOCIATES, INC.
155 EAST 55TH ST.
NEW YORK, NY 10022
(212) 838-7373

[L] KETAY, JOYCE AGENCY, INC., THE
1501 BROADWAY, #1908
NEW YORK, NY 10036
(212) 354-6825

KING, ARCHER, LTD.
10 COLUMBUS CIRCLE, #1492
NEW YORK, NY 10019
(212) 765-3103

[L] KINGDOM INDUSTRIES LTD.
118-11 195TH ST.
P O BOX 310
SAINT ALBANS, NY 11412-0310
(718) 949-9804

[L] KMA AGENCY
11 BROADWAY, SUITE 1101
NEW YORK, NY 10004
(212) 581-4610

KOZAK, OTTO LITERARY &
MOTION PICTURE AGENCY
114 CORONADO ST.
ATLANTIC BEACH, NY 11509

[**] LASERSON CREATIVE
358 13TH ST.
BROOKLYN, NY 11215
(718) 832-1785

[L] LITERARY GROUP INT'L, THE
270 LAFAYETTE ST., #1505
NEW YORK, NY 10012
(212) 274-1616

[**] LORD, STERLING LITERISTIC, INC.
65 BLEECKER ST.
NEW YORK, NY 10012
(212) 780-6050

MARKSON, ELAINE LITERARY AGENCY
44 GREENWICH AVE.
NEW YORK, NY 10011
(212) 243-8480

[**] MATSON, HAROLD, CO., INC.
276 FIFTH AVE.
NEW YORK, NY 10001
(212) 679-4490

[L] McINTOSH AND OTIS, INC.
310 MADISON AVE.
NEW YORK, NY 10017
(212) 687-7400

[*] MEYERS, ALLAN S. AGENCY
105 COURT ST.
BROOKLYN, NY 11201
(718) 596-2490

MILESTONE LITERARY AGENCY
247 W. 26TH ST., #3A
NEW YORK, NY 10001
(212) 691-0560

[P] MORRIS, WILLIAMS AGENCY, INC.
1325 AVENUE OF THE AMERICAS
NEW YORK, NY 10019
(212) 586-5100

[*] MORRISON, HENRY, INC.
105 SOUTH BEDFORD RD., #306-A
MOUNT KISCO, NY 10549
(914) 666-3500

[**,L] OMNIBUS PRODUCTIONS
184 THOMPSON ST., #1-G
NEW YORK, NY 10012
(212) 995-2941

OMNIPOP, INC. TALENT AGENCY
55 WEST OLD COUNTRY RD.
HICKSVILLE, NY 11801
(516) 937-6011

[**] OSCARD, FIFI AGENCY, INC.
24 WEST 40TH ST., 17TH FLOOR
NEW YORK, NY 10018
(212) 764-1100

[**] PALMER, DOROTHY AGENCY
235 WEST 56TH ST., #24K
NEW YORK, NY 10019
(212) 765-4280

PARAMUSE ARTISTS ASSOCIATION
1414 AVENUE OF THE AMERICAS
NEW YORK, NY 10019
(212) 758-5055

PROFESSIONAL ARTISTS UNLTD.
321 WEST 44TH ST., #605
NEW YORK, NY 10036
(212) 247-8770

[S] RAINES AND RAINES
71 PARK AVE.
NEW YORK, NY 10016
(212) 684-5160

ROBERTS, FLORA, INC.
157 WEST 57TH ST.
NEW YORK, NY 10019
(212) 355-4165

[L] SANDERS, VICTORIA LITERARY AGENCY
241 6TH AVE., #11H
NEW YORK, NY 10014
(212) 633-8811

[*,L] SCHULMAN, SUSAN LITERARY AGENCY
454 WEST 44TH ST.
NEW YORK, NY 10036
(212) 713-1633

[L] SCHWARTZ, LAURENS R., ESQ.
5 EAST 22ND ST., #15D
NEW YORK, NY 10010-5315

[**] SEIGEL, ROBERT L.
67-21F 193RD LN.
FRESH MEADOWS, NY 11365
(718) 454-7044

[**] SELMAN, EDYTHEA GINIS LITERARY AGENT
14 WASHINGTON PL.
NEW YORK, NY 10003
(212) 473-1874

[*,L] STEELE, LYLE & COMPANY, LTD.
511 EAST 73RD, #7
NEW YORK, NY 10021
(212) 288-2981

STERN, MIRIAM, ESQ.
303 EAST 83RD ST.
NEW YORK, NY 10028
(212) 794-1289

[*] STRATA SPHERES INC.
205 MULBERRY ST., #5F
NEW YORK, NY 10012
(212) 625-0365

[*] SYDRA TECHNIQUES CORPORATION
481 EIGHTH AVE., #E24
NEW YORK, NY 10001
(212) 631-0009

[*,L] TALENT EAST
555 MAIN ST., #704
NEW YORK, NY 10044
(212) 838-1392

TALENT REPRESENTATIVES, INC.
20 EAST 53RD ST.
NEW YORK, NY 10022
(212) 752-1835

[L] TANTLEFF OFFICE, THE
375 GREENWICH ST., #603
NEW YORK, NY 10013
(212) 941-3939

[S] TARG, ROSLYN LITERARY AGENCY
105 WEST 13TH ST.
NEW YORK, NY 10011
(212) 206-9390

WRIGHT, ANN REPRESENTATIVES
165 WEST 46TH ST., #1105
NEW YORK, NY 10036-2501
(212) 764-6770

[P] WRITERS & ARTISTS AGENCY
19 WEST 44TH ST., #1000
NEW YORK, NY 10036
(212) 391-1112

Appendix C

Online Resources

Until you find your agent from the previous list, you may need other ways to break into the business. With networking becoming such an important element of the film business, you need to make contacts. Since writers might not be the best mixers, I suggest using Web pages to find film professionals and lists of producers to contact. I include just a few of the most popular and most promising sites here:

www.scriptmag.com
The magazine's full-service home page recently expanded to include a wealth of information for the independently minded writer. The site includes special articles not found on these pages and story-analysis services.

www.ifp.org
The home page for the Independent Features Project, West, is the essential first stop for writers looking to learn more about independent film development and production. The IFP home page offers a complete overview of the organization and its many services.

http://hollywoodnet.com/listserv/
This site registers screenwriters for an online movie-writing mailing list that could improve their chances for successful coast-to-coast networking.

http://screenwriters.com/

One of the longer-running and most popular screenwriting Web sites, this page offers a good list of links that can guide a writer around the world of Inter-networking.

www.screenwritersrm.com

As mentioned earlier, the Screenwriters' Room has experienced feature film executives who read and consult on screenplays for all writers and can provide personal referrals to agents, producers, and studio executives.

www.wordplayer.com

A film writing and production research site with independent production information.

www.inhollywood.com

The Web site for working Hollywood. This insider's page offers development information, directories, and coverage tracking.

While none of these sites will guarantee you success as a writer, they offer suggestions that can help steer you in the right direction.

In the end, as usual, it's a good news/bad news deal for the up-and-coming screenwriter. The good news is that markets develop and present excellent opportunities to screenwriters unable or unwilling to break into the agency maze on their first tries. The bad news is that becoming a successful film or television writer is no easier than breaking in as any other kind of industry professional. The paths into the separate arenas are different, but the amount of effort needed to make the journey is the same. It's never easy. But if you wanted easy, you should have gone into brain surgery or astrophysics.

Glossary

Throughout this book, entertainment professionals tossed around a lot of buzzwords. This list of terms should explain any insider lingo that baffled you. Most of these terms originated with the famous Hollywood trade newspaper "Daily Variety." From there, they found their way into Hollywood insider-speak and American pop culture.

A

ABOVE-THE-LINE—Concerning film budgeting costs, above-the-line refers to all the costs of a creative rather than technical nature—defined as the monies paid to the writer, director, producer, and talent.

ACADEMY AWARD—The "Oscar," presented to the best in motion pictures by the Academy of Motion Picture Arts and Sciences.

ACTION—Subject's motion within camera range.

ADAPTATION—The rewriting of fact or fiction for film presentation, usually in the form of a completed screenplay or treatment.

ADDED SCENES—Material, shots, sequences, or scenes written into a script during its filming.

AD LIB—Improvised lines, phrases, or action.

AGENT—A professional who represents artists or performers in contracts, sales, and other negotiations with production companies for a percentage of their salary.

AMPAS—The Academy of Motion Picture Arts and Sciences.

ANCILLARY RIGHTS—Rights that allow a screenwriter to receive a percentage of the profits generated by the film through collectibles, toys, books, records, T-shirts, etc.

ANGLE/CAMERA ANGLE—The spatial relationship between the camera and the subject of the shot.

ANGLE ON—Direction in a shooting script directing that another camera angle is to be made of a previous shot, usually to emphasize a specific object.

ANIMATION—Process of creating the illusion of motion by creating individual frames, as opposed to filming naturally occurring action at a regular frame rate.

ANIME—Animated movies produced in Japan.

ANKLE—To quit or be dismissed from a job.

ANNOTATION—Comment in a script indicating the source of each script element that is not fictional, including all characters, events, settings, and dialogue.

ANTAGONIST—The villain of the story, important to the PROTAGONIST (hero) because without the conflict provided by the villain, there is no story.

ANTICLIMAX—Anything that happens in the final moments of a film that dulls the excitement or drama, thus causing the audience to feel dissatisfied.

ANTIHERO—A male or female protagonist in a film with pronounced character defects.

ARCHETYPE—A story or character that typifies a specific genre or type classification in style, content, characterization, and presentation.

ARTHOUSE—A motion picture theater that shows foreign or nonmainstream independent films.

ASSOCIATION OF MOTION PICTURE AND TELEVISION PRODUCERS—The union for film and television producers.

ATMOSPHERE—The tone of the action, setting, or dialogue in a story.

AVANT GARDE—An experimental, independent film, the forerunner of a new genre.

B

BACK TO SCENE/RESUME—The camera returns from an angle to its original shot.

BACK END—A film's profit from theatre ticket sales, video rentals, and ancillary markets.

BEAT—A pause in an actor's speech or action. Alternatively, a plot point within a story structure.

BELOW THE LINE—All costs of a technical rather than creative nature. Everything except the monies paid to the writer, director, producer, and principal talent.

BIDDING WAR—What ensues when a spec script, book, or written material is pitched to several studios, all wanting to buy the work.

BIZ—Shorthand for show business.

BLACK COMEDY—Comedy dealing with subjects that are typically considered "serious," such as death, war, and misery.

BLOCKBUSTER—Movie that is a financial success, earning more than $100 million.

BLUE (OR COLOR) PAGES—Pages in a shooting screenplay revised and inserted into the script. [might be helpful if you included an example of a normal revision sequence—i.e., white for the first set of pages, blue for first revision, pink (or whatever) for third, etc.]

B.O.—Box office. Measure of the total amount of money paid by movie-goers to see a movie.

BUDGET—The funds required to produce a film or television production.

<u>C</u>

CAMP/CAMPY—A form of comedic parody in which the clichéd conventions of a dramatic form are exaggerated to the point of absurdity.

CAN (IN THE)—The metal or plastic containers used for the transport and storage of film, or a reference to completing work on a project.

CAST—The collective term for all the actors appearing in a film.

CASTING—The selection process of hiring actors to play the characters in a script.

CASTING COUCH—The term referring to the clichéd-though-real practice of casting agents, directors, and producers demanding sex in return for a role in a film.

CENSORSHIP—Changes required in a movie by some person or body other than the studio or the filmmakers, usually a national or regional film classification board.

CERTIFICATE OF AUTHORSHIP—A form signed by the author of a screenplay that guarantees that the author's work is original.

CHANGE PAGES—When a script is being edited during production, changes are distributed to the actors and crew on "change pages," which are generally a different color from the original pages of the script, and follow a hierarchy of color as to the revision number.

CHARACTER ARC—The line tracing the development of a character over the course of a screenplay.

CINEMA VERITÉ—"Cinematic truth." A documentary style in which no directorial control is exerted.

CLOSE-UP (C.U.)—A film shot in which an object or actor is photographed so that it/he/she fills most of the frame.

COMPENSATION (CONSIDERATION)—The money paid for services rendered, such as the writing or sale of a screenplay.

CONFAB—Convention or professional gathering.

CONTINGENT COMPENSATION—A form of payment or compensation received on contingency. The writer receives payment *only if* a stated, contracted factor comes to pass, such as the film actually getting made.

CONTINUITY—The degree to which a movie is self-consistent without error.

CO-PRODUCER—A person who works with a producer in the filmmaking process. Both have equal responsibilities for the completion of a film project.

CO-PRODUCTION—A collaborative effort between producers and production companies to synthesize a final product and reach a larger market.

CORNY—Obvious or old-fashioned.

COVERAGE—A report used by a production company or producer. A reader evaluates and breaks down a screenplay for story, character, plot, etc. If the script receives positive feedback, it moves on to someone of greater importance.

CUT TO—The point at which one shot or scene is changed immediately to another.

D

DEAL MEMO—A document sent out to confirm verbal agreements reached over the phone.

DEUS EX MACHINA—A plot device that provides an unfairly easy solution to the protagonist's dilemma, one that is inconsistent with any realistic probabilities. The term comes from Latin, meaning "God in the machine."

DEVELOPMENT DEAL (OR STEP DEAL)—The paid process by which a story becomes a screenplay.

DGA—Directors Guild of America, the union of film and TV directors, assistant directors, and unit production managers.

DISSOLVE TO—Used to indicate when the image on screen fades out while a new image fades in.

DISTRIB—Distributor.

DOC, DOCU—Documentary.

DP—Director of photography. The lead cinematographer responsible for the composition of everything the camera records, including mise en scene, lighting, film exposure, frame rate, etc.

E

EXEC, EXEX—Executive, executives.

EXT. (EXTERIOR)—Used in scene headings to indicate that a scene takes place outdoors.

EXTREME CLOSE-UP (ECU)—Camera cue in direction that is generally used to emphasize some particular detail.

EXTREME LONG SHOT—Camera cue in direction used to describe a shot taken at a long distance from the subject.

F

FADE OUT—Scene ending used in television at the end of an act, or at the end of a feature film.

FAST TRACK—A project good enough to go into production.

FEATURE—Motion picture more than an hour in length.

FIRST-LOOK—A deal allowing a studio the first option on a filmmaker's projects.

F.G. (FOREGROUND)—Objects or action that is closest to the camera.

FLASHBACKS—Scenes referring to events that happened in the narrative's past.

FREEZE FRAME—Camera direction indicating that the picture stops and becomes a still photograph. Sometimes used to end films or TV shows.

G

GREEN-LIGHT—The go-ahead for a film to be made.

H

HELM—To direct a film or TV program; Helmer (n.) a director.

HIGH CONCEPT—A phrase associated with scripts that have a premise or storyline easily reduced to a simple and appealing pitch.

HYPE—Manufactured promotional buzz.

I

INCITING INCIDENT—The scene at the beginning of the script that serves as a catalyst for the story's main action.

INDIE—Independent film, filmmaker, producer, or TV station.

INK—To sign a contract.

INSERT—A shot within a scene that calls our attention to a specific piece of information or object.

INT. (INTERIOR)—Used in scene headings to indicate that the scene takes place indoors.

L

LEGS—Stamina at the box office.

LENS—To film a motion picture.

LONG FORM—TV programming that is longer than an hour in duration.

LONG SHOT (L.S.)—Camera cue indicating a shot taken from a distance.

M

MADE-FOR—A TV movie (i.e., made-for-television movie).

MAJOR—One of the seven major film studios (Disney, MGM, Paramount, Sony—Columbia/Tri-Star—20th Century Fox, Universal, and Warner Bros.)

MATCH CUT—A transition from one scene to another, matching the same subject within the frame.

MEGAPLEX—A movie theater with more than sixteen screens.

MID-SIX FIGURES AGAINST HIGH-SIX FIGURES—The writer makes a deal in the $400,000.00 to $600,000.00 range, against around $750,000.00 if the film gets made. Parties involved often wish to keep the details of the deal secret.

MINI-MAJOR—Big film-production companies that are supposedly smaller than the majors, although such companies as Miramax, Polygram, and New Line compete with the big studios.

MED. SHOT (MEDIUM SHOT)—A camera angle used to describe a shot of a character from the waist up.

MISE-EN-SCENE—French phrase referring to the staging or positioning of scene elements.

MOGUL—The head of a major studio or communications company; from the title of the all-powerful emperors of India.

MONTAGE—A rapid succession of shots, often used to compress time and events in a script.

MOW—A TV movie of the week.

MPA—Motion Picture Association (international arm of Motion Picture Association of America, MPAA, representing the interests of the Hollywood studios abroad).

MPAA—Motion Picture Association of America (represents the interests of the major motion picture studios).

MULTIPLEX—A movie theater comprising more than two screens but less than sixteen.

N

NET—TV network.

NICHE PROGRAMMING—TV programming or channels targeting particular demographics or interests.

NIX—Reject, say no to.

NUT—Operating expenses to be recovered.

O

OFF-NET—Network TV series sold into syndication.

ON THE NOSE—Dialogue that too obviously reveals the author's intentions.

OPTION—Agreement 'renting' the rights to a script for a specific period of time.

O.S. (OFF SCREEN)—Dialogue or sounds heard while the camera is on another subject. Typed (O.S.) next to the character cue in the scene description.

OVER THE TOP—A scene or action in a script that goes too far in one direction and stretches believability.

P

PACT—(n.) A contract; (v.) to sign a contract.

PAGE ONE REWRITE—A new draft.

PAN—A slow, side-to-side camera movement.

PAR—Paramount.

PPV—Pay-per-view.

PEACOCK—The NBC television network, named for its colorful mascot.

PEN—(v.) To write.

PERCENTER (also TEN PERCENTER)—Agent.

PERCENTERY (also TEN PERCENTERY)—Talent agency.

PIC(S) (also PIX)—Motion picture(s).

PITCH MEETING—Meeting in which writers tell their story in person to producers, from start to finish, in an attempt to obtain a development deal.

PLEX—Multiplex theatre or cable channel.

POINTS—Percentage points. The percentage of the net profits of a picture.

POST-PRODUCTION—Stage at which editing is done, and scoring, and effects are added on a motion picture or TV production.

P.O.V.—Point of view.

PRE-PRODUCTION—Stage at which a motion picture or TV project is prepared to go into production.

PREMISE—The idea for a story.

PREXY (also PREZ)—President.

PRODUCER'S NOTES—A shorter form of story analysis in which development executives make comments about a script.

PRODUCT—Completed film or TV production.

R

REP—(n.) A representative; (v.) to represent.

REUP—To renew an employment contract.

RISING ACTION—When events in a story build upon one another with increasing momentum.

S

SAG—The Screen Actors Guild, the union for film and TV actors.

SASE—Self-addressed, stamped envelope.

SCREENPLAY   A script for a feature film, generally 90 to 120 pages in length.

SCRIBBLER—Writer.

SCRIBE—A screenwriter.

SCRIPTER—A screenwriter.

SET-UP—The function of the first act in posing the problem that the story will resolve.

SHOOTING SCRIPT—The script that includes scene numbers, camera angles, inserts, and certain directors/cinematographers' input.

SHOWBIZ—Show business.

SITCOM—A situation comedy TV series.

SPEC SCRIPT—A script shopped or sold on the open market, as opposed to one commissioned by a studio or production company.

SPIN—Indicates uniqueness that creates effective or appealing scenes.

SPINE—The essential events in a story.

STEP OUTLINE—An outline of a story made by numbering the major scenes and the order in which they occur.

STORY ANALYST—A script reader covering feature scripts.

SUBPLOT—The "B Story," the substory.

SUSPENSER—Suspense film.

SYNDIE—Syndicated television programming, those sold to stations, rather than provided by one of the networks or netlets.

SYNOPSIS—Summary of a story.

I

TAP—To select or name.

TELEFILM—(Also, TELEPIC, TELEPIX)—Feature-length motion picture made for TV.

TELEPLAY—A script for a television show or series.

TENTPOLE—A film (or a trademark character, a la Indiana Jones or James Bond) that helps finance other projects.

THEATRICAL—Describes a feature-length motion picture.

THREE-ACT STRUCTURE—The basic frame of fictional events including the set-up, the complication, and the climax.

TREATMENT—A movie plot written in present tense prose form.

TURNAROUND—No longer active; a project put into "turnaround" has been abandoned by one studio and may be shopped to another.

Index

Books from Allworth Press

So You Want to Be a Screenwriter: How to Face the Fears and Take the Risks by Sara Caldwell and Marie-Eve Kielson (softcover, 6 × 9, 224 pages, $14.95)

Writing Scripts Hollywood Will Love, Revised Edition by Katherine Atwell Herbert (softcover, 6 × 9, 160 pages, $14.95)

Selling Scripts to Hollywood by Katherine Atwell Herbert (softcover, 6 × 9, 176 pages, $12.95)

The Screenwriter's Legal Guide, Second Edition by Stephen F. Breimer (softcover, 6 × 9, 320 pages, $19.95)

Writing Television Comedy by Jerry Rannow (softcover, 6 × 9, 224 pages, $14.95)

Producing for Hollywood: A Guide for Independent Producers by Paul Mason and Don Gold (softcover, 6 × 9, 272 pages, $19.95)

Making Independent Films: Advice from the Filmmakers by Liz Stubbs and Richard Rodriguez (softcover, 6 × 9, 224 pages, $16.95)

Get the Picture? The Movie Lover's Guide to Watching Films by Jim Piper (softcover, 6 × 9, 256 pages, $18.95)

An Actor's Guide—Your First Year in Hollywood, Revised Edition by Michael Saint Nicholas (softcover, 6 × 9, 272 pages, $18.95)

The Health and Safety Guide for Film, TV & Theater by Monona Rossol (softcover, 6 × 9, 256 pages, $19.95)

Technical Theater for Nontechnical People by Drew Campbell (softcover, 6 × 9, 256 pages, $18.95)

Creating Your Own Monologue by Glenn Alterman (softcover, 6 × 9, 192 pages, $14.95)

Please write to request our free catalog. To order by credit card, call 1-800-491-2808 or send a check or money order to Allworth Press, 10 East 23rd Street, Suite 510, New York, NY 10010. Include $5 for shipping and handling for the first book ordered and $1 for each additional book. Ten dollars plus $1 for each additional book if ordering from Canada. New York State residents must add sales tax.

To see our complete catalog on the World Wide Web, or to order online, you can find us at *www.allworth.com*.